Glory in the Cross

Holy Week in the Third Edition
of The Roman Missal

Paul Turner

A PUEBLO BOOK

Liturgical Press   Collegeville, Minnesota
www.litpress.org

A Pueblo Book published by Liturgical Press

Cover design by David Manahan, OSB. Illustration by Frank Kacmarcik, OblSB. Background photo courtesy of Thinkstock.com.

Citations of Scripture in this work are taken from the *Lectionary for Mass for Use in the Dioceses in the United States*. Copyright © 2001, 1998, 1997, 1992, 1986, and 1970, Confraternity of Christian Doctrine, Washington, DC.

Excerpts from the English translation of *Rite of Baptism for Children* © 1969, International Commission on English in the Liturgy Corporation (ICEL); excerpts from the English translation of *Rite of Christian Initiation of Adults* © 1985, ICEL; excerpts from the English translation of *Ceremonial of Bishops* © 1989, ICEL; excerpts from the English translation of *The Roman Missal* © 2010, ICEL. All rights reserved.

Unless otherwise noted, all translations of non-English sources, including ICEL's Schematas, are the author's own.

Library of Congress Cataloging-in-Publication Data

Turner, Paul, 1953–
  Glory in the cross : Holy Week in the third edition of the Roman missal / Paul Turner.
    p. cm.
  "A Pueblo book."
  Includes bibliographical references (p.   ) and index.
  ISBN 978-0-8146-6242-7 — ISBN 978-0-8146-6258-8 (e-book)
  1. Holy Week services. 2. Catholic Church. Missale Romanum (1970)
3. Catholic Church—Liturgy—Texts—History and criticism. I. Title.
BX2015.8.H63T87   2011
264'.023—dc23   2011033415

Glory in the Cross

HVNC VOLVMEN
MARGARETÆ TVRNER
CVIVS LINGVA GLORIOSI CORPORIS MYSTERIVM PANGIT
ET QVI RESRVRRECTIONIS HOMO
AVCTOREM STVDIO MVSICÆ ET LITVRGIÆ
ATQVE CVRA EIVS IVRVM VIRVM FEMINARVMQVE SVSTENTA EST
ILLE FRATER OFFERT

Contents

Acknowledgments   xi

Abbreviations   xiii

Preface   xv

Palm Sunday of the Passion of the Lord   1

   The Commemoration of the Lord's Entrance into Jerusalem   2
      First Form: The Procession   3
      Second Form: The Solemn Entrance   11
      Third Form: The Simple Entrance   12

   At the Mass   14

Weekdays   21

   Monday of Holy Week   21
      Entrance Antiphon   21
      Collect   22
      Liturgy of the Word   22
      Prayer over the Offerings   23
      Preface   23
      Communion Antiphon   23
      Prayer after Communion   24
      Prayer over the People   24

   Tuesday of Holy Week   24
      Entrance Antiphon   24
      Collect   25
      Liturgy of the Word   25
      Prayer over the Offerings   26
      Preface   26
      Communion Antiphon   26

Prayer after Communion 26

Prayer over the People 26

Wednesday of Holy Week 27

Entrance Antiphon 27

Collect 27

Liturgy of the Word 27

Prayer over the Offerings 28

Preface 28

Communion Antiphon 28

Prayer after Communion 29

Prayer over the People 29

Thursday of Holy Week [Holy Thursday] 30

The Chrism Mass 30

Renewal of Priestly Promises 36

The Blessing of Oils and the Consecration of Chrism 39

Introduction 39

The Matter 40

The Minister 41

The Day of Blessing 42

The Place of the Blessing in the Liturgical Action 42

The Blessing of Oils and the Consecration of Chrism 42

Preparations 42

The Rite of Blessing 43

The Blessing of the Oil of the Sick 48

The Blessing of the Oil of Catechumens 50

The Consecration of the Chrism 51

The Sacred Paschal Triduum 55

Thursday of the Lord's Supper 57

At the Evening Mass 57

The Washing of Feet 63

The Liturgy of the Eucharist 66

The Transfer of the Most Blessed Sacrament 73

Friday of the Passion of the Lord [Good Friday]   78

    The Celebration of the Passion of the Lord   79

        First Part: The Liturgy of the Word   83

            The Solemn Intercessions   86

        Second Part: The Adoration of the Holy Cross   92

            The Showing of the Holy Cross   95

                First Form   95

                Second Form   97

            The Adoration of the Holy Cross   98

        Third Part: Holy Communion   103

Holy Saturday   111

Easter Time: Easter Sunday of the Resurrection of the Lord   113

    The Easter Vigil in the Holy Night   113

        First Part: The Solemn Beginning of the Vigil
                or Lucernarium   118

            The Blessing of the Fire and Preparation of the Candle   118

            Procession   124

            The Easter Proclamation (Exsultet)   127

        Second Part: The Liturgy of the Word   131

            Prayers after the Readings   136

        Third Part: Baptismal Liturgy   145

            Blessing of Baptismal Water   149

            The Blessing of Water   155

            The Renewal of Baptismal Promises   156

        Fourth Part: The Liturgy of the Eucharist   160

    At Mass during the Day   164

Afterword   168

Notes   169

Bibliography   197

Index   200

Acknowledgments

I wish to thank

Hans Christoffersen and Peter Dwyer, who agreed,

the International Commission on English in the Liturgy, which archived,

Steve Obarski and John Baldovin, who read,

the people of St. Munchin and St. Aloysius, who endure,

Jesus Christ, who died and is risen.

P. T.

Abbreviations

CL   Congregation for Divine Worship and the Discipline of the Sacraments. Circular Letter Concerning the Preparation and Celebration of the Easter Feasts. Prot. N. 120/88, 20 February 1988. In *The Liturgy Documents: A Parish Resource.* Vol. 2. Chicago: Liturgy Training Publications, 1999.

CB   Ceremonial of Bishops. Collegeville, MN: Liturgical Press, 1989.

GIRM General Instruction of the Roman Missal

PL   *Patrologia Latina.* Edited by J. P. Migne. Paris: Apud Garnier, 1844.

RBC   Rite of Baptism for Children. Collegeville, MN: Liturgical Press, 2002.

RCIA Rite of Christian Initiation of Adults. Collegeville, MN: Liturgical Press, 1988.

Preface

Time disappears when someone we love is dying. Day cedes to night without much notice. Activities we have promised to do we discard instead, like the sweater we doff on a slowly warming afternoon. Routines we never break cease. Something else has taken our attention, is sitting in our brain, has bound our legs and lowered our head. Nothing else is important but this person who gave meaning to our life and whose threatened passing wicks away the confidence that hitherto steadied our days. Yet no death completely surprises, and each one bestows a deeper understanding of the meaning of life.

Holy Week invites the entire church into the emotional experience of loss, fear, and redemption. We remember the One who died for us. We accompany his waning days, attentive to his final words and actions, discovering anew our love for one who is lost—and the joy of one who returns.

The risen Christ abides in the hearts of believers born generations after his days in Jerusalem. These same believers reconnect with him in the rituals of Holy Week. By their fecund endurance these rites have performed many services. They proclaim the Gospel as Jesus commanded. They reawaken the faith of believers. They frame these beliefs in the context that human beings most crave: narrative. The liturgies of Holy Week are not reenactments of the passion and resurrection of Christ. Rather, they are means by which the faithful enter these mysteries. Each participant will ultimately experience not just the death of a loved one but death itself. Through Holy Week, each believer prepares for the day of the body's destiny and the soul's soaring freedom.

This book offers a commentary on the rites of Holy Week found in the Roman Missal of the Catholic Church. It does not treat the other liturgical services found in the Liturgy of the Hours. It does cover each Mass of Holy Week, as well as the principal service of Good Friday, which is not, properly speaking, a Mass. The reader will find it most helpful to consult the Roman Missal together with this text or use this text as a companion to a direct study of the Missal. The numbers of the sections of this book match the numbers in the Missal's presentation of each day.

The third edition of the Missal has introduced quite a number of small changes to the rubrics of this week. Most of them import legislation from other sources or clarify former ambiguities. Some new material is based on practices prior to the Second Vatican Council. The revised texts should help the faithful enter into the mystery of dying with the timeless hope of resurrection.

Palm Sunday of the Passion of the Lord

The title of this day is commonly abbreviated to "Palm Sunday." The full title embraces the two distinctive features of the celebration: commemorating the entrance of Jesus into Jerusalem amid the crowds strewing cloaks on his path and holding palm branches in celebration and commemorating his death on the cross. In history, the day has gone by different names: "The Mass for Presenting the Creed to Catechumens," "Indulgence Sunday," and even "The Sixth Sunday in Lent."[1] Prior to the Second Vatican Council, the Roman Missal called it "The Second Passion Sunday" or "Palm Sunday of the Solemn Procession of Palms in Honor of Christ the King." The post–Vatican II Missal restored the title from the seventh-century Gelasian Sacramentary: "Palm Sunday of the Passion of the Lord."

Crosses and images may be covered if the conference of bishops so decides. The practice is not obligatory, but if it is observed, they are covered beginning on the Fifth Sunday of Lent. The timing better fit the preconciliar calendar, which regarded that Sunday as the beginning of Passiontide; however, that title is no longer retained in the liturgical calendar or texts. Nevertheless, crosses may be covered until the end of the celebration of the Lord's Passion on Good Friday; images remain covered until the beginning of the Easter Vigil.[2] The color of the veil is not noted, but violet is traditional.

1. The main focus of this day is to recall the entrance of Christ into Jerusalem, the holy city, in order to bring the paschal mystery to its completion. This focus widens with the proclamation of the passion, but the main focus is the commemoration that marks the opening minutes of this liturgy.

The community may choose from three forms of commemorating this entrance. The appropriate form should be chosen for each Mass when more than one Eucharist is celebrated in the same church that day. The Missal envisions that one celebration is the principal Mass, and the community chooses between the procession and the solemn entrance for that event. Other Masses follow the third form, the simple

entrance. However, realizing that some communities have large participation at these other Masses, the solemn entrance may be celebrated
at more than one. The procession, however, is to be done only once on
Palm Sunday.

It is desirable to have a word service of the Lord's entrance and passion in places where neither the procession nor the solemn entrance is
observed. This information used to appear at the end of the description of the simple entrance in previous editions of the postconciliar
Missal. It has been moved here to a more logical introductory place,
to help a community think through its options. The paragraph has not
changed in the third edition, though the Congregation for Divine Worship's Circular Letter Concerning the Preparation and Celebration of
the Easter Feasts[3] says the circumstance applies to situations "where
the Mass cannot be celebrated."[4] This is slightly different from what
the Missal says, even though the Circular Letter cites the Missal to
footnote this directive. The Missal also seems to allow a circumstance
where the Mass is celebrated, but without the procession or solemn
entrance, and hence no proclamation of the gospel of Jesus' entry into
Jerusalem. It permits a word service based on the gospel of the Lord's
entrance and on his passion. The Missal offers no outline for such a
service, so communities should feel free to devise an appropriate one.
The gospel of the first Palm Sunday is so important that if it is not read
at Mass over the weekend, the community may gather for a word service to hear it. As will be seen below, the earliest record of Palm Sunday seems to have established this pattern.

THE COMMEMORATION OF THE LORD'S ENTRANCE
INTO JERUSALEM

The first part of the service commemorates the first Palm Sunday.
The second part is the Mass proper. Designating this opening ritual
a "commemoration" is new to the post–Vatican II Missal. The same
word is used for the observance of All Souls Day on November 2 each
year. In this case, it evokes a participation in the events of Holy Week,
not a mere rehearsal of historical events.

The earliest record of such an observance comes from Egeria, a pil-
grim who kept a diary of her visit to the Holy Land in the late fourth
century.[5] The Eucharist was celebrated in the morning as usual, and
before the dismissal the archdeacon told everyone where and when to
meet later in the day. Egeria describes a subsequent event with hymns,
antiphons, and readings beginning around 1:00 p.m. on the Mount

of Olives, and then at 3:00 p.m., moving up to the place where Jesus ascended, more of the same, plus orations. Matthew's account of Palm Sunday was read around 5:00 p.m. A procession formed, and the people led the bishop to the Church of the Holy Sepulcher, singing with hymns and antiphons, "Blessed is he who comes in the name of the Lord." All carried palm or olive branches. The celebration concluded with Vespers. The separation of this observance from Mass may explain why the previous paragraph explains the circumstances in which such a separation may still happen today.

First Form: The Procession

2. The liturgy begins at an appropriate hour. This sounds like an unnecessary directive, but prior to 1957 this Mass took place exclusively in the morning. In 1955 the Pontifical Commission for the Reform of the Sacred Liturgy entertained suggestions that the Mass take place in the afternoon or even Sunday evening for the convenience of the faithful.[6] When requests continued to arrive the following year, the commission supported granting a concession for a serious reason.[7] In 1957 the *Ordinations and Declarations* of the Sacred Congregation of Rites Concerning Holy Week said the solemn blessing of palms, procession, and Mass would be held in the morning after the office of Terce,[8] but for pastoral reasons the bishop may permit the same celebration in the evening where a large gathering customarily meets.[9] The post–Vatican II Missal simplified all this by using an expression that covers any appropriate hour of the day.

The people gather in a smaller church or another suitable place outside the main church. Not many parishes have the option of a separate church building within walking distance. But any place outside the main church will suffice: a large gathering area or a space outdoors. Ideally, the location permits a procession of the faithful to the main church. For many centuries, the celebration of Palm Sunday never included a procession. When it entered the liturgy in 1955, the procession rubric appeared not in the first paragraphs, but in the seventeenth, after the blessing of palms.[10] The historical antecedent is Egeria's record of the Jerusalem liturgy, which began on the Mount of Olives and processed to the city gates. Here, the ideal procession begins somewhere outside the church and approaches the doors as if they were the gates of Jerusalem. It should not begin inside the church, go outside, and then return.[11]

The faithful hold branches. The gospel says that they were from olive trees, but Egeria mentions both olive and palm. Today, any branch will do. Traditionally, these are supplied by the local church, which has purchased them through a religious goods store. But in the Bible, people brought their own branches. This is why the elaborate preconciliar ceremonies for distributing the branches have been removed from the post–Vatican II liturgy.[12] In the preconciliar liturgy, branches were first blessed and then distributed to the people. In the mid-fourteenth century, one ceremonial says that the pope gave each cardinal and bishop a frond of palms, passed more out by hand, and then hurled the remaining branches and leaves out over the people.[13] Now, people hold them from the very beginning. They could certainly bring them from home—no rubric forbids that. But Catholics are accustomed to receiving a branch on this day, which they use as a sacramental at home throughout the year.[14] The Ceremonial of Bishops is of two minds about all this. It says that the faithful carry branches at the beginning,[15] but also that the bishop may distribute them to concelebrants, ministers, and the faithful after the blessing—and after he has personally received one from a deacon or concelebrant.[16]

3. The priest and deacon wear red. Some communities have no deacon; his service is not obligatory, but when he is present, he wears red. Throughout the third edition of the Missal, the role of the deacon in these ceremonies has been clarified.

Prior to the Second Vatican Council, Palm Sunday vesture in the Roman Rite was violet. In 1954 the Pontifical Commission for the Reform of the Sacred Liturgy proposed rose or red vesture; rose was already being used twice a year to indicate "a window of joy during a period of sorrow."[17] In the 1955 reform of Palm Sunday, the priest wore a red cope to open the liturgy but switched to a violet chasuble for the introit of the Mass. Deacons likewise switched colors.[18] The postconciliar liturgy simplified this to one color, demonstrating the unity of the rites. The priest may still wear a cope for this part of the service. If so, he switches to a chasuble at the entrance antiphon (see paragraph 11 below).

Accompanied by other ministers, the priest and deacon go to the place where the people have already gathered, as indicated in paragraph 2. Prior to the council, there was no separate place, so the priest conducted the ceremony in the sanctuary at a table covered with branches, and he faced the people.[19] Previous editions of the postconciliar Missal did not mention "other ministers," even though they had been included in the 1955 reform.[20] The third edition corrected this oversight.

4. "Hosanna to the Son of David" or another appropriate chant is sung. The earliest record of this comes from the mid-tenth-century Roman-Germanic Pontifical,[21] and it has enjoyed a place in the Roman Rite ever since. Previous editions of the postconciliar Missal offered no chant notation for this antiphon, but the third edition inserts it. This is the first of many chants for Holy Week newly notated in the Missal. Clearly, the singing of these is encouraged. However, another song may replace this one. It need not be long. It simply gathers the voices of the people as the ministers arrive.

5. All make the sign of the cross as they usually do to start a celebration of the Eucharist. The text for the priest is included, but the people's Amen is missing—probably an oversight. This entire rubric was missing from previous postconciliar editions of the Missal. Its insertion clarifies the way that the priest begins.

The priest then greets the people in the usual way. This rubric was also missing from previous editions of the postconciliar Missal, but deliberately so. When Study Group 17 worked on the Holy Week ceremonies for the postconciliar reform, its members explicitly desired that the greeting would be omitted because the faithful were greeted with the introduction that immediately followed.[22] The study group intended to retain the greeting only for the third option, the simple entrance, in which the introduction and other ceremonies went unused.[23] The greeting was inserted here for the first time in the third edition of the Missal.

The rubrics do not explicitly say who gives this introduction. They just say that it is supposed to happen. When the bishop presides, he may deliver the introduction, or he may assign the responsibility to the deacon or a concelebrant.[24] Logically, the deacon could deliver the introduction whenever a priest presides. For that matter, the parish director of religious education, a religion teacher in a Catholic school, or the director of faith formation for the community could effectively deliver it. This would underscore the catechetical nature of the introduction, which explains the proceedings to the community. However, if the introduction is regarded as an extension of the greeting, then it more naturally falls to the priest or deacon.

A text is supplied, but the one who speaks it may use "these or similar words." This has always been the case and does not change with the third edition of the Missal. New to this edition are the sense lines, which make it easier to proclaim if the speaker chooses to use the text provided. If similar words are chosen, they would profitably stress the entire paschal mystery, as those in the Missal do, and they would invite the people who have observed a holy Lent into a faith-filled participation in the dying and rising of Christ through the special ceremonies of this day and the week ahead.

By this introduction the faithful are invited "to participate actively and consciously." Pope Pius X first promoted active participation in the opening to his 1903 instruction on sacred music. The concept had been recovered by the Second Vatican Council's Constitution on the Sacred Liturgy.[25] It is also promoted in the General Instruction of the Roman Missal.[26] Here it was enshrined in the Missal's first instruction to the people at the very beginning of Holy Week. They were not to watch this ceremony as if it were a passion play. They were to participate in it actively and consciously, entering into the paschal mystery through the beauty of the liturgy.

6. The priest extends his hands and says one of two alternative prayers. If reciting the first, he makes the sign of the cross with his hand over the branches. After either prayer he sprinkles the branches with holy water in silence.

This is the first time the priest has been explicitly told to extend his hands for this prayer. The custom of joining hands for it dates back to the preconciliar Missal.[27] In fact, the priest joined his hands for the greeting that preceded the prayer as well. Prior to that time, one may assume that the priest extended his hands as he did for other prayers because no special rubric indicates otherwise. The postconciliar Missal omitted the greeting, as has been noted, but kept the practice of joining hands for the oration. The Ceremonial of Bishops instructed the bishop to extend his hands for this prayer, putting into place even on this special occasion the common practice.[28] The third edition of the Roman Missal now assigns every priest the same gesture recently given to bishops.

The oldest formula for blessing branches comes from the late seventh-century Bobbio Missal.[29] As the Roman Rite developed, the blessings became quite numerous. They were also accompanied by a preliminary exorcism of the branches,[30] a preface,[31] and a reading from Exodus.[32] The postconciliar Missal simplified the number and length of the prayers, providing only two from which one is chosen. Both prayers are new, though they are inspired by texts from *Ordo Romanus* 50.[33] The first follows the tradition of blessing the branches with a sign of the cross. The second has the feel of a prayer over the people.[34] The third edition of the Missal has increased the usage of prayers over the people throughout the season of Lent.

At the conclusion of the prayer, the priest sprinkles the branches with blessed water, saying nothing. His silence is important to note because prior to the reforms of Holy Week he recited the antiphon *Asperges me*.[35] The former rubrics asked him to sprinkle the branches three times and to follow it up with an incensation. All these instructions were dramatically simplified in the postconciliar Missal.

The reforms of the Palm Sunday liturgy transposed the blessing of branches and the proclamation of the gospel. Prior to the Second Vatican Council, the gospel of Palm Sunday preceded the blessing of branches. In this way, the people acted upon the proclamation of the gospel and entered the church as the crowd accompanied Jesus on his entry to Jerusalem. Now they hold branches from the very beginning, as if they had brought them in imitation of the crowd, and they hear the gospel of Palm Sunday with branches in hand. The results strengthened the active participation of the people in the flow of the liturgy.

7. The deacon, or in his absence the priest, proclaims the gospel of Palm Sunday in the usual way. Incense may be used. Both points should have been understood, but they are included now in the third edition of the Missal for clarity. The "usual way" probably refers to the use of candles and the dialogue between the deacon and the priest, or the priest's private preparation.

In preparing the postconciliar Missal, Study Group 17 said that this gospel is necessary because it is in the form of a memorial in an excellent sense, and it is at the same time an interpretation of the whole rite.[36]

As noted above, this is one of the oldest parts of the ceremony. Even Egeria mentioned hearing excerpts from Matthew's account. Evidence for reading John's account comes from northern Italian notes on the gospels from the seventh, eighth, and ninth centuries.[37] Although Matthew's account has the longest usage in the Roman Rite, the postconciliar Missal allowed a rotation of the gospels to match the distribution of readings in the three-year cycle. Hence, Matthew's is read in Year A and Luke's in Year C. Year B offers a choice of either Mark or John. In this way, all the accounts can be proclaimed over a stretch of years in the same community.

All the gospel passages now appear in the Missal. They have always been in the Latin Missal, but the English translation of the third edition includes them for the first time. This provides a practical solution by simplifying the number of liturgical books needed for the opening rite, though it may diminish the sense of the gospel because people are used to seeing it proclaimed from a book designated for this purpose. Nonetheless, the Book of the Gospels could still be used instead since it is to be proclaimed "in the usual way," and since the deacon will carry it in the procession, according to paragraph 9 below. When a bishop presides, he holds a palm branch while the deacon proclaims the gospel.[38]

8. A brief homily may be given. Then the procession begins with an invitation from the priest, deacon, or a lay minister. These two events are deliberately linked.

The English translation of the second edition of the Missal gave similar instructions about the homily, but the Latin said *pro opportunitate*—if it seems appropriate. That expression no longer appears in the third edition, but English speakers will not notice its absence. It was likely omitted because the main verb of the sentence already states that a homily is optional. The 1956 reform of this liturgy makes no mention of a homily here.[39] Study Group 17 discussed it. Some wanted an admonition, or an explanation and invitation, to put into practice what the gospel had just proclaimed. Others thought that a homily would serve better—but *pro opportunitate*. A homily would contribute much to the active and conscious participation of the people, "upon which almost all spiritual fruit depends."[40] As the revised liturgy took shape, the rubric expressed this option: "After the gospel if it seems appropriate a short homily may take place, or the people may be invited [to process] with a few words."[41] The intent of the proposed homily was to invite the participation of the people.

The third edition of the Missal clarifies that a priest, deacon, or lay minister may give the invitation. The explicit mention of the deacon is new. This was probably inspired by the occasions when a bishop presides: he may entrust this invitation to a deacon.[42] This was already the case in the 1956 reform of Holy Week.[43] Perhaps whoever gives the address in paragraph 5 above would also issue this invitation.

The invitation may be given in "these or similar words." However, musical notation appears here in the third edition of the Missal for the first time, suggesting appropriately that the invitation be sung. If the minister is using similar words, singing them becomes more challenging. Two options are provided, the second a much shorter form of the first and simpler in musical notation. That is the one that generates a sung reply from the people. This brief dialogue recaptures the one from the preconciliar Missal and reform of Holy Week.[44] It had been omitted from the postconciliar Missal but has been restored in the third edition, recapturing a time-honored text.

9. The procession begins as usual. It enters the church where the Mass will be celebrated—distinct from wherever the blessing took place. The thurifer leads the way, and two ministers with lighted candles flank the person carrying the cross, which may be decorated with palm branches. The deacon carries the Book of the Gospels, then the priest follows with any other ministers, and the people enter as well, all carrying branches. The choir and the people sing a song in honor of Christ the King. Texts are proposed, but others may be used.

The third edition has lightly retouched this paragraph, indicating that the procession forms as usual, an acolyte could carry the cross, a deacon carries the Book of the Gospels, and the cross should be decorated. The 1956 Rite called for a subdeacon or acolyte to carry the cross, which accounts for the reappearance of the acolyte as the suggested minister for this role.[45] The same rite specified that the cross should be unveiled, which would have distinguished it from other crosses veiled during the last two weeks of Lent.[46] Decorating the cross is a logical amplification. The seventh-century *Liber Ordinum* may have the earliest record of a procession from one church to another,[47] but the most probable source for the evolution of this procession in the Roman Rite comes from the tenth-century Roman-Germanic Pontifical.[48] Prior to the 1956 reform, the priest and ministers processed outside and back inside the church, and the people did not actually take part in the procession. In preparing the postconciliar liturgy, Study Group 17 wanted the procession to begin outside the building and go in, saying furthermore that it should not start from the sacristy.[49] In one draft, the group explained that the crowd brought the priest "as a type of Christ" into the church,[50] an expression found in Egeria's description of the event,[51] but this was eliminated from the final rubrics.

There are three recommended chants for this procession. The first two have similar antiphons and are assigned Psalm 24 (23) and Psalm 47 (46), respectively. The third is the hymn *Gloria, laus*, again in a structure using an antiphon. This structure favors the processional nature of the action that this music accompanies. All these antiphons can be found in the Roman-Germanic Pontifical,[52] though the last of them had been composed by Theodulph of Orleans (+821) a century earlier.[53] These chants were originally sung during a veneration of the cross that used to take place near the start of the Palm Sunday liturgy, then in later centuries the first two accompanied the distribution of blessed branches to the faithful before the proclamation of the gospel, and the last accompanied the procession that followed the gospel. In the post–Vatican II reform, these chants were all assigned to the entrance procession. These three were retained; others of more recent vintage were eliminated.

Even with those removals, it still seems like a lot of music for this part of the Mass. That is partly because the elimination of the distribution of palms caused the rubrics to bunch together the oldest antiphons the church wanted to retain, and partly because of the psalms. The 1956 reform of Holy Week introduced the complete text of Psalms 23 and 46.[54] The 1974 and 1985 Sacramentary in English provided the text for the two antiphons only, indicating the usage of Psalms 23 and 46 in the rubric. Now the complete psalm verses have been restored in the English edition; they were never missing from the Latin. The third edition has made slight changes to sense lines and punctuation of these antiphons.

People take for granted that these antiphons are sung by the whole community, but they used to be assigned to the choir. In 1956, for the first time in history, the third chant, *Gloria, laus,* was offered to the people to sing.[55] Now people may sing all three of them. The third edition of the Missal now states that other songs "in honor of Christ the King" may replace these antiphons. Prior to the council, this same rubric applied to the hymn *Christus vincit,* which could be sung just before the procession entered the church. The rubrics today specify the theme for this hymn partly to honor the previous custom and partly to keep the procession focused on Christ. The popular hymn setting "All Glory, Laud and Honor" is a strophic version of *Gloria, laus.* Still, it would be good for parishes to learn a common repertoire of key chants such as those supplied in the Missal.

10. A sung responsory is proposed as the procession enters the church. The text has been part of the Palm Sunday liturgy ever since the Roman-Germanic Pontifical.[56] It has always come at the end of the chants as the procession crosses the threshold of the church. In the solemn procession, it also serves as the entrance antiphon for the Mass. The procession keeps moving throughout this music. In practice, some communities tend to simplify the music that is here, and, in fact, the rubrics allow these texts to be substituted by others.[57] However, in the first form of the procession, the liturgy envisions a series of musical offerings to accompany the participants from one building to the other.

In many parishes people hear several separate pieces of music to accompany a wedding procession; the same concept is at work here.[58]

11. When the priest reaches the altar, he venerates it. He may also incense the altar if this seems appropriate. He goes to his chair. If he has been wearing a cope, he removes it now and puts on a chasuble, signifying a switch from the processional rites to the Mass proper. If appropriate, the *Kyrie* may be sung. The priest says the collect, and Mass continues as usual.

When a bishop presides, and if he has been wearing a cope, he may remove it before venerating the altar.[59] It is not clear why a bishop and not a priest has this option, or even if it is preferable. The long tradition has the presider changing vesture after reverencing the altar. However, by changing before doing so, the presider wraps the greeting of the altar into the start of the Mass. Prior to the council, the priest and deacons changed from red to violet vestments at this point,[60] highlighting the distinction between these two parts of the service and turning the Mass into more of a memorial of the passion. However, the single vestment color unifies the purposes of the celebration as well as one's experience of the complete paschal mystery.

The reference to the *Kyrie* is new to the third edition of the Missal. However, it can be found in the Roman-Germanic Pontifical as the last music before the responsory that accompanies the entrance into the church (see paragraph 10 above).[61] It is optional, but there appears to be now some desire to retain it, perhaps because of the practice in the tenth century, and perhaps because it comes somewhere between the entrance antiphon and the collect in a typical Mass.

Second Form: The Solemn Entrance

12. Where a procession from outside the church is not possible, the principal Mass may begin inside with the solemn entrance. When this version of the procession came under discussion after the Second Vatican Council, this form emerged for the situation in which the procession starts inside the church and when not all the people may participate in the procession.[62] Earlier, the study group had regarded the first circumstance (starting inside) to be a minor difference between this form and the first form of the procession, while the second circumstance (the people not actually processing) to be the major difference.[63] As indicated in paragraph 1 above, this solemn entrance may be repeated at other Masses, whereas the first form, the procession, may be done only once.

13. The faithful gather either outside the door of the church or inside, holding branches. The priest and the ministers and some representatives of the faithful go up to a place in the church outside the sanctuary where most of the others can still see them.

If people are gathering outside, this will naturally involve them in the procession; but some churches do not even have space for that much to happen. In some years, even those who do may have unfavorable weather, making an outdoor gathering impractical. In such cases, the ceremony takes place completely inside, where all can see— but outside the sanctuary, so that the priest and ministers make even the briefest of processions.

14. The priest and deacon wear the vestments for Mass; the option of the priest wearing a cope is not mentioned in the second form of the entrance. When the priest arrives, all sing Hosanna or another appropriate song. The ceremony takes place as described in paragraphs 5–7 above, including the gospel of Palm Sunday. The invitation to the procession and most of the musical suggestions are omitted. Then the procession moves into the sanctuary, and at that point the people sing the responsory designated for entry into the church in the first form of the procession (paragraph 10). Another appropriate song may be sung.

15. The priest approaches the altar and venerates it. This form does not mention the use of incense, but incense is always optional.[64] He does not change vestments because he has worn the chasuble throughout. As in the first form, the *Kyrie* may be sung before the collect (see paragraph 11).

Third Form: The Simple Entrance
16. The simple entrance is used at Masses that do not have the procession or the solemn entrance. Above, paragraph 1 envisions that one of the first two forms (procession or solemn entrance) will take place at some Mass this weekend. Therefore, the use of the simple entrance implies that one of those other forms happens at a different Mass in the same church.

In 1956 the commission working on the revision of Holy Week considered having a blessing of palm branches without any kind of procession, but its members believed strongly that these two elements belonged together. "The blessing of palms is closely connected with the procession which is [the main] characteristic of this Sunday. A blessing [of palms], without a procession would reduce it to a simple sacramental. This would be to the detriment of the rite which would lose much of its forcefulness."[65] The commission was considering a request to have the blessing of branches the evening before, freeing up Sunday morning to celebrate hourly Masses more expeditiously. They did agree to the option of having the blessing outdoors in order to accommodate the crowds attending Mass that day.[66]

In 1968 Study Group 17 considered a request to blend the gospel of Palm Sunday with the reading of the passion, but this was outside the tradition of the Roman Rite and posed practical difficulties.[67] To accommodate the pastoral desire for a simpler way of celebrating Palm Sunday, the simple entrance was developed. It does not include the gospel of Palm Sunday at all. Instead, it relies on the entrance antiphon to bring that gospel text into the community's celebration of the day.[68]

Communities today will be attracted to the third form at Masses that pose practical difficulties because of the hour of the day, the schedule of other Masses, or the shortage of assisting ministers. However, a thorough celebration of Palm Sunday will prefer one of the previous two forms of the entrance.

17. While the priest goes to the altar, the entrance antiphon and its psalm or another chant of the same theme is sung. He venerates the altar and goes to his chair. He makes the sign of the cross, greets the people, and Mass continues as usual. In other words, this Mass omits the blessing of palms, the gospel of Palm Sunday, and the procession of people and ministers. It does include the act of penitence before the collect.[69]

If no one can sing the entrance antiphon, the priest reads it after he greets the people. This is in keeping with an option he has at any Mass.[70] In the previous editions of the postconciliar Missal, this rubric also applied to Masses the priest celebrated without a congregation. The 1985 Sacramentary in English did not translate that option in this paragraph, but the third edition of the Missal has removed it anyway.

If the entrance chant is replaced with another text, it would be important to draw on this passage from the gospel of Palm Sunday, if possible. It is the only part of this Mass that permits the people to commemorate the Lord's entrance into Jerusalem.

18. The entrance antiphon for the simple entrance comes from John 12 and Psalm 24 (23). The text appears only in this third form of the entrance rites because on that occasion it is the only opportunity

people have to hear or sing anything from the story of Palm Sunday. The text first appeared in the Roman-Germanic Pontifical at the conclusion of the lengthy blessing and distribution of palms.[71] It was retained in the Roman Rite up until the 1956 revision as a processional antiphon.[72] The post–Vatican II Roman Missal has put it into service as the antiphon for the simple entrance.

AT THE MASS

19. After the procession or the solemn entrance, Mass begins with the collect. The simple entrance is not mentioned in this rubric, presumably because Mass has already begun. Once the collect begins, all the prayers and antiphons refer to the suffering, death, and resurrection of Christ. There is no longer any reference to the biblical events of Palm Sunday. The liturgy takes a realistic view about the lives of Catholics this week: not as many will participate in the Good Friday liturgy as are present today.[73] Consequently, the focus of the Mass is on the passion, a prelude to next week's celebration of Easter.

20. In the collect, the community prays that it might share in the patient suffering of the Savior and enjoy a share in his resurrection. The revised translation sounds Pelagian, as though the faithful can merit the resurrection by heeding the patient suffering of Christ, but the Latin word rendered "merit" here has more a sense of receiving something as a gift. The prayer first appeared in the Gelasian Sacramentary exactly in this position, and it has remained virtually unchanged since the seventh century.[74]

When the 1955 revision of Holy Week was under discussion, many people thought the Palm Sunday liturgy should be reduced in length. Because the blessing of palms had taken on the weight of a complete liturgical action, one proposal would have moved immediately from the collect to the offertory of the Mass, omitting the other readings, including the passion. However, no such elaborate change happened.[75]

21. The reading of the passion takes place without processional candles or incense, without the greeting of the people, their response, or the signing of the book.[76] A deacon reads it, or in his absence a priest does. It may also be read by lectors, reserving the part of Christ to the priest, if possible. Only a deacon asks the priest for a blessing, as he does on other occasions.[77]

The other readings from the Lectionary for Mass are Isaiah 50:4-7; Psalm 22 (21):8-9, 17-18a, 19-20, and 23-24; and Philippians 2:6-11.

Because the Lectionary includes the four options for the first gospel of Palm Sunday as well as three versions of the Passion, this one day consumes fifty pages in a typical lectionary, far more than any other day of the year, including the Easter Vigil.

The passage from Isaiah 50 was newly added to the Palm Sunday liturgy in the post–Vatican II Lectionary. There is no evidence for any Old Testament reading on Palm Sunday prior to the Second Vatican Council, and one had to be chosen in accordance with the revised schema for Sunday readings. The group preparing the revised Lectionary chose this third of four oracles of the servant of the Lord from the book of Isaiah, which is repeated on Wednesday of Holy Week with a few extra verses. Only this oracle enjoys an ancient usage during Holy Week: it appears on Monday in the seventh-century Wurzburg Lectionary, one of the oldest collections of readings known to Christianity.[78] It had been retained on that day up to the preconciliar liturgy. That may have influenced its choice for the first reading on Palm Sunday, especially since a different reading was being assigned for Monday of Holy Week (see below).

Verses from Psalm 22 (21) served as the tract for this Mass as early as the eighth century antiphonals[79] and continued through the usage of the preconciliar Missal.[80] An abbreviated version remains in the current Liturgy of the Word, serving now as the responsorial psalm because the tract has been discontinued. The reason for its selection is obvious. Jesus quotes the text just before his death on the cross in Matthew 27:46 and Mark 15:34. It therefore looks forward to the passion more than it echoes the first reading.

Whereas the first reading is a relative newcomer to the Palm Sunday liturgy, the second reading from Philippians has been associated with this day for as long as there have been lectionaries. It appears as the only reading in the Wurzburg Lectionary.[81] In this passage, Paul is likely quoting an early Christian hymn about the abasement and exaltation of Christ.

The verse before the gospel comes from the same passage in Philippians. It formerly served as the gradual for the Holy Thursday Mass, and, in increasing lengths, as the antiphon for the *Benedictus* at Lauds on Holy Thursday, Good Friday, and Holy Saturday. It appeared on Holy Thursday as early as the eighth-century *Ordo Romanus* 27.[82] It was moved here for the Palm Sunday liturgy in the post–Vatican II reform.

For pastoral reasons, one or both of the readings may be omitted, and even the short form of the passion may be used.[83] The reasons are left to the discretion of those responsible for the local liturgy. However, the Circular Letter says, "For the spiritual good of the faithful, the Passion should be proclaimed in its entirety, and the readings that proceed it should not be omitted."[84]

Palm Sunday sermons delivered by Pope Leo the Great prove that the passion was proclaimed on this day as early as the fifth century. This makes the mid-twentieth-century discussion about eliminating the passion at some Masses on this day all the more surprising.[85] Prior to the 1956 reform, the passion extended from Matthew 26:1 to 27:66. It was abbreviated to Matthew 26:36 to 27:54, eliminating the plot to kill Jesus, the anointing at Bethany, the conversation between Judas and the chief priests, and the events pertaining to the Last Supper, as well as the burial of Jesus and the posting of the guard at the tomb. For the sake of priests celebrating a second or third Mass, the passion of the 1956 liturgy could be abbreviated to Matthew 27:45-52, the few verses relating the death of Jesus.[86] A short form is still provided in the Lectionary for Mass, but without any restriction. The judgment for its usage is completely in the hands of the parish. In most congregations, people expect the reading of the passion to take some time, but in certain pastoral circumstances— Mass at a nursing home, or where several celebrations need to take place within a short space of time—the shorter form may be chosen.

The post–Vatican II Lectionary for Mass extended the passage from Matthew almost to the length it enjoyed before the reform. Then it did something new. It put Matthew's account into Year A of the three-year cycle of Sunday readings, to be followed by Mark's and Luke's accounts in Years B and C. In the past, these two accounts were read on Tuesday and Wednesday, respectively.[87] In at least one eighth-century lectionary, the passions of Mark and John may have served as alternatives on Palm Sunday,[88] but otherwise the idea of cycling through the Synoptic accounts of the passion was unknown prior to the post– Vatican II reforms. The decision has allowed Sunday worshipers to hear three accounts over time, broadening their experience of the testimony from the apostolic church.

The rubrics that lend honor and celebration to the usual proclamation of the gospel are much simplified for the passion out of respect for its unusual nature. Prior to 1956, the book was incensed before and after the proclamation of the passion,[89] but this is now expressly forbidden.

Regarding the dialogue before the passion, evidence from the eighth to the tenth century shows no common practice. Some communities omitted the greeting and its response. Others included it. Many used the formula, "The Passion of our Lord Jesus Christ according to Matthew," but not everyone encouraged the people to respond to it with "Glory to you, O Lord." Some congregations remained silent.[90]

Although a deacon or a priest may read the passion alone, the text is traditionally divided among four participants: the priest reading the part of Christ, a narrator, a reader of other solo voices, and the crowd. In the past, these roles were sometimes marked with + for the role of Christ, C for the narrator (the *Chronista*), S for an individual speaker (*Synagoga*), and SS for the crowd (indicating the plural of S). The *Chronista* traditionally stood in the middle, the *Synagoga* on the left, and the *Christus* on the right. Two acolytes without candles stood to the left of the *Synagoga* and the right of the *Christus*.[91] A choir could sing the part of the crowd, but it was not to be assigned to nuns.[92] Today, when a bishop presides, the passion is proclaimed by deacons. They all ask and receive the blessing from him. He does not take part in the proclamation.[93]

The kissing of the book after the passion was discontinued in the 1956 reform,[94] but it is no longer listed among the excluded reverences. The deacon or priest would therefore continue the practice, as was done prior to the 1956 reform.[95]

22. A brief homily may be delivered after the proclamation of the passion. Alternatively, or along with a homily, a period of silence may be observed. The option of replacing the homily with silence is new to the third edition of the Roman Missal. It follows an opinion from Study Group 17: "The reading of the passion is itself a preaching of such intensity that it seems unusual for one to profit as much from the words of a preacher."[96] Still, a preacher who works hard on a homily for this day will reward his congregation, and the Circular Letter states more strongly, "After the Passion has been proclaimed, a homily is to be given."[97]

The Creed and the universal prayer follow. Drafts of the post–Vatican II Palm Sunday liturgy called for the omission of the Creed,[98] but it was included in the final version. Although today's liturgy makes no reference to the custom, this was one of the days on which the Creed was presented to catechumens of old.[99] Today, it is presented during a weekday gathering in the third week of Lent.[100] The Creed became a kind of textbook for those preparing for baptism. They were to commit it to memory and return it to the community from memory.

Today they still respond to questions based on the Creed before they are baptized.

A sample prayer of the faithful was included in the 1968 draft of this liturgy, but it did not survive. Here is the text:

> Let us beseech our crucified Lord Jesus Christ, most beloved brothers and sisters.
>
> Save your Church, Lord, endangered in this age.
>   Kyrie, eleison.
>
> Have mercy, Lord, on our pope N., that he may have strength to comfort his brothers and sisters.
>
> Grant light, Lord, to our bishop N. and all the bishops, together with the priests, that they may wisely direct your flock.
>
> Direct, Lord, the Christian people and all the peoples of the earth, as well as those who lead them, in the way of justice, charity and peace.
>
> Almighty Father, who did not withhold your own Son for the sake of our salvation, let your kingdom come. Through Christ our Lord.[101]

The post–Vatican II Missal has always included a sample prayer of the faithful for weekdays in Holy Week, which now appears in the fifth appendix. But its petitions are completely different.

23. The prayer over the offerings asks that God's atonement may be near at hand for the community. The prayer is based on one from the Verona Sacramentary, where it appears as a prayer over the offerings for the month of July.[102] It is new to the post–Vatican II Missal. The original prayer from the Verona Sacramentary did include the word "sacrifice," but the opening phrase referring to the passion of the only-begotten Son was newly added to this prayer in order to make it fit more properly the celebration of this day. It replaces a prayer that had a more generic content.[103]

24. The preface recalls the innocence of Christ, who suffered to save the guilty. His death washes away the sins of others, and his resurrection has purchased justification. In the third edition of the Missal, the text and music appear among the pages dedicated to Palm Sunday. It is no longer necessary to look for and mark the preface in a different part of the book. Its usage is still limited exclusively to today's Mass.

In the preconciliar Missal, the preface of the holy cross was used on this day. It was not replaced until after the Second Vatican Council, even though a new preface had been proposed in 1950.[104] Today's preface is based on one for Wednesday of Holy Week in the Gregorian Sacramentary's Hadrian Supplement.[105]

The other postconciliar prefaces concerning the passion are the one for the holy cross, which used to be heard on Palm Sunday, and the one for weekdays of Holy Week. In the 1968 draft of the post-conciliar Palm Sunday liturgy, all three of these were listed as options.[106] Now only the new preface, the one recovered from its eighth-century source, is prayed. The *Sanctus* follows as usual.

25. The communion antiphon is the traditional one for this day and has not been changed. It can be traced back to the eighth century.[107] Of course, in the post–Vatican II liturgy, any communion antiphon may be replaced with a different one.[108] Throughout, the Missal keeps to the occasional custom of drawing the text of the communion antiphon from the gospel of the day. Because the traditional version of the passion proclaimed today was Matthew's, his gospel supplies this day's antiphon. The relationship works in Year A of the lectionary cycle.

26. The prayer after communion asks that those who have hope because of their belief in the death of God's Son may arrive at their eternal destination by his resurrection. The prayer succinctly applies the belief in the paschal mystery to the Communion just received and the hope of eternal life.

In the post–Vatican II Missal, this prayer replaced an earlier one that had a more generic content. This one was created from two different Palm Sunday prayers in the Gelasian Sacramentary: the post-Communion prayer and one that preceded the reading from Exodus.[109] The combination of these two ancient prayers enriched the creation of the one now in force.

27. The prayer over the people concludes the special texts for this Mass. It asks God to look upon the family for whom Jesus did not hesitate to be handed over to his enemies and to submit to the agony of the cross.

This prayer is new to the third edition of the Missal. To find a precedent, one has to go back to the preconciliar Missal, where all the Masses of Lent concluded with a prayer over the people. The third edition of the Missal has restored the custom, and this is the first instance of it in Holy Week. Ever since the Second Vatican Council, the Sacramentary in English has concluded this Mass with the solemn blessing for Passiontide. It appeared among other solemn blessings in the appendix to the Order of Mass in the second edition of the Latin

Missal, so it was logical for the English Sacramentary to move it to a more easily located spot. The solemn blessing still appears in the appendix to the Order of Mass in the third edition of the Missal, but apparently it has been retained for other occasions—not Palm Sunday.

This prayer over the people was drawn from the liturgy of Wednesday of Holy Week in the Gregorian Sacramentary's Hadrian Supplement,[110] the same Mass that supplied the preface for the postconciliar Palm Sunday liturgy.

Weekdays

The table of liturgical days in the Roman Catholic Church, located in the introductory sections of the Missal, places the paschal Triduum at the top of the list. Just under it come other days such as Christmas, Epiphany, Ascension, and Pentecost. In the same group can be found the weekdays of Holy Week. They rank higher than any other feast or solemnity on the calendar. So do the weekdays of the Easter Octave. If a solemnity such as St. Joseph or the Annunciation or even the parish's patron saint should fall during Holy Week in a given year, the celebration is postponed to the nearest open date on the calendar, usually Monday of the Second Week of Easter. These three days are that important to observe.

Baptisms and confirmations should not be celebrated on weekdays of Holy Week.[1] In practice, some parishes refuse to baptize during the season of Lent, but the prohibition only applies to the weekdays of Holy Week.

The Circular Letter recommends a penitential celebration to conclude the season of Lent, to help people prepare to celebrate more fully the paschal mystery. These celebrations should take place before the Triduum, but not immediately before the evening Mass of the Lord's Supper.[2] Many communities offer a communal celebration of the sacrament of reconciliation at this time. However, a "penitential celebration" need not be the sacrament of penance.

As late as the fourth century, there was still no celebration of the Eucharist on these days.[3] Within the next few centuries, evidence for texts of Masses on these days appears in the Gelasian and Gregorian Sacramentaries.[4]

MONDAY OF HOLY WEEK

Entrance Antiphon

This antiphon asks God to arise to the defense of the singers, who sound as Jesus may have sounded in the days before his passion. This is the traditional antiphon, and the third edition of the Missal continues using it, but with sense lines and a clarified citation indicating that it is not a direct quotation of Psalms 35 (34):1-2 and 140 (139):8, but is rather inspired by those verses. Actually, the difference is slight. The earliest record of an antiphon for this day, dating to the eighth century, cites Psalm 34:1.[5] It was expanded by one verse in the Missal prior to the Second Vatican Council, and the final reference to God as "mighty help" comes from the postconciliar Missal. Gradually this antiphon has expanded to show God's power over enemies, in order to set a confident tone at the beginning of Holy Week.

When this liturgy was under redevelopment after the Second Vatican Council, the study groups considered replacing it with one from the New Testament relating to the Eucharist or the mystery of redemption in general.[6] However, the traditional antiphon was retained.

Collect

In the collect the community prays for revival from weakness through the passion of God's only-begotten Son. This collect is traditional for this day. It has been in continuous usage since its appearance in eighth-century editions of the Gelasian and Gregorian Sacramentaries.[7] Because there is no earlier record of a Mass on this day, this is the only collect ever to be associated with today's Eucharist. The only change in the third edition of the Missal in Latin is the capitalization of the word *Unigeniti*, which accounts for the extra capital letters in the revised English translation of "Only Begotten" in this prayer.

Liturgy of the Word

The Lectionary for Mass assigns to this day Isaiah 42:1-7; Psalm 27 (26):1-3, 13-14; and John 12:1-11. The only passage that enjoys antiquity is the gospel; the other citations are new to the post–Vatican II liturgy.

As indicated above in the discussion on Palm Sunday, there is a history to hearing Isaiah 50:5-10 on this day. That reading has been reassigned to yesterday's Mass. This opened up a plan in which the four servant oracles from Isaiah could all be read on weekdays of Holy Week. The first three are proclaimed on Monday, Tuesday, and Wednesday respectively, and the fourth is the first reading each year on Good Friday. Although this first reading is relatively new to the history of the liturgy, it fits a broader plan in which those who attend daily Mass can experience more fully the prophecies pertaining to the ministry of Jesus.

The responsorial psalm was chosen because it resonates with the first reading. God calls the servant "a light for the nations," and the psalmist sings that the Lord is "light and salvation." The concluding verses offer hope of deliverance; the revised Holy Week liturgy never wallows in despair. It always holds the entire paschal mystery. There is no precedent for this psalm on this day in the history of Holy Week, but it forms a unit with the new first reading.

Evidence for reading from John 12 first appears in the earliest lectionary tradition, dating to the seventh century.[8] The first verse begins with the words "Six days before Passover," making it the obvious choice for Monday's gospel. Its placement on Monday accounts for the previous custom that deferred the passions according to Mark and Luke to Tuesday and Wednesday of this week. There was some discussion about moving this gospel to Saturday of the Fifth Week of Lent,[9] adjusting the chronology of events, but the traditional day prevailed.

Prayer over the Offerings

The community prays for the fruit of eternal life through the same gift God provided in mercy to cancel the judgment against their sins. The reference, of course, is to Jesus Christ, whose suffering wins redemption. This prayer first appeared in the Gelasian Sacramentary on Monday of Holy Week.[10] A different prayer appeared in the Gregorian Sacramentary, and that one enjoyed usage throughout the long history of the preconciliar Missal.[11] However, the Gelasian prayer, which is more expressive of this day's themes, was restored to this position after the Second Vatican Council.

Preface

The victory of the passion is proclaimed in the preface assigned to Monday, Tuesday, and Wednesday of this week. It acknowledges the approaching days of the Triduum, days of triumph over the ancient foe and of celebrating the mystery of redemption. This preface is based on one from the late Gelasian and Gregorian traditions[12] and was newly added to the Missal after the Second Vatican Council.[13]

Communion Antiphon

The psalmist asks God not to hide his face but to turn his ear and speedily answer in this day of distress. Nearly the entire history of this antiphon before the Second Vatican Council lists Psalm 35 (34):26, a verse that asks for retribution on the enemy.[14] It was replaced with a less vindictive verse. The third edition of the Missal leaves it unchanged, except that it refers the reader to Psalm 102 (101):3, rather than claim to be citing it exactly. The Vulgate updated the wording, but the Missal retains the former tradition. There is virtually no difference in meaning.

Prayer after Communion

The community prays that God will look upon the hearts of those dedicated to the sacred mysteries. This prayer originated in the Verona Sacramentary[15] and became a prayer over the people during Lent in the Gelasian Sacramentary.[16] The post–Vatican II Missal used it to replace the previous post-Communion prayer, which had been in force for many centuries.[17]

Prayer over the People

Although there had been a custom for concluding this liturgy with a prayer over the people, the first editions of the post–Vatican II Missal did not include one. This prayer was added to the third edition of the Missal. It was newly composed from two in the Verona Sacramentary, one from September[18] and one from July.[19] The community prays that it may celebrate the paschal festivities not only with bodily observance but with purity of mind.

This prayer is optional. It may be replaced with any other prayer over the people, or it may be omitted. However, using it continues the practice of offering a prayer over the people throughout the season of Lent.

TUESDAY OF HOLY WEEK

Entrance Antiphon

One can almost hear Jesus quoting this psalm, asking his Father not to hand him over to the foes pursuing him. The text is a slight variation from the new Vulgate, which accounts for the "cf." at the start of the citation. This antiphon replaces one that had been used on this day throughout its history prior to the Second Vatican Council, from Galatians 6:14, about glorying in the cross of the Lord Jesus Christ. That text is still used for the Holy Thursday evening Mass of the Lord's Supper. It was also sung on this day, probably because the passion according to Mark used to be proclaimed at this Mass.

Study Group 17 considered requiring red vesture on all the days from Palm Sunday through Good Friday,[20] but this was not accepted.

It would have created a passion time, a new designation for the final week of Lent. However, in keeping with the desire to move the Synoptic accounts of the passion to Palm Sunday, to redraw the Lectionary for these weekdays, and to highlight the entire paschal mystery, this decision gave Tuesday its own character, preliminary to the coming of the Triduum.

Collect

The community prays for a celebration of the Lord's Passion that will gain pardon for sins. This is the traditional collect for this day, in continuous use for many hundreds of years,[21] and originating in the eighth-century Gelasian tradition.[22] It made a little more sense as a prelude to the passion according to Mark, but its sentiments still apply to Tuesday's position within the flow of this week.

Liturgy of the Word

The readings for this day were new to the post–Vatican II Lectionary for Mass. The first reading is the second oracle of the servant of the Lord (Isa 49:1-6). It is read today as part of a sequence of the four oracles proclaimed throughout Holy Week. The first oracle was yesterday's first reading. This one replaces Jeremiah 11:18-20.[23] That reading was moved to Saturday of the Fourth Week of Lent to make room for Isaiah's oracle. Other passages have been heard on this day throughout history; the study group preparing the postconciliar Lectionary knew of an early tradition that used Wisdom 2:12-22, about the wicked plotting against the just, but this was assigned to Friday of the Fourth Week of Lent.[24]

The responsorial psalm (Ps 71 [70]:1-2, 3-4a, 5ab-6ab, 15, and 17) is also new to the Lectionary. It echoes the themes of rescue, as presented in the first reading. Its final stanzas indicate that God has provided strength since the time the psalmist spent in the womb and throughout the period of youth. It recalls the statement in the oracle that God called the servant from birth, even from the mother's womb.

The gospel (John 13:21-33, 36-38) announces Judas' betrayal. It concludes the readings from John's gospel that have dominated the weekday Lectionary throughout the second half of Lent. A similar passage appeared in a seventh-century Roman listing for the gospel on this day.[25] The current text replaces the passion according to Mark, which had been proclaimed on this day for many centuries. Mark's passion was abbreviated in the reforms of 1956.[26] But it eventually became

assigned to the Palm Sunday Mass in Year B of the post–Vatican II
Lectionary.

Prayer over the Offerings

The community members ask God to look favorably upon the offerings and to grant them a share in the fullness of the sacred gifts. This
prayer was new to the post–Vatican II Missal, but it was taken from
the formula for this day in the Gelasian Sacramentary.[27] It replaces one
that had been in use more recently for several centuries.[28]

Preface

The preface from yesterday is repeated today.

Communion Antiphon

Citing Paul's Letter to the Romans, the community sings that God
handed his only Son over for the sake of all. This antiphon was new to
the post–Vatican II Missal and replaced one that had been in use from
ninth-century records of antiphons for this day.[29] Psalm 69 (68):13-14
contrasted the enemy's threat with the psalmist's prayer for God's
mercy. It was replaced perhaps in favor of a New Testament passage
highlighting the salvific mission of the Son.

Prayer after Communion

The community prays that the gifts they have received as nourish-
ment will make them partakers of life eternal. The prayer was new to
the post–Vatican II Missal, replacing one that had been used for many
centuries.[30] The study group considered replacing it with the one from
the Gelasian Sacramentary for Tuesday of Holy Week,[31] but even that
was replaced with this one, whose origins are not clear.

Prayer over the People

The third edition of the Missal has added prayers over the people
throughout the weekdays of Lent. These may be used, replaced, or
omitted. The one that appears on this day is a slight reworking of the
prayer over the people in the Hadrian Supplement of the Gregorian
Sacramentary for the same occasion.[32] It prays that the people may
be cleansed of every seduction of former ways and made capable of
new holiness. The postconciliar study group had considered using the
prayer over the people from the Gelasian Sacramentary,[33] but it never
appeared in the post–Vatican II Missal.

WEDNESDAY OF HOLY WEEK

Entrance Antiphon

The antiphon invites all creation to bend the knee at the name of Jesus, who was obedient unto death, even death upon the cross (cf. Philippians 2:10, 8, 11). The "cf." indicates that the Latin text is the traditional antiphon for this day, but the new Vulgate has slightly altered it. This antiphon has been in place here ever since the earliest records of this liturgy.[34] The verses have always followed this nonsequential order.

Collect

The community prays for the grace of the resurrection from God, whose Son suffered on the cross to drive away the power of the enemy. This prayer has a long history in the Roman Rite, having been used on this day at least since the eighth century[35] at a Mass that included a scrutiny of catechumens. This may account for its exorcistic content. It may also explain why people used to be invited to kneel for silent prayer after the words "Let us pray," standing then for the text of the collect. For many centuries, it was the second of two collects assigned to this day, separated by a reading from Isaiah and a gradual.[36] The first collect did not carry over to the post–Vatican II Missal.

During the development of the revised English translation of the Mass, this became one of the most controversial prayers because it translated the Latin word *patibulum* as "gibbet," referring to the crossbeam and coming from the Latin words for putting something on display. The word appears only three times in the entire Missal: here, in the Good Friday reproaches, and in one of the appendix's optional private prayers that a priest may say before Mass. Still, some people regarded the word "gibbet" as a threat to one's comprehension of the entire translation. It has been replaced with the word "yoke."

Liturgy of the Word

The first reading (Isa 50:4-9a) is basically the passage that served on Monday of Holy Week for many centuries. Moved here, it continues the sequence of the oracles of the servant. This is the third, and it appears here following the previous two proclaimed on Monday and Tuesday of this week. It depicts a servant who receives blows without rebelling, not trying to avoid buffets and spitting. This passage replaces a reading that had been proclaimed for many centuries on this day: Isaiah 62:11; 63:1-7. That text, which proclaims God's vengeance on Edom, and whose usage on this day can be traced all the way back to the sixth century,[37] was removed not just from Holy Week but from the entire Lectionary. The study group felt that it could not be retained because of its wrath and vindictiveness.[38]

The verses of Psalm 69 (68):8-10, 21-22, 31, and 33-34 come from one who has borne insults and finds no support. The second stanza of this responsory contains the prophetic text about receiving vinegar to drink. It stands behind the actions of those who offered vinegar to Jesus on the cross (Matt 27:48; Mark 15:36; Luke 23:36; and John 19:29). It was added to the liturgy of this day in the post–Vatican II Lectionary.

The gospel (Matt 26:14-25) continues the sequence of events from yesterday's gospel of the betrayal of Judas and serves as a bridge to Thursday's account of the Last Supper. Egeria mentions the use of this passage in Jerusalem already in the fourth century. She says that when it was proclaimed, the people reacted with much groaning and weeping.[39] The same passage was in use on this day in an Ambrosian Rite Lectionary from the turn of the first millennium.[40] Today it replaces the passion according to St. Luke, which had been used on this day in the Roman Rite possibly from the fifth to the twentieth centuries.[41] The 1956 reform of Holy Week had abbreviated some of the verses. Now Luke's passion is heard on Year C of the Palm Sunday Mass.

There was a Roman custom in the eighth century to offer the same solemn intercessions from the Good Friday liturgy on this day as well.[42] This did not continue, but a sample form for the prayer of the faithful during Holy Week can be found in the appendix of the Missal.

Prayer over the Offerings

The community asks God that it may experience the grace of the Son's passion. This is the same prayer from the pre–Vatican II Missal. It originated in the Gelasian Sacramentary on this day.[43]

Preface

The same preface from Monday and Tuesday this week is repeated today.

Communion Antiphon

The Son of Man came to give his life as a ransom for many (Matt 20:28). This antiphon replaces the one from Psalm 102 (101):10, 13, 14, which had been in use for many hundreds of years, from the earliest record of antiphons to the twentieth century.[44] The text calls upon God's mercy in a time of human suffering. The revised antiphon fits the Missal's apparent desire to present the saving mission of Jesus as the subject of this communion song. It keeps the entire paschal mystery in view.

Prayer after Communion

The community prays for the conviction that it has received perpetual life through the death of Jesus Christ. This is the same prayer that appeared in the pre–Vatican II Missal.[45] Its earliest appearance is in the Gregorian Sacramentary.[46] Its theme has always been appropriate to this day.

Prayer over the People

The priest asks God that the people may partake of the paschal mysteries and await the gifts to come. Although this prayer is new to the third edition of the Missal, it originated in the Gelasian Sacramentary, but on Tuesday of Holy Week.[47] As with the prayers over the people on the preceding two days, it may be offered, replaced, or omitted.

Thursday of Holy Week [Holy Thursday]

1. All Masses without people to participate in them are forbidden. This most ancient tradition is retained. This rubric was in the second edition of the Roman Missal, but in a different location: just before the descriptions of the evening Mass of the Lord's Supper. It is moved here to govern the description of any Mass celebrated on this day, including the chrism Mass.

A funeral Mass may not be celebrated on Holy Thursday.[1] If a parish needs to celebrate a funeral, people may gather for a Funeral Outside of Mass.[2] It still includes the Liturgy of the Word and the various prayers for the deceased, but omits the Liturgy of the Eucharist.

THE CHRISM MASS

2. During this Mass the bishop blesses the oil of the sick and the oil of catechumens, and he consecrates the oil of chrism. The difference in the verbs indicates a hierarchy of the oils. Chrism is the most sublime of them all. Under other circumstances, a priest may bless the first two oils before he uses them. But only a bishop may consecrate chrism.

The texts are found in two different books. The main prayers over the oils come from the Roman Pontifical. The Roman Missal traditionally retains the parts that pertain to the Mass—the presidential prayers and the preface, for example. In previous English editions, the Sacramentary contained both groups of these texts. Although the prayers for the oil have always appeared in the *Pontificale Romanum*, previous editions of the Missal never said this. The third edition states explicitly for the first time that that is where the oil texts are to be found. However, the English-language Catholic Church does not have a separate Roman Pontifical. The prayers over the oils had been folded into an appendix of the Sacramentary to make them accessible. In truth, the only person who needs those prayers is the bishop, and it is therefore not necessary to include them in the Missal of every parish church.

Traditionally this Mass is celebrated in the morning hours. Here, the rubric means the morning hours of Holy Thursday. The 1956 reform of Holy Thursday called for the celebration to take place after Terce,[3] the first of the middle hours in the Breviary. That may have been influenced by evidence that the Mass was celebrated at the sixth hour (noon) in the time of Gregory the Great. The time after Terce was explicitly mentioned in the Roman-Germanic Pontifical.[4]

Early evidence for a blessing of oils can be found in the *Apostolic Tradition* 21:6-7.[5] The bishop gives thanks over one oil and calls it the oil of thanksgiving, and he exorcises another and calls it the oil of exorcism. These prayers immediately precede baptism; nowhere does the *Apostolic Tradition* state that the rites take place at the Easter Vigil. Still, it established a sequence in which the bishop prays over the oil soon to be used in the rites of initiation. The fifth-century *Life of Sylvester* says that chrism was consecrated on Holy Thursday, though it is not clear if it took place during the Eucharist.[6] The Gelasian Sacramentary provides separate texts for the chrism Mass and the evening Mass,[7] but the Gregorian Sacramentary combines them both: when the bishop presided for the Mass of the Lord's Supper, he consecrated chrism and blessed oil.[8] This custom eventually prevailed[9] until the 1956 reform, which restored the chrism Mass.[10] A draft of the postconciliar reform considered changing the title from "Chrism Mass" to "Morning Mass in the Cathedral Church" or even "Cathedral Mass,"[11] but the traditional title from the Gelasian Sacramentary held, which also accented the difference between this Mass and that of the Lord's Supper.

3. If the clergy and the people find it difficult to gather with the bishop on Holy Thursday, the chrism Mass may be anticipated on some other day near Easter. Some dioceses exercise this option earlier in Holy Week; others choose Thursday of the previous week. In this case, "near to Easter" means "before Easter," as the Circular Letter indicates, "The chrism and the oil of catechumens is to be used in the celebration of the sacraments of initiation on Easter night."[12] The previous editions of the Missal said the "blessing" could be transferred to another day, but the third edition clarifies that the "Mass" may be transferred.

The idea of transferring the Mass to a different day came from mission countries. "Since today, especially in regions of the missions, it may not be possible for the clergy and the people to gather on the morning of Holy Thursday for the chrismal Mass, and again in the evening for the Mass of the Lord's Supper, it pleases the Relators to allow bishops, for submitted reasons, to consecrate chrism on another day, but near and before Easter."[13] The permission was perhaps easy to grant because the earliest evidence for blessing oils from the *Apostolic*

Tradition was not connected to a particular day, but rather connected to baptism. In practice, the idea of transferring the chrism Mass to another day has appealed to first world countries, where parish staffs embrace the demands of the Triduum so vigorously that celebrating the chrism Mass at another time relieves some stress for them.

4. The bishop concelebrates with his priests, showing their common priesthood with him. It is appropriate for all priests to participate and receive communion at this Mass under both kinds. The unity of the priesthood is best shown when priests come from different regions of the diocese. Even though the focus of the Mass is on the chrism and the other oils, another dynamic is introduced through them: the ministry that priests share with the bishop. The Mass is not just about oils but about those committed to serving the community through their use. The bishop has the fundamental responsibility to administer the initiation rites, and priests share this task with their bishop. Although many have accused this liturgy of being too clerical a celebration, it should manifest a spirit of service through the unity of the presbyterate in the mission of the local diocese gathered under its head, the bishop. Some priests have opted not to concelebrate the chrism Mass in order to counteract the perceived clericalism of the celebration. However, if there is one Mass priests should concelebrate each year, this is it.

The first indication of concelebration comes from Amalarius of Metz (+ ca. 850). Commenting on the blessing of the oil of the sick, he notes the rubric "The Holy Father and all the priests bless" and explains: "It is the custom of the Roman Church that in the consecration of the sacrifice of Christ the priests are present and consecrate at the same time with the pontiff in their words and with their hands. And, because the consecration of this oil is included in this rubric, the priests and the pontiff must consecrate the oil in the same way as the others."[14] The exact meaning of this is not clear, but it opened the way for the practice that has become common: priests concelebrating with their bishop at the Eucharist and joining him in the consecration of chrism (see p. 52 below). In 1952 the Pontifical Commission for the Reform of the Sacred Liturgy discussed the possibility of concelebrating the chrism Mass, but they could reach no consensus. Even so, the possibility opened.[15] Concelebration was to become more common after the Second Vatican Council, but Pope Paul VI gave permission to concelebrate the chrism Mass in 1965.[16] This started to change the perceived meaning of the celebration from the oils to priesthood. The

Ceremonial of Bishops says that the practice manifests the communion of priests and bishop, as well as their shared ministry to build up, sanctify, and rule the people of God.[17]

It seems unusual for the rubrics to tell the concelebrants to receive Communion, even under both kinds. This clarification was needed after the Second Vatican Council because prior to this time only the bishop received Communion at the chrism Mass. None of the priests did. None of the people did. And the bishop was instructed to receive both the Body and Blood of Christ.[18]

5. According to a custom handed down through many generations, the blessing of the oil of the sick takes place before the end of the eucharistic prayer. Prayers for the other two oils take place after Communion. However, for pastoral reasons, the entire rite may be conducted after the Liturgy of the Word. This permission has always been in the post–Vatican II Roman Pontifical, but it is clarified here in the Missal's third edition.

The traditional arrangement seems almost illogical to those familiar with the post–Vatican II rites of baptism, confirmation, ordination, marriage, and anointing of the sick. In every case, the featured ritual takes place after the Liturgy of the Word. That is why the rubrics now permit the prayers over the oils to follow that model.

Nonetheless, the traditional arrangement has its own internal logic. To start at the end, the relationship between the oil of catechumens and the oil of chrism has been obvious ever since the *Apostolic Tradition*, which indicates that the bishop prays over both of them, though in the reverse order, starting with chrism, the more important one, and then proceeding to the oil of exorcism or the oil of catechumens. The placement of these two prayers after Communion has more to do with the chrism, which is consecrated rather than blessed. It seemed appropriate that the Eucharist should be consecrated before anything else. The order of the oils was reversed, making chrism the climax of the three. The oil of the sick was incorporated into the Roman Canon just before its close, near the words where the community thanks God for many other gifts, not just the bread and wine. The *Apostolic Tradition* knew a custom of blessing foodstuffs, including an oil for health, and the instructions were included right after the eucharistic prayer.[19] There seems to have been a custom of blessing other foods and oils before the eucharistic prayer was over. The blessing of the oil of the sick naturally slipped into that position at a Mass dedicated to prayers over other oils.

The Gelasian and Gregorian sacramentaries do not agree on the sequence of events. In the Gelasian, the blessing of the oil of catechumens precedes the consecration of chrism, whereas these are reversed in the Gregorian. The Gelasian puts them both after the breaking of the bread and before Communion. Its consecration of chrism is extended with an exorcism and another prayer.[20]

After the Second Vatican Council, Study Group 21, which worked on the revised Pontifical, considered many changes to the chrism Mass. In an early meeting, a bare majority—eight of fifteen—strongly requested that the "consecration of the three oils happen at the same time in the Mass," namely, before the end of the Canon. They gave theological reasons: it would give clarity to the liturgy and express the unity of the oils instituted for the salvation of the faithful. They also wondered why the noblest oil was consecrated outside the Canon. They gave historical reasons: the medieval sacramentaries bear witness to a variety of practices; in the past, the length of the prayers prohibited including them all in the Canon. The Canon would not be interrupted as much as it would unify the sacraments of the church with the Eucharist itself.[21] Eventually the option for praying over all the oils together prevailed, but it was placed outside the eucharistic prayer.

There was some discussion about whether or not the oil of exorcism would be kept at all. The study group considered making it optional before the baptism of infants. If its use was retained, a priest could bless it before using it, making its inclusion in the chrism Mass unnecessary. Similarly, could not the oil of the sick be removed from the chrism Mass because a priest could bless it as he needed it?[22] These ideas did not override the long tradition of having the bishop bless the oils of the catechumens and of the sick during the chrism Mass.[23]

The study group considered several options for the time to consecrate the chrism: within the Canon, after Communion, or after the Liturgy of the Word.[24] The participants were aware of a variety of traditions but settled on the options of retaining the present order or putting the oils together after the Liturgy of the Word.[25] Those alternatives remain.

6. Jesus Christ has made a kingdom and priests for his God and Father. To him be glory for ever and ever. Citing the book of Revelation, the entrance antiphon has the community singing, "Christ has made us priests." This replaces the historical antiphon for this day from Exodus 30:25, 31 and Psalm 89 (88):2, in which God gives Moses

instructions for mixing the aromatic oil with which Moses will anoint Aaron and his sons as priests. The group preparing the 1956 reform considered replacing the introit with a passage from St. Paul, but no decision was made.[26] The first meeting of the study group on the liturgical year likewise made no change to the introit or the offertory antiphon because "the allusions to anointings can be understood equally toward the anointing of the baptized-confirmed faithful and of the anointing of priests."[27] Still, it was replaced with a New Testament text that probably strove to achieve the same meaning through having the community recall its own priesthood.

The Gloria is sung. This was also true in the pre–Vatican II Missal.[28]

7. In the collect the members of the community pray that, as sharers in the same consecration that made Jesus Christ and Lord, they may be witnesses in the world to the redemption. This was a newly composed prayer for the post–Vatican II Missal. It alludes to Acts 2:33-36, where Peter proclaims that the Holy Spirit has been poured out upon the community and that God has made Jesus both Lord and Christ. The prayer's references to a New Testament passage and to the Holy Spirit made it a stronger prayer than the one it replaced, which spoke of two priesthoods, even though that one had been used on this day ever since the Gelasian Sacramentary.[29]

Some people have wondered if the prayer refers to ordained priests or to the entire Christian community. In context, it can only refer to the community. The prayer is in the first person plural. The consecration to be like Christ comes with baptism and confirmation.

8. After the reading of the gospel, the bishop delivers the homily based on the readings from the Liturgy of the Word. He addresses the people and the priests about the priestly anointing and exhorts his priests to be faithful in their ministry, inviting them to renew their promises in public. This rubric has been relocated in the third edition of the Missal from its place in the introductory remarks of this Mass in the previous editions. It fits more logically here. The study group preparing the post–Vatican II liturgy imagined that the homily would treat the mystery of the oils, making it the fitting prelude to the blessing of the chrism.[30]

The readings in question are new to the post–Vatican II Lectionary. Prior to the council, the readings were James 5:13-16, concerning the anointing of the sick; Psalm 28 (27):7-8, praising God as the refuge of salvation for his anointed one; and Mark 6:7-13, in which Jesus sends out the twelve to anoint the sick. The emphasis was placed on the one oil that was arguably not at the center of the celebration.

By 1966 already, these readings had changed to Isaiah 61:1-4, 6, 8-9; Ps 27:7-8; and Luke 4:16-22.[31] The post–Vatican II Lectionary for Mass retained the first reading and the gospel with minor variations (Isa 61:1-3a, 6a, 8b-9; Luke 4:16-21), exchanged the gradual psalm with Psalm 89 (88):21-22, 25, 27, and added Revelation 1:5-8, which had also supplied the entrance antiphon. The gospel tells of Jesus reading about his mission as God's anointed one, and one of the passages he cites is the prophecy in the first reading. The psalm tells of David's anointing, a foreshadowing of the anointing of Jesus and of his followers. History records other readings that were proclaimed on this day, some of which were influenced by the story of the Last Supper.[32] But in the early days the chrism Mass and the Mass of the Lord's Supper were the same celebration. The current Lectionary opts for a theological reflection on the mystery of anointing: what it is for the followers of Christ to be called Christians, a priestly people.

Renewal of Priestly Promises

9. After the homily, the bishop speaks to the priests and invites them to renew their promises. He also asks the people to pray for the priests and for him as their bishop.

Pope Paul VI added this to the chrism Mass at the suggestion of Cardinal John Wright, Prefect of the Congregation for Clergy. After the Council, a great many priests and religious were leaving active ministry. This dialogue was added in an attempt to stabilize the faithfulness of priests and to challenge them to renew their commitment each year. This Mass was chosen because Holy Thursday is regarded as the anniversary of the day Jesus instituted the priesthood by instituting the Eucharist, and because of a practical matter: priests and the bishop were gathering on this day for the chrism Mass. The insertion of this dialogue has been criticized because it confuses the purpose of the chrism Mass, which is primarily to consecrate chrism and bless the other oils for the administration of sacraments for the sake of the faithful. The chrism Mass manifests the unity of priests and bishop around this ministry, but the renewal of promises has seemed to some as an introspective intrusion on a liturgy struggling to reclaim its purpose. Concerns were raised as early as 1964 by the study group assigned to the liturgical year:

> To commemorate the institution of the priesthood in the chrismal Mass is to separate it from its essential root, i.e. from the institution of the

Eucharist. . . . The priesthood (in the hierarchical sense) has no stronger connection with chrism (and the other oils) than the priesthood of the baptized and confirmed. . . . Such commemoration of priesthood does not pertain to the historico-mystical celebration of salvation history, which Holy Week precisely and eminently intends, and which the modern liturgical restoration desires (cf. Constitution on the Liturgy n. 6 and 107). If a so-called ideological celebration of priesthood is desired, would it not suffice to have this on the feast of Corpus Christi?[33]

Some dioceses have expanded the focus on priesthood by hosting a day of renewal for priests in conjunction with the chrism Mass. All these customs have merit, but they demand extra care to the overall celebration of the liturgy, so that priesthood does not draw attention away from the oils.

10. The Creed is not said. This has always been the case. This paragraph makes no mention of the prayer of the faithful, which has had a curious history. The first editions of the post–Vatican II Missal said explicitly that the prayer of the faithful was also omitted. However, the Ceremonial of Bishops refers to the intentions that are found in the Roman Missal (Sacramentary).[34] In 2002, the third edition of the Roman Missal said in this paragraph that the prayer of the faithful follows the renewal of promises and that the Creed is omitted. But the 2008 reprint of the third edition omitted any reference to the prayer of the faithful.[35] It appears then that the reference in the Ceremonial of Bishops remains in force. The final part of the renewal, which is addressed to the people and invites their prayer, is the prayer of the faithful. Most unusually, it is led by the bishop, not by another minister, and it is only two petitions long.

It is permitted to have the blessing and consecration of oils at this point in the Mass. Commentary on that section of the Pontifical will follow these paragraphs on the texts in the Roman Missal.

11. In the prayer over the offerings, the community prays that their old way of life may be replaced with newness and salvation. This same prayer can be found in the Gelasian Sacramentary for this day.[36] The study group on the liturgical year considered replacing it with a prayer from the Verona Sacramentary, one that highlighted the ministerial priesthood, but it was not advanced into the post–Vatican II Missal.[37]

The previous editions of the post–Vatican II Missal carried a heading here to indicate the Liturgy of the Eucharist. This has been removed. The heading for the renewal of priestly promises seems to stand over the rest of the Mass, but it pertains only to paragraph 9.

12. The preface was newly composed for the post–Vatican II Missal. It is the same one used in the ordination rites. It praises God for sharing the ministry of Christ's priesthood with human beings. The choice of this theme again tipped the meaning of the chrism Mass away from the oils. The complete text of the preface appears here together with the notes for singing; this will make the preface easier to find and should encourage chanting it.

When the first eucharistic prayer is used at this Mass, the inserts for Holy Thursday's Mass of the Lord's Supper are not included.[38] They were not in the Gelasian Sacramentary's presentation of the chrism Mass, but the Gregorian Sacramentary did put them there. At the time, however, there was only one Mass on Holy Thursday, so the inclusion was necessary. Even if the chrism Mass is celebrated on Holy Thursday, the insertions belong more properly to the evening liturgy.

In 1965, some changes were made to reduce the theme of peace from the Liturgy of the Eucharist at the chrism Mass. The third petition of the *Agnus Dei* was changed from "grant us peace" to "have mercy on us," as had been the custom at funeral Masses. The prayer recalling Jesus' gift of peace was omitted.[39] These recalled similar practices in the Gelasian Sacramentary, which forbade the bishop to give the greeting of peace and the sign of peace before receiving Communion.[40] These changes, which probably intended to dramatize the day on which Judas betrayed Jesus with a kiss, did not last when the postconciliar Missal was published.

In the pre-1956 version of this celebration, which combined elements of the Mass of the Lord's Supper, the bishop alone received Communion.[41] The deacon placed another host in a chalice or another vessel, which was to be reserved for the bishop's Communion in the Mass on Good Friday.[42] Today these practices have been abolished. All the faithful are encouraged to participate in Communion at this Mass.

13. In the communion antiphon the psalmist sings of the mercies and fidelity of the Lord. A number of other antiphons had been suggested or used throughout history. The pontifical commission preparing the 1956 reform adopted a gospel verse about Jesus sending the apostles out to anoint the sick.[43] In 1965 this was replaced with Psalm 45 (44):7, about God anointing the one who loves justice and hates wickedness. The study group on the liturgical year proposed an antiphon that would be taken from one of its recommended Scripture passages in the Lectionary for this day: John 17:12-13, 15, from the High Priestly Prayer of Jesus; or 1 Peter 2:9, concerning the royal priesthood

of the faithful.[44] In the end, the post–Vatican II Missal chose the opening verse of Psalm 89 (88), which seems nondescript by itself, but introduces the same psalm that serves as the responsorial for this Mass, one that concerns the anointing of David.

14. In the prayer after Communion, the community prays that those renewed by these sacraments may become the pleasing fragrance of Christ. This prayer was newly composed for the post–Vatican II Missal. The first part of it is a prayer that concluded two Masses in the Gregorian Sacramentary,[45] whereas the conclusion refers to 2 Corinthians 2:15, where Paul calls Christians the pleasing fragrance of Christ. The prayer it replaces had been in force for several hundred years but lacked antiquity with the earliest sources.[46] The current prayer's sentiment resembles the prayer over the offerings, asking for a renewed mind, passing from old to new things.

15. The reception of the sacred oils may take place in individual parishes either before the evening Mass of the Lord's Supper or at another time that seems more appropriate. This rubric is new to the third edition of the Missal. In the United States, the Sacramentary Supplement has included a brief service for this presentation, to take place during the presentation of the gifts. However, these oils are not the equivalent of the bread, wine, and gifts for the poor that typically make up the elements of the procession. They are in a sense a gift of the bishop to the parish, not an offering of the parishioners to God. It is not clear if the "reception" of the oils implies anything formal or liturgical. In all practicality, they just need to be delivered to the parish before they can be used at the Easter Vigil.

The Blessing of Oils and the Consecration of Chrism

INTRODUCTION

1. The bishop is to be regarded as the high priest of his flock, whose life in Christ in some way derives from and depends on the bishop. The chrism Mass is among the principal expressions of the fullness of the bishop's priesthood. It signifies his unity with his priests, especially by means of their concelebration. The newly baptized and confirmed are anointed with chrism consecrated by the bishop. In addition, the oil of catechumens and the oil of the sick are prepared respectively for those preparing for baptism and those seeking relief in their sufferings.

These opening paragraphs focus on the bishop, partly because he presides over this liturgy, but also because the instructions for its execution are found in the Roman Pontifical, the book of ceremonies over which a bishop presides. This introduction will be read principally by a bishop, and it explains to him the significance of the liturgy he is about to oversee. It does not mention the upcoming renewal of priestly promises because that practice was appended to the liturgy, but that renewal is best seen within the framework of the association the priests have with the bishop's ministry.

2. The Old Testament states that kings, priests, and prophets were anointed, and Christians believe that these events prefigured Jesus Christ, whose title means "Anointed of the Lord." Each Christian is incorporated into the paschal mystery of Christ through baptism, thus sharing in his royal and prophetic priesthood. In confirmation they receive the anointing of the Holy Spirit. The oil of catechumens strengthens the effect of the exorcisms, helping those preparing for baptism to renounce Satan and sin before they are reborn. The oil of the sick helps Christians seek healing, bear evils, and obtain forgiveness.

Immediately, the introduction shifts its focus from the ministry of the bishop to the benefits offered the people of God. This paragraph concerns each Christian, for each one shares in the priesthood of Jesus Christ.

THE MATTER

3. Olive oil or oil from other plants is used. This represents a shift in the tradition. Formerly, only olive oil was proper for sacramental anointings. However, as the church has spread throughout the world, believers populated regions where olives were scarce. As the post–Vatican II study group on the Pontifical was preparing its work on this liturgy, it opened with this general principle: "Any oil fit for anointing the human body is appropriate matter of the sacrament."[47] The wording did not enter the final version of the rite, which chose to specify the source of oil (plants) rather than its purpose (anointing). In the end, it reaffirms the close link between Catholic sacramental practice and the world of nature.

The heading for this section, "oils" in the first translation, is more properly "matter," referring to the scholastic term still used in sacramental theology.

4. Chrism is a mixture of oil and some fragrant substance, such as perfumes. The traditional recipe of mixing olive oil and balsam is no longer required, probably again because of the difficulty in obtaining these elements in certain areas of the Catholic world. Similar freedoms

have never been offered for the bread and wine of the Eucharist, by contrast, but the sacramental oils may now come from regional substances.

5. Mixing the chrism may be done privately or by the bishop in the public liturgy. The wording implies that anyone can mix the perfume with the oil if it is desirable to do so in advance. But during the liturgy, the responsibility falls to the bishop. Traditionally, the bishop has mixed the chrism just before consecrating it during the Mass, but the symbolism has not been readily apprehended or appreciated by all. In fact, the ceremony was ridiculed during the Protestant Reformation.[48] The option for private preparation responds to such sensibilities.

THE MINISTER

6. Only a bishop may consecrate chrism. This preserves a long-standing practice of the church. Although the other two oils may be blessed by priests, chrism must be consecrated by a bishop. This shows the universality of his ministry throughout the diocese. Whenever a priest baptizes or confirms under the proper circumstances, he does so with chrism consecrated by the bishop.

7. The oil of catechumens is blessed by the bishop during the chrism Mass if the conference of bishops retains its use. As indicated above, there was some dispute after the Second Vatican Council about continuing the use of the oil of catechumens. This paragraph indicates that a conference of bishops may abandon it altogether, in which case the blessing is omitted from the chrism Mass.

Priests may bless this oil in the case of the baptism of adults in the liturgy in which the anointing takes place.[49] The same permission does not appear in the Rite of Baptism for Children. Apparently, anointing an infant moments before baptism seems significantly less important than anointing an adult for whom the oil's purpose could be extended through a longer period of preparation for baptism. The anointing with the oil of catechumens is always optional, but if the oil is inaccessible for an infant baptism, the priest omits the anointing; he does not bless new oil.

8. The oil of the sick is to be blessed by a bishop or a priest. It is included in the chrism Mass, but in cases of true necessity, any priest may bless this oil. This permission exemplifies the church's pastoral care for the sick. So anxious is the church to offer this sacrament that permission is granted to a priest to bless the oil if none is available at the moment he needs it.[50]

THE DAY OF BLESSING

9. Ordinarily, the bishop presides over this celebration on the morning of Holy Thursday. The 1956 revision of the liturgy specified that it should take place "after Terce," or not before 9:00 a.m.[51] This is the old tradition, which allows those to be baptized at the Easter Vigil to be anointed with the freshest chrism possible. There is perhaps a secondary symbol of the bishop gathering with his priests and people for the Eucharist on Holy Thursday, the day Jesus instituted the Eucharist at table with his disciples. However, this symbol works more naturally with the evening celebration of the Lord's Supper.

10. Another day may be chosen if it is difficult for the priests and people to gather with their bishop on Holy Thursday, but it should be a day near Easter. The chosen date should be "near" Easter, but the implication is "shortly before" Easter. It would be disadvantageous to the celebration of initiation if the consecration of new chrism took place afterward. See comments on paragraph 3 of the chrism Mass above.

THE PLACE OF THE BLESSING IN THE LITURGICAL ACTION

11. Traditionally, the oil of the sick is blessed before the end of the eucharistic prayer, but the other two oils are blessed and consecrated after Communion. As stated above in the comments on paragraph 5 of the chrism Mass, the reason has to do with the historical evolution of these rites.

12. However, the entire rite may take place after the Liturgy of the Word. This permission, new to the history of the chrism Mass, was accepted after the Second Vatican Council in the light of other ceremonies taking place at a similar moment in different Masses. All one needs are "pastoral reasons," and these are not specified. However, in the pastoral-friendly postconciliar era, this permission conceded that the spiritual formation of the people would probably be enhanced if they witnessed special rituals taking place at a consistent place within the liturgical action. The historical reasons for the traditional arrangement of the blessings are obscure, and the transposition of the ceremonies to this part of the chrism Mass fit the generic postconciliar sequence of liturgical events.

The Blessing of Oils and the Consecration of Chrism

PREPARATIONS

13. The rubrics divide the preparations between those outside and inside the sanctuary of the church. This distinction is new to the

postconciliar liturgy, but the preconciliar liturgy began with a very similar list of preparations.[52] Outside the sanctuary, the sacristy may be used, but another appropriate place is acceptable. What makes it appropriate? The rubrics do not say, but the location of the sacristy will probably influence the determination that another site should be used. All the items set aside in this place are the elements to be brought forward in the procession of the gifts. This suggests that the usual location for setting items for that procession is the best starting point for the procession of the oils, and these should be placed there before the Eucharist begins. The sacristy is mentioned because it was the traditional place to prepare the oils prior to the celebration in the preconciliar ritual. Perfume is also set with these elements if the bishop is to mix it with the oil during the Eucharist.

The elements carried in the procession of the gifts are listed as "bread, wine, and water," but other liturgical documents are not consistent about including water in the procession of gifts. The Order of Mass 22 and GIRM 73 do not mention it; however, GIRM 118c permits water in the procession, and GIRM 72.1 says that "wine with water" is brought to the altar, though this could refer to the practice of the deacon preparing the wine with the water at a side table and then bringing that vessel to the altar. The custom of carrying to the altar some bread and wine mixed with water can be traced to the second-century Justin Martyr,[53] but in that case the water was already mixed with the wine. The custom endures in many places, though other churches restrict the procession of the gifts to the bread and wine, the principal symbols of the Eucharist.

Two items are to be set in the sanctuary: a table for the oils and a chair for the bishop. Note that the table is to be set where the people can see it and take part in the liturgical action. Once again, the active participation of the people is stressed as one of the key elements in the observance of Holy Week. The chair for the bishop, also known as the faldstool, is used only if he presides for this part of the ceremony in front of the altar. Arguably, if his normal chair, the cathedra, is situated where people can see him and the action, he could be seated there. Setting out the faldstool was part of the preconciliar preparations, so its usage is still permitted.[54]

THE RITE OF BLESSING

14. Not only is the chrism Mass to be concelebrated, but the priests who come should represent different regions of the diocese. If not

every priest can be there, representatives should be. This rubric describes priests as witnesses and coworkers with the bishop. These same words appeared in the Roman-Germanic Pontifical and have been retained to tell of the relationship between priest and bishop.[55] Priests testify to the bishop's ministry, and they share in it.

15. The preparation of the ministers and the execution of the Liturgy of the Word take place according to the Rite of Concelebration. This was the wording in the preconciliar rubric of 1966;[56] today it probably refers to the GIRM, where such instructions are found in 209–13. This reference avoids the creation of new rubrics and keeps consistent the practices pertaining to concelebration. Earlier drafts of this work still mentioned the role of the subdeacon,[57] but Pope Paul VI eliminated the subdiaconate in 1973 with his apostolic letter *Ministeria Quaedam*.

In the entrance procession, the deacons who will assist with the oils precede the concelebrating priests to the altar. This clarification was needed because different deacons precede and follow concelebrating priests when the bishop presides. Two deacons walk with the bishop, but the deacon who carries the gospel book and any other deacons present precede the concelebrating priests, who also walk in front of the bishop.[58] It appears that the deacons who will assist with the oils would follow the one who bears the Book of the Gospels.

16. Whether or not the blessing and consecration take place immediately after the Liturgy of the Word, the vessels are carried to the altar after the renewal of priestly promises during the procession of the gifts. Prior to the council, each oil was carried forward immediately before the bishop's prayer over it; first the oil of sick near the end of the Roman Canon, and then the other two oils together after Communion.[59] The postconciliar liturgy moves the procession of oils to this point, drawing together instead the procession of the oils with the procession of the gifts.[60] One of the first drafts of the postconciliar rite carries this note: "Although the procession of the oils does not have an ancient or a Roman origin, it pleases nevertheless to preserve it for a pastoral reason, and it becomes as it were a solemn procession of the oblation. For like the bread and wine, the oils are matter for consecration—though certainly not for the same reason—and therefore for offering."[61]

GIRM 73 says that a typical procession of the gifts includes the elements that will become the Body and Blood of Christ; money or other gifts for the poor or for the church are also appropriate. To include the oils in this procession may seem to blur its purpose and bears some evidence of an expedient solution to the need of bringing them forward without unnecessarily complicating the liturgy. However, the long tradition concerning the oil of the sick is that its blessing was included right within the eucharistic prayer, recalling an even earlier tradition that the faithful carried forth various gifts for a blessing. The congruence of these elements in this particular procession says more about how they will be treated within this liturgy than it says about their function in the eucharistic sacrifice.

Deacons carry the oil, but if there are no deacons, then priests do. In either case, ministers assist. The faithful bring forward the bread, wine, and water. The rubric seems to distinguish ministers from faithful. In practice, some communities have members of the faithful assist deacons in carrying forward the oils. This was explicitly promoted in an early draft of the preconciliar liturgy, which said, "There is no objection if the oil that is to be blessed for the sick or for catechumens is carried by the faithful themselves."[62] The idea of having presumably vested ministers assist with the oils stems from the preconciliar practice.[63] The only explicit requirement today is that the oil for chrism be carried not by a layperson but by a deacon or a priest, to heighten the significance of that particular oil. One suspects that the church permits the involvement of various lay ministers in the procession for the sake of areas where the bishop may not have access to many deacons and priests; however, communities promoting the involvement of lay ministers in preparing people for the sacraments have profitably included them in the procession of oils.

The rubric describes the complete procession in two movements: first the participants go to the place where the oils have been prepared, and then they process to the altar. The sacristy is still mentioned as one option for the location of the vessels, but this is influenced by the preconciliar custom. Although the rubric clearly says that the ministers carry the vessels to the altar, it probably means the sanctuary, where a table for the oils has been prepared (see paragraph 13). However, paragraph 18 says more specifically that they bring the vessels to the altar or the chair, wherever the bishop is at the time.

The order of procession is noteworthy. If the bishop is going to mix the chrism, the vessel of perfume comes first. In the preconciliar liturgy, this vessel arrived after Communion.[64] The oil of the sick had already been carried in, blessed, and carried away. In the procession, a subdeacon carried the vessel of balsam, and then deacons followed him with the oils to be used for chrism and the oil of catechumens. In the revised liturgy, which has no subdeacon, a minister bringing the vessel of perfume leads the way. This perhaps heightens anticipation around the mixing of the chrism, while keeping the three oils together in better visual balance. The vessel for the oil of catechumens comes next if the conference of bishops has approved its use. Then comes the one for the oil of the sick, and finally the one for chrism. The order of these oils differs from the one in the preconciliar liturgy, which put the oil of catechumens last, perhaps because it was blessed last, in keeping with the practice from the *Apostolic Tradition*,[65] and perhaps because it kept the elements for mixing chrism together.

Theoretically, the procession can be simplified. Someone may have mixed perfume into the oil for chrism before Mass began; the bishops of a conference may have discontinued the use of the oil of catechumens. There may be only two vessels involved. But it is common to see four—three for oil, one for perfume.

In the preconciliar liturgy, a thurifer led the two processions of the oils.[66] The revised liturgy omits any reference to incense in this procession, probably because it now takes place with the procession of the gifts. At a typical Mass, incense may be used once the gifts have been placed on the altar, but not during the procession. Furthermore, the oils have not yet been blessed and consecrated. They are just oil at this point.

17. The hymn "O Redeemer" or another appropriate song is sung as the procession moves through the church. This replaces the offertory chant. However, most people are unaware that there is an offertory chant at all, much less that one is being replaced here. Offertory chants for the entire liturgical year can be found in the *Graduale Romanum* and the *Graduale Simplex*, books that few parishes have within reach; the texts for these antiphons do not appear in the postconciliar Roman Missal. These chants are usually quite florid, and each text represents a verse or two of Scripture. "O Redeemer" actually appears in both versions of the *Graduale* as the text to be sung on this day. The difference is that it is a hymn, not a chanted biblical verse. Prior to the council, there was an offertory antiphon for this day: "You love justice and hate wickedness; therefore God, your God has anointed you with the oil of gladness" (Ps 45 [44]:7).[67] However, also prior to the council, there was no procession of the gifts, and the procession of the oils took place in two steps—one before the end of the Roman Canon and the other after Communion. "O Redeemer" used to be sung for the second of these, the procession of the oils for chrism and catechumens.[68]

The refrain simply asks the Redeemer to receive the song of those joining their voices. The verses, however, all refer to chrism. The faithful sing of the oil they present to God, oil made from trees that God created. They ask God to consecrate the oil for its purposes: protection from the Evil One, the renewal of people in baptism, the bestowal of holy gifts, and light for their lives. They also pray that this feast may be a day free from the corruption of time, a day made holy by God. The hymn has been part of the liturgy at least since the Roman-Germanic Pontifical.[69] It seems not to be older than Carolingian times.[70] The text of the hymn did not appear in the 1985 Sacramentary in English. Any other hymn may replace this one, but there is a long tradition behind its association with the chrism Mass.

18. The bishop receives the gifts when the bearers reach the altar or the chair. Under normal circumstances, the gifts are carried to "an appropriate place."[71] In the preconciliar liturgy, the vessels were carried to the bishop, who was sitting on the faldstool in front of the specially prepared table, facing the altar.[72] Although it is permissible for the bishop to be at the altar, it is more in keeping with the nature of the procession and the purpose of the altar if he receives the gifts at the chair.

The deacon (or priest) carrying the oil for chrism presents it first, probably because it is the most significant of the oils. This happened in the second procession of the oils in the preconciliar liturgy also, but of course the oil of the sick had already been presented and blessed.[73] Revised preconciliar rubrics had the oil of the sick coming after the other two, and the vessel of balsam was presented to the bishop last without any announcement.[74]

The deacon announces the name of the oil to the bishop. He does this in a loud voice, presumably so that all can hear. The same instruction about volume appears in the very first record of this announcement from the thirteenth-century Pontifical of William Durandus.[75]

The bishop takes the vessel and hands it to a deacon. In practice, some dioceses have the oil in extremely large vessels, and the bishop symbolically and momentarily grasps the vessel before others take it away. It is placed on the table that was prepared in the sanctuary before the service begins. It is not placed on the altar. The other vessels are brought forward, first the oil of the sick, then the oil of catechumens, and a similar procedure unfolds. In each case, the one who carries the oil announces its name to the bishop. Oddly, the oils are presented in a different order from the one in which they were processed, different again from the order in which they will be blessed and consecrated. In practice, this is not always observed.

According to the notes of an early draft of the preconciliar liturgy, this presentation of the oils was retained in the revision because "it enlivens and procures the active participation of the people."[76] It also says that the presentation of the oil is "the most recent element of the entire rite," but it still refers to a thirteenth-century practice.

19. If the traditional sequence of events happens, in which the oil of the sick will be blessed at the end of the eucharistic prayer, the Mass continues as indicated in the rite of concelebration. This copies the rubric from the revised preconciliar liturgy of 1966,[77] but the rubrics for concelebration, as indicated above, are found in the postconciliar GIRM.

Alternatively, the blessing and consecration of all the oils may take place immediately, in which case the liturgy is interrupted at this point for the blessing of the oil of the sick.

The Blessing of the Oil of the Sick

20. If the blessing of the oil of the sick takes place at the end of the eucharistic prayer, it comes before the doxology unless Eucharistic Prayer I is being offered, in which case it precedes the words, "through whom you continue to make all these good things," the brief section that precedes the doxology. That is its traditional location, where the oil probably becomes included in the "good things" to which that line refers. In its origins, this section of the prayer probably acknowledged other gifts that had been brought forward, not just the bread and wine. By placing the procession of the oils together with the procession of the gifts, the postconciliar liturgy has brought more coherence to these words in those places where the blessing of the oil of the sick takes place at this time.

The bishop remains at the altar, and the one who carried the vessel to him now returns to hold it as he offers the prayer. In the preconciliar liturgy, the bishop left the altar and took up a position at the faldstool, where he received the oil and then blessed it, turning toward the altar. In the revised preconciliar liturgy, because the oils had already been brought forward with the bread and wine, all he had to do was bless it. This required the deacon to bring the vessel to the bishop's left side and for the bishop to turn away from the altar and toward the deacon.[78] Today, with a freestanding altar, the person carrying the oil can hold it "in front of the bishop." The bishop need not leave the altar but may continue praying from there, facing the minister with the oil and facing the people.

The prayer is based on one from the Gelasian Sacramentary.[79] It carries a new introduction, a simpler conclusion, and some light retouching throughout, but on the whole, this is the prayer that has been offered over the oil of the sick at least since the seventh century. The Ceremonial of Bishops says the purpose of the prayer is to comfort and support the sick,[80] and indeed it should. It calls for the Holy Spirit under the title of Paraclete or Consoler; prays for protection in body, soul, and spirit; and requests freedom from pain, infirmity, and sickness. The optional concluding formula is omitted only when this blessing is inserted into the eucharistic prayer.

The Roman-Germanic Pontifical said that this oil would be used not only for the sick but also for energoumens,[81] those who probably suffered from some mental illness. In the preconciliar liturgy, this blessing was preceded by an exorcism.[82] This has been eliminated. One of the postconciliar drafts for the blessing of this oil presented as an alternative a newly composed text, punctuated by acclamations by the people:

—Blessed are you, O God, the Father almighty, who sent your Son into the world, that he might heal our wounds.

℟. Blessed be God.

—Blessed are you, O God, the only-begotten Son, who, coming down to our human conditions, went about doing good and healing all people.

℟. Blessed be God.

—Blessed are you, O God, the Holy Spirit, the Paraclete, who are strengthening the weaknesses of our body with everlasting power.

℟. Blessed be God.

—Draw near, Lord, in your kindness,

and by your blessing sanctify this oil prepared to heal the torments of your faithful,

so that, as faithful prayer makes its request,

all those anointed by it

may be set free from every infirmity that lays hold of them.

Through Christ our Lord.

℟. Amen.[83]

This option did not survive into the final version of the postconciliar liturgy. There is only one prayer that may be offered. However, its antiquity justifies its usage.

The newly blessed oil of the sick is returned to the table, and—if this has taken place at the conclusion to the eucharistic prayer—Mass continues through the entire Rite of Communion.

The Blessing of the Oil of Catechumens

21. If the oils are not all blessed together at the end of the Liturgy of the Word, and if the oil of catechumens has not been removed from usage by the conference of bishops, it is blessed following the prayer after Communion. The rubric says that the ministers now place the vessels on a table in the center of the sanctuary, but they were placed there at the end of the procession (paragraph 18). The preconciliar liturgy had a similar instruction because these two oils were just now being brought from the sacristy to the sanctuary and they had to be placed on a table there.[84] But the revised preconciliar liturgy, which put the three oils in the procession of the gifts, says here that the *table* was placed in the middle of the sanctuary.[85] This presumes either that the table had been moved aside for the communion rite or that it needed to be placed where the people could better see what was happening. This actually made more sense than the current rubric does. In any case, the table should be in the center of the sanctuary, and the oils should be on the table.

The bishop probably stands behind the table, though this is not explicitly stated. The concelebrating priests stand around him on either side like a crown. Other ministers stand behind the bishop, and he proceeds with the prayers. Many historical descriptions envision an elaborate arrangement of ministers carrying candles, crosses, thuribles, and even the Book of the Gospels.[86] But the image of priests standing "like a crown" was new to the revised preconciliar liturgy[87] and was retained after the council.

The blessing for the oil of catechumens precedes the consecration of chrism, but this was not the case prior to the council. The former liturgy began with a blessing of the balsam, then the consecration of chrism, and finally the blessing of the oil of catechumens.[88] The revised order imitates the once-abandoned structure of the Gelasian Sacramentary.[89]

All this takes place following the prayer after Communion, but in the preconciliar liturgy it happened after Communion,[90] and the post-Communion prayer followed the consecration of chrism.[91]

22. The bishop says the prayer facing the people. This was important to state because the preconciliar liturgy had him facing the other direction.[92] The revised preconciliar liturgy already had him facing the people.[93]

The preconciliar liturgy did not explicitly state what the bishop should do with his hands, though he made several signs of the cross during these prayers,[94] so he may have kept them folded throughout. Most of these signs of the cross have been eliminated, and the prayers are now to be said with hands extended.

In the preconciliar liturgy, the bishop breathed on this oil before offering the prayer,[95] but this action has been removed from the rite.

The text for this prayer is new to the liturgy. Previous versions were set aside. Others were considered during the development of the revised rite. In the end, the prayer that appears here is the same one placed in the final version of the postconciliar Rite of Christian Initiation of Adults. Throughout the development of drafts for that rite, no text for blessing the oil of catechumens ever appeared.[96] The rite for blessing oil at the chrism Mass states that priests are granted the faculty of blessing the oil of catechumens in the case of adult baptism (paragraph 7), so this text was probably composed to suit both rituals. This was the first time that a priest would be able to bless the oil of catechumens and for the blessing to take place outside the chrism Mass. The text prays that catechumens may have fortitude, understand the gospel, undertake the labors of the Christian life, and rejoice to be born anew and to live in the church.

The Consecration of the Chrism

23. If the oil for chrism has not yet been mixed, the bishop pours perfume into the oil. He does this silently. Formerly, he offered several prayers of exorcism and blessing over the balsam.[97] These have been eliminated so that the emphasis is placed upon the mixed oil, not on the perfume.

24. The bishop invites everyone to join him in prayer that those who are signed outwardly may be inwardly anointed and worthy of redemption. This is a much abbreviated version of the invitation from the preconciliar liturgy.[98] It first appeared in the Roman-Germanic Pontifical.[99]

25. If it seems appropriate, the bishop may breathe over the opened vessel of chrism. This used to be obligatory, and evidence for it is also

in the Roman-Germanic Pontifical[100] and in the *Ordines Romani* 27 and 31.[101] However, the symbol could be easily misunderstood, so it has been made optional. At a preparatory meeting for the revised rite, Francois Vandenbroucke said, "The breathing should be suppressed; indeed, it is a medieval rite that appears to endure today without any pastoral purpose." Cyrille Vogel added, "It seems to me that the whole rite should be omitted. What can it still represent today for the religious sensibilities of the faithful?"[102] Still, the long tradition has found it an apt expression of the action of the Holy Spirit upon the prayer of consecration.

The bishop extends his hands. He used to say this with hands extended before his breast,[103] but now he makes the same gesture he commonly uses when offering any prayer.

There are now two options for the prayer of consecration; formerly there was just one, though it was preceded by a prayer of exorcism and a preface dialogue.[104] The first option reworks the traditional prayer that served the preconciliar liturgy and dates back to the Gelasian Sacramentary.[105] It praises God as the creator of the olive tree. It recalls David's song that oil would gladden the face (probably referring to Ps 104 [103]:15); it recalls as well the dove that announced peace on earth by presenting an olive branch to Noah when the floodwaters had receded (Gen 8:11). These events foreshadow baptism, in which sins are washed away and faces are joyful and serene. Moses anointed Aaron a priest after he had been washed in water (Lev 8:6, 30), and the Holy Spirit came upon Jesus at his baptism in the Jordan (Matt 3:16; Mark 1:10; Luke 3:22; John 1:32; and Acts 10:38). These show the fulfillment of another passage from David, that Christ was anointed with the oil of gladness (Ps 45 [44]:7; and Heb 1:9).

At this juncture, the prayer is paused as the concelebrants raise their right hands toward the chrism. This gesture was newly added to the liturgy after the council; there is no precedent for it. However, it strengthens the idea that priests are witnesses and coworkers with the bishop in the ministry of chrism. In one of the drafts of the postconciliar rite, the study group said that some of the old *Ordines Romani* suggested that this part of the prayer contained its essential words.[106]

The bishop resumes the prayer, which finally comes to its point. He asks God to sanctify this rich oil, giving it the strength of the Holy Spirit, making it a sacred sign of salvation for those born in baptism. He prays that those anointed with it may be fragrant with the innocence of a life pleasing to God, wear their dignity unstained, and become partakers of eternal life. Sections of this final part had been eliminated from the prayer immediately before the council because they duplicated lines from the preface.[107] The preface has completely changed in the postconciliar rite, so the lines in question have been restored to this part of the prayer.

What is often overlooked in this prayer is that it deals entirely with baptism. Some people may assume that the prayer has to do with priesthood. After all, the priests are concelebrating with the bishop, they have just renewed their promises, and their hands are raised as the bishop invokes the Holy Spirit. The entire liturgy makes many people think that priesthood is its central theme, but this prayer is completely concerned about baptism and how the faithful anointed with chrism will serve as priest, prophet, and king in the church.

As an alternative, the bishop may offer a prayer that thanks God who gave the oil of sanctification to foreshadow and shine forth in Christ. When Jesus saved the human race, he filled the church with the Holy Spirit, endowing it with heavenly gifts. Now, through the mystery of chrism, God dispenses grace to the world so that those born again in baptism are strengthened by the anointing of the Spirit and share in the prophetic, priestly, and kingly office.

Here again, after giving God praise for wondrous deeds, the prayer pauses so that the concelebrants may raise their right hands toward the chrism, saying nothing.

The bishop continues, asking God that the mingling of perfume and oil may be a sacrament of blessing. He asks God to pour out the gifts of the Holy Spirit upon those who will be anointed with this oil, to adorn with the beauty of holiness the places and things signed by sacred oils, and to give growth to the church.

This text, too, has little to do with priesthood, everything to do with baptism, and some nuances suggesting the conferral of confirmation and the anointing of a church's walls and altars. Chrism is used on rare occasions, but this prayer draws them together to state the purpose of its consecration. It asks for the coming of the Spirit not just upon the oil but upon those anointed with it. This prayer appears to be a reworking of a text authored in French by Pierre Jounel.[108]

In the preconciliar rite, following the prayer of consecration, the bishop said, "Hail, holy Chrism!" This was echoed by the priests.[109] In the revised preconciliar liturgy, even the people saluted the chrism.[110] This was removed from the liturgy, probably because the practice could be easily misunderstood. At an early meeting of the study group preparing the revised text, Aimé Georges Martimort said the greeting should be eliminated because it was recent and it would seem ridiculous in modern languages.[111]

26. If the entire rite of blessing and consecrating the oils takes place after the Liturgy of the Word, the bishop and concelebrants go to the specially prepared table and then follow the liturgy as described in paragraphs 20–25 above. This has become a very popular way to celebrate the chrism Mass, but because the former distribution of the ceremonies has the longer history, it is the first method described.

27. After the final blessing of the Mass, the bishop puts incense in the thurible and the procession to the sacristy is arranged. It is rare to see incense in the rubrics for the recessional. Normally, when Mass is ended, there is no such indication, even though it is often carried in practice. Normally, though, there is nothing left to incense. As will be seen, the evening Mass of the Lord's Supper on Holy Thursday calls for incense in the recessional, but there it precedes the Blessed Sacrament. Here, the incense will precede the blessed and consecrated oils.

The oils are carried immediately after the cross, while people sing more verses of "O Redeemer" (paragraph 17) or some other song. In the preconciliar liturgy, the last four verses of this hymn were reserved for this part of the Mass.[112]

The minister who carried the oil in procession to the bishop during the Mass also carries it out. In actual practice, some dioceses do not carry the oils out at the end of the service because they have workers pouring the oil into smaller vessels so that priests and parish representatives can carry them home. When the oils are blessed and consecrated together in the Liturgy of the Word, it provides more time for workers to perform this service.

28. After the celebration, the bishop instructs the priests how to treat, honor, and store the oils. This is a rubric that has been retained from the preconciliar liturgy. In fact, the bishop used to give this instruction from the faldstool.[113] In practice, the bishop may omit this or send the information to his priests through some other medium.

The Sacred Paschal Triduum

1. In the Sacred Paschal Triduum the church celebrates the memorial of the crucified, buried, and risen Lord. The introductory paragraphs of this section are new to the third edition of the Roman Missal. They set forth the purpose of these celebrations. The Triduum actually begins with the observance of the Lord's Supper, which serves as a prelude to the memorials mentioned in the opening sentence of this introduction.

The word "Triduum" appears in the writing of St. Augustine, where he says, "The very three days [*Triduum*], on which the Lord died and rose, cannot be correctly understood except in that way of speaking in which the whole is understood from the part."[1] Originally, then, the three days were the ones referred to in the first sentence of this introduction, counting the day of Jesus' death, the day he lay in the tomb, and the day of his resurrection, even though these events probably spanned less than thirty-six hours. However, in the revised liturgy the observance of the Triduum now begins with the Holy Thursday Mass of the Lord's Supper, so that it is included in the observance of the one event of the dying and rising of the Lord.[2]

Ambrose also used the word in one of his letters: "Since therefore that sacred Triduum nearly occupies the final week; within which Triduum he suffered, rested, and rose; of which Triduum he said, 'Destroy this temple, and in three days I will raise it up' (John 2:14), what can bring the bother of doubt to us?"[3]

The fast should be kept on Good Friday everywhere and on Saturday where possible. According to the Code of Canon Law, Good Friday is a day of fast and abstinence. Abstinence from meat applies to everyone who has passed his or her fourteenth birthday. There is no upper age limit to abstinence. Fasting from food applies to those who have passed their eighteenth birthday. To fast is to eat one full meal and no more than two smaller meals not equaling a second meal that day. The obligation ends at the conclusion of one's fifty-ninth birthday.[4]

Few Catholics realize that they are encouraged to observe the laws of fast again on Holy Saturday. This is not new to the third edition of the Missal; it has been promoted in the Rite of Christian Initiation of Adults (185/1) and even in the Second Vatican Council's Constitution on the Sacred Liturgy (*Sacrosanctum Concilium* 110). The practice can be found at the turn of the first century in the *Didache* (7). With Saturday's fast, the community supports those who are to be baptized by joining them in heightened anticipation of the moment of their rebirth. If the purpose of the Good Friday fast is penitential, the Holy Saturday fast is communitarian and anticipatory. People fast the same way, but with a slightly different spirit.

The season of Lent comes to an end before the evening Mass of the Lord's Supper. With that liturgy, the Triduum begins.[5] Because the sacrament of marriage cannot be celebrated on Friday and Saturday, this is the last possible day to convalidate the marriage of those joining the church at the Easter Vigil.[6]

2. The celebration of these ceremonies requires the assistance of a number of lay ministers. They must be carefully instructed so that they know what to do. Although this new rubric does not say so, it would be charitable also to acknowledge the expertise and spirit of service that they bring.

Singing is key to these celebrations. The Triduum is a good example of how singing the service is more powerful than just singing at the service. That is, singing the texts of the Triduum is more powerful than adorning them with additional songs. The dialogues, acclamations, and hymns of the Triduum are particularly expressive when sung. The revised chant settings should inspire a common repertoire among English-speaking Catholics around the world.

To help people engage in active and fruitful participation, pastors should explain the celebrations to them. They will also naturally exhort the faithful to come, for the meaning of the Triduum is best experienced by the community at worship.

3. The celebrations should take place in cathedrals and parish churches large enough to present them well. Although some smaller associations of the faithful may desire to celebrate these days together, they will derive more benefit if they participate with a larger ecclesial community. This seems to come from a concern about some associations that prefer to celebrate their own Sunday Eucharist apart from the parish at large.

Thursday of the Lord's Supper

AT THE EVENING MASS

The Triduum begins with the evening Mass of the Lord's Supper. This heading, "At the Evening Mass," is new to the third edition of the Missal. It is inserted here for clarity.

1. All the faithful are invited to participate in the evening Mass together—those from the local community and all priests and other ministers exercising their office. This Eucharist should demonstrate the unity of the church at prayer, all the ministers present, gathered at one table, offering one sacrifice.

This paragraph used to begin with the reminder that any Mass without the people is forbidden on this day. The instruction is still in force, but because it refers to the entire day, not just the start of the Triduum, it was moved to the introductory comments for the chrism Mass. The word order of the new first paragraph in Latin was reworked so that it now begins with the words, "The Mass of the Lord's Supper."

Many people take it for granted that this Eucharist is celebrated in the evening, but this was not always the case. The earliest records tell of an evening celebration; by the fourth century, Epiphanius says that some places celebrated the Eucharist at 3:00 p.m. on Thursday;[1] Egeria says it took place in the first hour of the night;[2] Augustine also knew multiple practices, including an evening celebration.[3] The custom was honored, obviously, because the New Testament records that the Last Supper of Jesus took place in the evening. Nonetheless, "it is not likely that the Evening Mass survived the ninth century."[4]

However, the viewpoint changed after the reform of the Easter Vigil in 1951. The Pontifical Commission for the Reform of the Sacred Liturgy accepted a motion already in 1952 to move the Holy Thursday Mass to the evening as well.[5] Eventually the commission settled on a recommended hour sometime between 4:00 and 9:00 p.m.[6] Today's parish may choose its time for the evening celebration.

The introductory paragraph says that the priests should participate, but it says nothing of the color of their vesture. It is to be white. This was explicitly stated in the introductory paragraphs to the preconciliar rite.[7] White vesture appears as early as the eighth-century *Ordo Romanus* 23.[8]

Among the ancient customs lost was the lighting of a fire at the start of the Holy Thursday liturgy. Evidence for this is not widespread, but it did exist by the eighth century in some Roman practices.[9] It foreshadowed the light ceremony that opened the Easter Vigil, and it served the practical need of providing light for the services that preceded the blessing of the Easter fire. It may also have supplied the fire used in the divine office for these days in which the candles in a candelabrum were extinguished one by one, a service that came to be known as Tenebrae, but which—like lighting a fire to start the Holy Thursday Eucharist—has been discontinued from the official books of the Roman Rite.

2. Priests concelebrate, even if they have done so earlier in the day. In some places, they may have concelebrated the chrism Mass. In others, they may have celebrated an earlier Mass for the good of the Christian faithful, described in the next paragraph. The reformed preconciliar chrism Mass had given permission to the local ordinary (the bishop) to celebrate more than one Mass on this day,[10] but the permission for any priest to do so was new to the postconciliar Missal.

3. The local ordinary may permit more than one evening Mass in the same church or oratory where there is a pastoral need, and in genuine necessity he may even permit a morning Mass on this day. However, such celebrations should not draw people away from the evening service or show favoritism to individuals or groups.

The third edition of the Missal has removed a reference to public and semipublic oratories. The possibility of priests celebrating more than one Mass on this day with the permission of the ordinary became a reality in 1955 and 1957.[11]

4. Those who are sick may receive Communion at any time on this day, but the faithful who are healthy may only receive it during the celebration of the Eucharist. This permission appeared in 1957.[12] New to the third edition of the Missal is the sending of communion ministers from the evening Mass to the sick.[13]

5. Flowers may adorn the altar with moderation. This is new to the third edition of the postconciliar Missal. It fits with the only mention of flowers in the GIRM,[14] which says that they should not be used

during Lent at all, except on the Fourth Sunday and on feasts and solemnities. The GIRM states in the same place that flowers should be placed around the altar, not on its top. So when this paragraph says that the altar may be decorated with flowers, it probably means on the floor or raised on stands at the sides of the altar.

The tabernacle should be completely empty. The same instruction appeared in the preconciliar liturgy.[15] Although the rubric does not say so explicitly, the sanctuary light should be extinguished and the doors of the empty tabernacle should be flung wide, giving a further visual sign of how different this Eucharist shall be. Whatever remains of the Blessed Sacrament before this Mass could be stored in a ciborium in the sacristy or another suitable place out of view—and reach. All participants will receive from the bread consecrated at this Mass, not from the bread of a previous sacrifice. The priest is obliged to receive that way at every Mass, and the people should ideally do the same.[16] The focus of this Mass will be on sharing communion from the bread and wine consecrated here. There was no tabernacle at the Last Supper.

As this liturgy was being revised, the study group stated that the tabernacle should be empty if it is located on the altar.[17] Apparently, the members saw no problem with a full tabernacle located apart from the sanctuary. Now, however, any tabernacle, no matter where it is located, is to be empty as the Triduum begins.

There will be no consecration at all on Good Friday, so a sufficient amount of bread needs to be consecrated at this Mass so that those who participate in the Good Friday liturgy may also share Communion. In the preconciliar liturgy, the pyx containing the bread for tomorrow was placed on the altar before Mass.[18] Today it is prepared before Mass but brought to the altar with the other gifts.

This is a small matter, but the third edition of the Missal eliminated a subheading before this paragraph. It used to indicate that this was the beginning of the section treating the initial rites and the Liturgy of the Word. Other subheadings in this liturgy were retained, but this one has been removed.

6. The entrance antiphon for the Mass is inspired by Galatians 6:14, where Paul says he does not boast except in the cross of Jesus Christ. The community makes Paul's statement its own declaration. The antiphon shows how the cross is a source of glory. It blends the elements of the paschal mystery—the suffering and glorification of Jesus. This antiphon has introduced this celebration of the Eucharist at least since

the eighth century.[19] In various sources there was some variation in the verse that was sung together with this antiphon. Some used Psalm 96 (95):1, which invited people to sing a new song to the Lord. Others used Psalm 67 (66):2, which asked God to show mercy and to bless and shed the light of his face upon those who sing this chant.[20] The second is the one that has survived in the *Graduale Romanum* of the postconciliar church.

This antiphon was also used on Tuesday of Holy Week in the same eighth-century sources. However, the revision of the Holy Week liturgies after the Second Vatican Council replaced the antiphon on that day,[21] thus making unique the entrance of the Holy Thursday liturgy. This is now the only appearance of this antiphon in the entire Roman Missal.

The 1956 liturgy had the choir chant the entrance antiphon for this Mass as the procession moved to the altar.[22] This seems self-explanatory, but at the time the introit was often read or chanted somewhere within the introductory rites, not necessarily to accompany the procession. This provided a small indication that the liturgical renewal was paying closer attention to the function of the individual parts of the Mass. The postconciliar Missal did not carry over this instruction, which has become unnecessary.

7. The Gloria, which has been omitted on the Sundays of Lent, returns for this celebration. Its inclusion dates at least to the eighth century, yet there were some places at the time where it seems to have been omitted.[23] The Gloria may be recited, but especially on an occasion like this, it begs to be sung.

Bells are rung during the singing, and they are silenced for two days at the end. This tradition entered the Roman Rite with the preconciliar Missal and remains in force to this day.[24] The rubric implies that bells are rung throughout the Gloria. These need not be restricted to the sanctuary bell: the tower bells—or any bell—may be rung at this time as well.

The first postconciliar Missal said the bells remain silent until the Easter Vigil, but the third edition now specifies that they are silent until the Gloria of the vigil. The diocesan bishop may decide otherwise, though it is hard to imagine why he might, unless to toll someone's death or rejoice at some historic event. The postconciliar Missal at first assigned this authority to the conference of bishops, and the Ceremonial of Bishops expanded the authority to include the diocesan bishop;[25] but the third edition now specifies that the diocesan bishop—not the conference—makes the call.

The organ and other musical instruments also remain silent for the same period except to support the singing. The 1954 Rite mentioned the bells but not the organ; the 1956 Rite added the reference to the organ.[26] Similar instructions appeared in the Instruction on Sacred Music from the Sacred Congregation of Rites in 1966.[27] The first postconciliar Missal mentioned only the bells again, but the third edition gives instructions concerning not only the bells but also the organ, and now for other musical instruments as well.

It was customary in some places to replace bells with wooden clappers during the period when the bells were silenced, but the official rubrics for the principal Holy Week liturgies never indicated this. Certainly today there is no call for clappers anywhere in the Missal.[28]

8. In the collect the community prays that those who participate in the supper that Jesus entrusted to the church may have the fullness of charity and life.

The collect was newly composed for the post–Vatican II church, and as with some other new compositions, it is grammatically complex. A formal translation defies the expertise of those wanting a smooth prayer in English that remains faithful to the structure of the original Latin. The new composition shares the themes of the gospel soon to be proclaimed, as well as the double eucharistic emphasis on meal and sacrifice.

Although the text is dense, the preconciliar prayer it replaced presented its own difficulties. That text, which can be found even in the Gelasian Sacramentary,[29] contrasted the punishment of Judas with the reward of the good thief, while asking that Christ who judges justly may bestow the grace of his resurrection upon those offering the prayer. The name of Jesus' betrayer appeared near the very beginning of that prayer, prompting the postconciliar group revising the texts for the liturgical year to note, "The received prayer concerning the betrayer Judas does not pertain to the Eucharistic Mystery. Therefore a more appropriate text is proposed by the pertinent study group."[30] That text, which was very lightly based on a preface from the Easter season in the Verona Sacramentary, was itself completely rewritten to produce the prayer that first appeared in the postconciliar Missal.

The Scripture readings for this day are Exodus 12:1-8, 11-14; Psalm 116:12-13, 15-16bc, 17-18; 1 Corinthians 11:23-26; and John 13:1-15. The first reading, concerning the origins of the Passover meal, seems like an obvious choice, yet prior to the council it was one of several passages proclaimed on Good Friday.[31] It was moved to this day with the postconciliar Lectionary, where it sets the tone for the celebration to follow. Two verses (9 and 10) from the former Good Friday reading were removed because they were rather difficult, instructing people to roast the head, feet, and intestines of the lamb, not to eat any of it raw or boiled, to eat all of it, and to burn whatever was left over.[32]

The psalm replaces the gradual, well known by its Latin title *Christus factus est* (Phil 2:8-9). The passage tells of the obedience of Christ unto death on a cross, so it was moved after the council to the Palm Sunday Mass and replaced here with a psalm that is new to the Holy Thursday liturgy. Psalm 116 says, "The cup of salvation I will raise," and "How precious in the eyes of the Lord is the death of his faithful" (Grail). This foreshadows the events of the night Jesus shared a final meal with his disciples and entered upon his passion. To these select verses has been appended a refrain inspired by a passage from the New Testament, picking up the theme of the cup from the psalm: "Our blessing-cup is a communion with the Blood of Christ" (cf. 1 Cor 10:16). In Paul's letter, this verse is a rhetorical question; here it is a statement of faith.

The second reading presents the earliest record of the Last Supper. Paul's First Letter to the Corinthians predates any of the gospels and was probably composed less than twenty years after the Last Supper. This is the same passage that served as the epistle in the preconciliar liturgy, and there is a clear record of it in the Roman tradition at least back to the seventh century.[33] Egeria, who offered one of the earliest records of this liturgy, says appropriate readings were proclaimed at the evening Mass,[34] but she does not say what they were. It is hard to imagine that this passage would have been neglected.

The gospel tells of Jesus washing the feet of his disciples. John's Gospel includes the discourse on the bread of life in chapter 6, but his account of the Last Supper does not have Jesus saying the famous words of institution recorded in 1 Corinthians and in the Synoptics. Instead, just when the reader expects Jesus to pick up bread, he picks up a towel and a basin to wash the feet of his disciples. The Eucharist is not just about eating and drinking; it concerns service. This passage was also proclaimed in the preconciliar liturgy. It has a long history in the Roman tradition, and evidence for it appears in the very earliest lists of Holy Week readings from at least the seventh century.[35]

9. The priest gives a homily about the institution of the Eucharist, the priesthood, and the new commandment of love. Rarely do the rubrics suggest a specific theme for the homily of the day, but here the suggestions explicitly appear. Those familiar with the 1985 English

Sacramentary will notice little difference here, but in Latin the second edition of the Missal combined the themes of the homily with the rubric introducing the washing of feet. The Sacramentary separated these into two paragraphs, and now the third edition of the Missal has done the same.

The first suggestion for a homily appeared in the 1956 revision of this Mass, and the same three themes were proposed.[36] In 1957 the *Ordinations and Declarations* from the Sacred Congregation of Rites requested a homily even at Holy Thursday Masses without music.[37] In 1969 one of the last drafts for the revised liturgy omitted the reference to the homily's content,[38] but it was restored when the postconciliar Missal was published. Today, most of those participating at the Holy Thursday Mass expect a homily, but the two suggestions that there be one and that it have a specific content are both relatively new.

The Washing of Feet

10. If a pastoral reason suggests it, the washing of feet follows the homily. No further insight into the "pastoral reason" is given, but this has been the criterion ever since the Holy Thursday liturgy was revised in 1956.[39] A draft of the revised liturgy in 1969 changed the wording to "if it seems to be appropriate,"[40] but the previous wording prevailed when the postconciliar Missal was published.

There is clear evidence for the practice of washing feet on Holy Thursday as far back as the seventh century.[41] Earlier, it had been part of the baptismal liturgy in Milan.[42] Its first appearance in a major Roman liturgical rite is in the Roman-Germanic Pontifical,[43] where it seems to have arrived because it already existed in monasteries. In that Pontifical, the washing took place after Mass and Vespers, before or after dinner. By the twelfth century, there is evidence of a double washing—one for the feet of the poor and the other for members of the community.[44] Eventually the washing of feet took place in the Roman Rite at the conclusion of the Holy Thursday Eucharist, following the stripping of the altar. During the footwashing ceremony, the schola sang the appropriate antiphons, and then a deacon read the account from John 13, and immediately afterward the celebrant washed, dried, and kissed the right foot of the individuals.[45] The Pontifical Commission for the Reform of the Sacred Liturgy looked favorably upon suggestions to improve the footwashing ceremony in 1952.[46] And in 1956 it was assigned a prominent place within the evening Mass for the first time, though it was then (and has been ever since) an optional rite.

11. Ministers lead the men chosen for the footwashing to seats prepared in a suitable place. If necessary, the priest removes his chasuble. He goes to each person. Ministers assist him as he washes and dries each person's feet.

The rubric says that "men" are chosen, and the word in Latin, *viri*, does indeed mean "males." In 1987, the chairman of the Bishops' Committee on the Liturgy for the United States Conference of Catholic Bishops wrote, "it has become customary in many places to invite both men and women to be participants in this rite in recognition of the service that should be given by all the faithful to the church and to the world. Thus, in the United States, a variation in the rite developed in which not only charity is signified but also humble service."[47] Because the entire ceremony of washing men's feet is optional, it is difficult to say what must be done.

Although the 1956 liturgy called for "twelve men,"[48] the postconciliar Missal has never given a number. Perhaps it realized that some communities were too small even for twelve men to be found.

Seats are to be prepared in a suitable place. This probably means a place where the congregation can see and where the priest has room to stoop down and move around from one person to the next.

Ministers help the priest, but it is not clear what they do. They may, as in the past, hold vessels and towels;[49] however, the priest should be demonstrating the giving of service, not the receiving of it.

The priest need not remove his chasuble, but he may if it could get in the way, get soiled, or even make him look less like a servant as he performs this action. The bishop may remove his miter and chasuble; however, if he is wearing a dalmatic, the diaconal sign of service, he leaves it on.[50]

He pours water over each one's "feet." Although in the past he washed the right foot of the individuals, the implication now is that he washes both their feet. It no longer calls for him to kiss the feet he washes.[51]

In 1955 the Sacred Congregation of Rites issued *A General Decree by Which the Liturgical Order of Holy Week is Renewed*. It said of the footwashing that "the faithful should be instructed on the profound meaning of this sacred rite and should be taught that it is only proper that they should abound in works of Christian charity on this day."[52]

Some communities have experimented with the footwashing. It is such an unusual gesture that it has tolerated a wide variety of interpretations. Some have washed hands instead of feet. Some have deacons or lay ministers in addition to the priests do the washing. Or they invite those who have had their feet washed to wash the feet of others. However, staying close to the rubrics will usually generate the best results. It seemed odd to the disciples that Jesus would wash their feet; it still feels odd today. If the priest enlists the help of others, he may diminish the symbol of service that he is called to give to his community. And if people who have had their feet washed literally wash the feet of someone else, they run the risk of missing the point made in the 1955 decree: "they should abound in works of Christian charity on this day." When Jesus told his disciples to wash one another's feet, he surely did not mean this literally. He wanted more than that: a true and active spirit of service. That is what the footwashing should inspire.

12. While feet are being washed, antiphons should be sung. The postconciliar Missal includes a variety of these, and it permits other songs as well. Six antiphons were proposed in the second edition, and a new one has been added to the third. It now occupies the second place in the list of antiphons.

The idea of singing antiphons dates to the Roman-Germanic Pontifical, the first major Roman liturgical book to include the washing of feet.[53] It lists dozens of antiphons. The Roman Rite eventually settled on seven, though one (John 13:12, 13, and 15) was removed from the postconciliar Missal. The other six were all carried over. The missing antiphon, however, is the one restored to the third edition of the Missal.[54]

The traditional list of antiphons began with John 13:34, in which Jesus gives a new commandment to his disciples: that they love one another as he has loved them. As the first antiphon in the list, its first word gave the name to the action of washing feet, *mandatum*, meaning "commandment." Some people still refer to the footwashing as the *mandatum*; and this is the word that influenced a popular title for the whole day: Maundy Thursday.

For better or worse, the postconciliar Missal rearranged all these antiphons, so that the first one no longer begins with that traditional word. However, the antiphons have been arranged in biblical order, forming now a sequence of passages to help people move from one to the next. That is why the restoration of the seventh antiphon places it second in the list—it appears in the Bible earlier than most of the others. The *mandatum* is still in there, but it is now the sixth antiphon of the suite.

Traditionally, many of these antiphons also carried a verse from a psalm to be sung between repetitions of the antiphon. These verses have been eliminated from the Missal. However, the Simple Gradual, which presents only one antiphon for washing feet, the most traditional of them all—the *mandatum*—employs the first ten verses of Psalm 119 (118). In the preconciliar Missal, the first verse of that psalm appeared with the same antiphon at the start of the footwashing ceremony.

13. The priest washes and dries his hands, puts his chasuble back on (if it has been removed for the footwashing), and returns to his chair for the universal prayer.

New to the third edition is that the priest washes his hands. This hygienic action serves a practical purpose, but it also restores a custom that existed in the preconciliar Missals.[55] Also new is the instruction to put his chasuble back on (though this should have been understood) and return to his chair. His position at the chair was probably included for the sake of clarity. The second edition of the Missal said here that he leads the prayer of the faithful *statim*, or "immediately." That word has been removed because he now washes his hands before starting the next section of the liturgy. (*Statim* had not been translated in the 1985 Sacramentary.)

In the 1969 draft of this rite, it was proposed that the prayer of the faithful follow the homily and precede the washing of feet.[56] This opinion did not prevail.

There is no Creed at this Mass. This should be obvious, but prior to the 1956 reforms, the Creed was included in the Mass of Holy Thursday.[57]

The Liturgy of the Eucharist

14. During the procession, gifts for the poor may be presented together with the bread and wine. The third edition clarifies this point. Previous editions of the postconciliar Missal just mentioned gifts for the poor. It should have been understood that these are brought forward together with the bread and wine, but this had not been explicit. Preconciliar editions of the Missal had nothing resembling this rubric. The postconciliar GIRM 73 permits gifts for the poor at any Mass. They are especially recommended for Holy Thursday. Drafts of this liturgy in 1968–69 stated that the procession of gifts for the poor was "laudably" formed,[58] but this adverb did not survive. The Circular Letter goes further to say, "Gifts for the poor, especially those collected

during Lent as the fruit of penance, may be presented in the offertory procession."[59]

Meanwhile, an appropriate chant is sung. The recommended text is the traditional one for this occasion, *Ubi caritas*.

The text comes from the Benedictine monastery at Reichenau about the year 800. Several verses are inspired by sections from the Rule of St. Benedict.[60] This hymn appeared in the Missal of the Roman Curia from the fourteenth to the sixteenth century,[61] and it has been part of the liturgy ever since. One significant change happened after the Second Vatican Council. Prior to that time, *Ubi caritas* was the last of the antiphons sung during the washing of the feet, and even though other antiphons could be omitted, this one was obligatory.[62] Now it has been moved to the preparation and procession of the gifts, and it may be replaced by another song. Still, it is a classic piece of chant, and its inclusion would help preserve a long and beautiful tradition of the Holy Thursday liturgy. The English language third edition includes a translation of this hymn.

15. In the prayer over the offerings the community asks to participate worthily in these mysteries. This prayer replaces the one from the preconciliar Missal.[63] The new text actually comes from the Verona Sacramentary, where it is listed among prayers for April,[64] and has a richer content than its predecessor for this day. The revisers of the liturgy were familiar with the now-current text because the preconciliar liturgy had used it on the Ninth Sunday after Pentecost. The same prayer now also appears on the Second Sunday in Ordinary Time and in the votive Mass for Our Lord Jesus Christ, the High and Eternal Priest.

16. The preface acclaims Christ as the true and eternal priest, who instituted the Eucharist, offered himself as a victim, and commanded his followers to make this offering. By sharing in Communion, the community is made strong and washed clean. This preface replaced the one for the Holy Cross that was in use before the Council.

Previous editions of the Missal in Latin and in English simply referred the presider to the correct preface from the collection later in the book, but the third edition has inserted on this page the entire text together with its title, "The Sacrifice and Sacrament of Christ." It even gives the first line of the Sanctus.

The preface appears here only in its sung form. It may be spoken, of course, and for that the priest needs to turn to a different section of the

Missal to find the words without the notes. The editing implies that this preface should be sung if possible.

17. If the Roman Canon is selected as the eucharistic prayer for this Mass, the special inserts are to be used in three of its sections. These inserts for this day have remained virtually unchanged for 1500 years.[65] Other eucharistic prayers may be used, especially Prayer III, but the antiquity of the custom surrounding these inserts suggests a deference to Prayer I.

18. New to the third edition of the Missal in Latin and in English is the complete text of Eucharistic Prayer I in this place. It appears again in the Order of Mass and in the appendix with chant notation.

The 2002 third edition of the Missal in Latin was reprinted in 2008 with a few changes, and one of them affected this section. The footnote used to say that mention may be made of the coadjutor and auxiliary bishops and of some other bishop, but now the "other bishop" is no longer listed among the options. If other bishops are present, their names are not mentioned in the prayer. Even the names of the co-adjutor and auxiliaries may be omitted—their inclusion is permitted, not obligatory. If the presider is a bishop from another diocese, he mentions "me, your unworthy servant," but, new to the third edition, he does so after praying for the bishop who is the ordinary, not before.[66]

19. There is no change to the commemoration of the living. This section of the prayer is the same whenever it is used.

20. This section, subtitled "Within the Action," has always been one of the most fluid sections of the Roman Canon. On certain festal days of the liturgical year, this section expresses the nature of the celebration. The title probably comes from this practice of making a reference to the feast within the action of this prayer.

This is probably the most important of all the inserts. In the Order of Mass, Eucharistic Prayer I has always included a list of occasional inserts for "Within the Action." This one has been removed from that section in the third edition of the Missal and moved here to a more prominent place, making it easier for priests to read the sentence without referring to a footnote to find it. The prayer remembers the day "on which our Lord Jesus Christ was handed over for our sake." There are other ways of noting the significance of Holy Thursday, as the homily suggestions have stated, but here in the eucharistic prayer, the lordship, betrayal, and salvific mission of Jesus Christ are neatly summarized for those engaging in the sacrifice and eschatological meal of this Eucharist.

21. This is another section of the Roman Canon that has always allowed some variation. Apart from the special mention of the day, the rest of this section does not add much new to what the prayer has already said. Consequently, one theory holds that in the development of the canon this section began as a special insert and then was made generic to justify its regular inclusion. During the discussions prior to the revisions of the Order of Mass in 1969, some theologians argued that this section should be removed except on those days that retained a special formula for it.[67] The entire section remained, however, probably due to the long tradition of keeping it here. In any case, this part still contains a special formula during Easter week and in certain ritual Masses such as the one for marriage. At the evening Mass on Holy Thursday, it focuses on the events being commemorated, "the day on which our Lord Jesus Christ handed on the mysteries of his Body and Blood."

22. This section, which asks God to approve the offering, is identical to its counterpart on any other occasion when the first eucharistic prayer is used.

23. This is the third section of the Roman Canon that has long contained a special insert for the Mass on Holy Thursday. It is perhaps the most dramatic. When remembering the day on which Jesus suffered, it adds "for our salvation and the salvation of all, that is today."

Joseph Jungmann notes that the expression "for our salvation and the salvation of all" appears only on this day in the Roman tradition but was used more broadly in Gallic versions of the canon. He theorizes that it "may originally have been incorporated to underscore the all-embracing character of the redemption as a protest against the gloomy predestinationism rampant in the fifth and sixth centuries."[68] This may have counterbalanced a false interpretation of the words concerning the Blood of Christ, "which will be poured out for you and for many." Jesus died for all people, and this insert on Holy Thursday says so explicitly.

The words "that is today" are obviously designed to underscore the significance of celebrating the Eucharist on the anniversary of its institution. The rubric that the priest should pronounce the formulas clearly and distinctly is identical to the one that appears in all the eucharistic prayers of the Roman Rite.

24–32. The rest of Eucharistic Prayer I appears without any change from the way it looks in the Order of Mass. However, to make it easier on the priest who wishes to use this prayer with its inserts on this day, the entire text is presented for the sake of completion.

The 1956 revision of the service noted that the incensation during the elevations should always be done at this Mass,[69] but it is optional today, as it is for any other celebration of the Eucharist.

For the Lamb of God, the 1956 revision also called for the third petition to conclude the same way the others do: "Have mercy on us." The kiss of peace was omitted, as was the prayer recalling that Jesus said to his apostles, "Peace I leave with you." If the bishop distributed Communion to the faithful, they were instructed not to kiss his ring before receiving on this day.[70] It is generally thought that these words and actions were struck from the service because this was the night on which Judas betrayed Jesus with a kiss. Such rubrics do not appear now because of the belief that the paschal mystery overpowers all evil.

The third edition indicates here the page number for the communion rite. This helps the priest who finds a similar instruction at the conclusion of every eucharistic prayer in the Order of Mass. In 1966, the revisions to the liturgy were expected to draw so many people that a rubric was added to the communion rite: "If, however, the crowd of the faithful coming to the sacred table is large, other priests may also distribute Communion together with the celebrant at the edge of the sanctuary area or in some other suitable place. Care must be taken to preserve good order and the devotion of the faithful."[71]

One of the last drafts of the postconciliar liturgy included a rubric stating that, according to the judgment of the ordinary, "it is permitted to all the faithful to receive communion under both kinds."[72] This did not carry over into the final text, probably because it is always true.

33. New to the third edition of the Missal is an instruction to bring Communion to the sick, "so that in this way they may be more closely united to the celebrating church," as the Circular Letter states.[73] The priest entrusts the Eucharist to those who will carry it on his behalf. He does this at "an appropriate moment during Communion." No further information is given, and this is probably wise because the practice will vary considerably. The goal is to get into the hands of each minister a pyx with the appropriate number of hosts and to do this preferably during the communion rite of the Mass. On a practical note, someone should probably contact the sick in advance to arrange this. Some may find the hour too late to receive a visitor. Others will be

delighted. Communion ministers will find this a particularly beautiful night to share this apostolate.

The priest entrusts the Eucharist that is on the altar. Practically speaking, he has no other choice. This Mass begins with an empty tabernacle. But ritually, the rubric wants the Eucharist of this celebration to be shared with those who could not otherwise come. The full symbol is that they share in the Communion from the Mass of the Lord's Supper.

The rubric refers to "the Eucharist," not to "the Body of Christ." Some who are sick may only be able to swallow liquids. They may receive Communion under the form of wine alone.

The ministers in question are deacons, acolytes, or other extraordinary ministers. Few parishes have installed acolytes; usually the only ones are seminarians preparing for ordination to the priesthood or candidates for the permanent diaconate; the installation of acolytes requires a bishop, and he may confer this ministry only upon males. Extraordinary ministers of Holy Communion, however, may be both men and women, and they usually provide this service for a typical parish.

In the past there were some variations in the communion rite of this Mass. For example, in 1954 the priest consecrated one extra host for him to consume the next day, along with some smaller particles that could be shared with the sick. The deacon placed these in a separate chalice, not a ciborium, covered it with a pall and an inverted paten, and then stretched a veil over the top, leaving the ensemble on the center of the altar before the distribution of Communion.[74] In the middle of the eighth century, *Ordo Romanus* 24 instructed the bishop to give himself the consecrated bread in the usual way but to receive the cup from the deacon—only on this day.[75] Perhaps this stressed that everyone receives Communion as a gift.

34. The communion antiphon is lifted directly from the second reading, the earliest record of the Last Supper. If the communion antiphon quotes one of the readings, normally the gospel supplies the text. Prior to the council, the communion antiphon for this Mass was John 13:12, 13, and 15. Having washed the feet of his disciples, Jesus says he gave them an example and he asks them to imitate it. This antiphon was paired with Psalms 23 (22), 72 (71), 104 (103), and 150.[76] In the postconciliar liturgy on this night, as Communion is being shared, the antiphon selects the words of the Lord Jesus announcing that the bread and wine are his Body and Blood.

Throughout the Missal, many of the antiphons that quote a saying of Jesus include a phrase such as "says the Lord," as this one does. Hence, this is not a direct quote from Paul's letter but a very close derivative. In the Latin original, internal punctuation is missing in all the instances where this pattern appears, so no quotation marks surround the words of Jesus to separate them from the clause that names the speaker.

35. A ciborium with hosts for the following day is left on the altar after Communion. The priest offers the prayer after Communion from the chair. Previous editions of the postconciliar Missal in Latin said here that the Mass is finished with that prayer, but this has been removed in the third edition. The phrase had never been translated into English. The preconciliar Missal considered the transfer of the Blessed Sacrament a ceremony that took place once the Mass was over.[77]

The ciborium replaces the chalice that had been used for this purpose in the past. It is more in keeping with the purpose of the ciborium to store the consecrated bread. The rubric indicates that the ciborium is to be used "on the following day," which the previous English translation rendered with the equivalent phrase, "on Good Friday." It is left on the altar because the procession will start from there. A monstrance is not to be used. In fact, the Circular Letter expressly forbids the use of a monstrance.[78]

The priest says the prayer after Communion from the chair. Normally he has an option of using the altar or the chair, and the third edition has the order in that way in one place[79] and in the reverse order in a different place.[80] On this day, however, because the Blessed Sacrament stands on the altar, the priest offers the prayer from the chair.

36. The community prays that it may enjoy the eternal banquet as it is renewed by the Supper of God's Son in this present age. This replaces the prayer in use for hundreds of years before the council, which asked that what the people pursue in the time of their mortality they may obtain with the gift of God's immortality. This prayer echoes the theme but is a bit richer and derives from the prayer after Communion for this day in the Gothic Missal.[81] The postconciliar Roman Missal incorporated a wider variety of Western sources for its prayers, and this is a good example. The only change is that where the present text refers to "the Supper of your Son," the Gothic Missal had "the Supper of your Son's Passion." Perhaps the elimination of the word "Passion" keeps the focus on the heavenly banquet.

The greeting, blessing, and dismissal are all omitted in this celebration. The 1966 revision replaced the dismissal formula with "Let us bless the Lord." It also instructed the celebrant and the ministers to remove their maniples and the celebrant to exchange his chasuble for a white cope.[82] Today, the celebrant concludes the service in his chasuble.

The Transfer of the Most Blessed Sacrament

37. Standing at his chair, the priest puts incense in the thurible, blesses it, and kneels. He incenses the Blessed Sacrament three times. He puts on a white humeral veil, stands, takes up the ciborium, and covers it with the ends of the veil.

The third edition specifies that this all takes place after the prayer after Communion. Previous editions simply said "after the prayer." The third edition also removes the instruction that he places incense in the thurible while standing "before the altar," a holdover from the preconciliar Missal.[83] Now he is at the chair for this action. Throughout the third edition, whenever the priest adds incense to the thurible, he blesses it. This is to be done without words;[84] a simple sign of the cross over the smoke is enough. Perhaps it was important to clarify the blessing at this point because the preconciliar Missal said the priest added incense without any blessing here.[85]

The priest incenses the Blessed Sacrament while kneeling. Presumably he has now moved from the chair to a place in front of the altar. He swings the censer three times. This is the same number of swings used on other occasions for a relic of the cross, images of the Lord, the offerings for the Mass, the altar cross, the Book of the Gospels, the paschal candle, the priest, and the people.[86] The swings have been simplified in the postconciliar Missal.

Previous editions of the Missal did not stipulate the color of the humeral veil. Now it notes that the veil is white, though that should be obvious. The Missal does not explain how he puts it on, but it is customary for servers to bring him the veil from behind so that he can clip it in front. The third edition also specifies that the priest stands up after putting on the veil. This should have been obvious, but for the sake of thoroughness, the posture is now indicated. It was specified in the preconciliar Missal.[87]

The priest takes the ciborium. The previous Latin editions of the postconciliar Missal said he did this "with his hands," but this should be obvious. The same editions simply said he covered the ciborium "with the veil," but now the third edition specifies "with the ends of the veil." Again, this should be obvious, but perhaps the practice had become unknown in some places. The priest had been told to use the ends of the veil in the preconciliar liturgy.[88] They were still included in the rubric in the 1969 draft of this liturgy,[89] but they did not appear in the first editions of the postconciliar Missal.

38. The priest carries the Blessed Sacrament through the church. A cross-bearer and two persons carrying lighted candles lead the way. Others may follow, carrying more lighted candles. The thurifer follows them, and then comes the priest. A hymn is sung. Traditionally, it is *Pange lingua*, but without the final two stanzas, which are sung later.

This paragraph in Latin now names the Blessed Sacrament first. The previous postconciliar Missal mentioned the cross-bearer first; after all, that minister leads the procession. But because the procession is all about the Blessed Sacrament, it occupies a more dominant place in the first line of the rubric.

Prior to the council, two thuribles[90] and a baldachin[91] joined the procession. Now it is just one thurible, and the reference to the baldachin has been removed. The previous editions of the postconciliar Missal said that candles accompanied the cross, but the third edition now specifies two lighted candles with the cross and even more following it. Egeria said two hundred candles accompanied the Holy Thursday procession at Gethsemane.[92] Throughout this paragraph, the third edition is much clearer than earlier editions about the complete sequence of ministers in this procession.

When a bishop presides, a minister carries the pastoral staff for him.[93] The bishop usually carries the pastoral staff in a liturgical procession, but because his hands are holding the Blessed Sacrament, another minister must carry the staff if it is to accompany the bishop.

The procession goes "through the church." Some communities lengthen the procession by having it snake through the building, but that is not necessary. The point is to move to the place of repose either in the church or a chapel. The previous editions of the postconciliar Missal only indicated the use of a chapel; the third edition now permits a part of the church and lists it as the first option, perhaps because of the history of this part of the ceremony. The 1966 revised liturgy listed both options, but in the reverse order: a chapel or an altar of the church.[94] The Circular Letter calls for "a place . . . prepared and adorned in such a way as to be conducive to prayer and meditation; . . . When the tabernacle is located in a chapel separated from the central part of the church, it is appropriate to prepare there the place of repose and adoration."[95] If the procession comes to its end within the church, ordinarily the Blessed Sacrament should not be placed in the usual tabernacle; that is done only if there are no Good Friday services in the church the next day.[96] It should be set in a place apart. Someplace outside the nave would still seem to be ideal, if such a location is available. Wherever the procession ends up, the place should be "suitably decorated." This is often done with candles, cloths, and whatever else will lend dignity to the space.

Any eucharistic hymn may accompany the procession, but the traditional *Pange lingua* is still recommended. Although the Missal does not provide the text as it does for *Ubi caritas*, it is easily found in many hymnals. Venantius Fortunatus (+609) composed it on the occasion of a procession of the relic of the true cross to the Gallic Queen Radegunde (+587).[97] It entered the liturgy as part of the Good Friday service, but it has a hallowed place here in the Holy Thursday procession.[98]

39. At the place of repose the priest places the ciborium in the tabernacle, leaving the doors open; a deacon may assist. Still standing, the priest adds incense to the thurible, then kneels and incenses the Blessed Sacrament. Any eucharistic song may be sung, but *Tantum ergo Sacramentum* is traditional. These are the final two stanzas of *Pange lingua*. The deacon or the priest places the Blessed Sacrament in the tabernacle and closes the door.

The English rubrics have the minister place the Blessed Sacrament in the tabernacle twice, but in Latin it is only once: upon arrival at the place of repose. The deacon may help, but the rubrics do not say how. Perhaps he may actually place the ciborium in the tabernacle, which was his responsibility in the preconciliar liturgy.[99] New to the third edition is the mention of the deacon and the instruction that the doors to the tabernacle should be left open. This should have been obvious because they are not closed until after the incensation, but the clarification will probably help.

Previous editions of the postconciliar Missal allowed no option for the music here. It was to be *Tantum ergo*. The third edition permits a different song.

The third edition also indicates for the first time that the deacon may close the door to the tabernacle, and this possibility is mentioned first, before the permission that the priest may do it. This action was not mentioned in the preconciliar liturgy, though the deacon probably closed the door when he placed the Blessed Sacrament in the tabernacle.

40. A period of silent adoration follows. Then the priest and ministers genuflect to the tabernacle and return to the sacristy.

The third edition of the Missal has made no change to this rubric. The practice of reservation goes back to the Middle Ages. Even the Gelasian Sacramentary indicates that the Holy Thursday service concluded with Communion and reservation.[100] When a bishop presides, he carries the pastoral staff himself as he returns to the sacristy.[101]

41. The service has concluded at this point. At some convenient time, the altar is stripped and crosses are removed from the church—if they can be. Any that remain are covered. The Circular Letter says that they should be covered in red or violet, unless they were already veiled on the Saturday before the Fifth Sunday of Lent. Candles should not be lit before images of saints.[102]

In the past, the stripping of the altar was a ceremony all its own. The priest changed into violet vesture for the event.[103] The stripping happened for a practical purpose: the Eucharist would not be celebrated there on Good Friday.[104] Because the altar is a symbol of Christ, its stripping provided an allegorical comparison to the stripping of Christ before his crucifixion.[105] Similarly, Isidore of Seville says the altar, walls, and floors of the church were washed, probably to clean things up for Easter, but these actions became "consonant with the atmosphere of desolation"[106] in this part of Holy Week.

Holy water stoups may be emptied at this point.[107] They are to be refilled after the Easter Vigil with newly blessed water.

At best, the entire sanctuary will look bare. Anything not needed for the Good Friday liturgy would be put into the sacristy or another appropriate place following the celebration of the Mass of the Lord's Supper.

42. Those who participate in the Mass of the Lord's Supper do not celebrate evening prayer. The extra length of the service and the hour of the day in which it is celebrated make Vespers unnecessary.

43. Adoration may extend into the night. The faithful are invited to spend some time before the Blessed Sacrament. After midnight adoration may take place without solemnity.

This was the night on which Jesus asked his disciples to stay awake and pray with him, but they kept falling asleep.[108] The faithful should be encouraged to spend an hour in response to Jesus' request, but any time they can give will enrich their spiritual lives.

This rubric used to say that the faithful "should be encouraged" to come; it has now been changed to "invited." Even the Latin verb has been softened in the third edition of the Missal. The verb uses the passive voice. It does not say, "the priest invites the people," but simply that "the people are invited." It may not require a public announcement. While the adoration is going on, it is appropriate to read parts of the Gospel of John, chapters 13–17.[109] These chapters were part of the lengthy Holy Thursday liturgy in the Roman-Germanic Pontifical, to be read after the washing of feet.[110]

Midnight divides adoration with solemnity from adoration without solemnity, but it is difficult to know what this means. It is fine to close the period of adoration at midnight as Good Friday begins.

44. If the Good Friday service does not take place in the same church, the Mass is concluded in the usual way—with the greeting, blessing, and dismissal. The Blessed Sacrament is placed in the tabernacle without a procession or a period of adoration.

This situation exists in some parts of the world where the priest has charge of more than one church and moves the location of the Triduum ceremonies from one location to another. This direction is new to the third edition of the Missal, though it appeared in the Circular Letter, which cited an instruction from the Vatican in 1956.[111] However, the Circular Letter cautions, "where there are small parishes with only one priest, it is recommended that such parishes should assemble, as far as possible, in a principal church and there participate in the celebrations" of the Triduum. Nonetheless, "where the celebrations can be carried out with the requisite care and solemnity, the celebrations of the Easter Triduum may be repeated in accord with the given norms."[112]

Friday of the Passion of the Lord [Good Friday]

1. The church does not celebrate the sacraments on Good Friday or Holy Saturday. The only exceptions are penance and the anointing of the sick. These are newly noted in the third edition of the Missal.

The Missal indicates that the tradition behind this practice is ancient. It is referring to the letter of Pope Innocent I (+417) to Decentius of Gubbio, where the exact phrase the Missal uses to describe these two days ("the Church does not celebrate the Sacraments at all") can be found.[1] The 1969 draft of the revised liturgy explains that the context for this is that "the spouse has been taken away,"[2] but this was not retained in the final text, perhaps because Innocent did not make that association and because the biblical reference has more to do with the fast.[3]

The permission to celebrate penance and the anointing of the sick enshrines what had become pastoral practice. Even Pope John Paul II heard confessions in St. Peter's Basilica on Good Friday, on a day when the rubrics said the sacraments are not celebrated "at all."

The Circular Letter recommends the common celebration of the Office of Readings and Morning Prayer on this day and on Holy Saturday.[4] It says that this office was formerly called Tenebrae, but the former practices of methodically extinguishing candles and beating hymnals on pews in the dark are no longer part of the Liturgy of the Hours. These liturgical offices incorporate the singing of hymns and psalms.

Surprising, then, is the instruction concerning funerals on these two days. The Circular Letter says that they may be celebrated without Mass, which is understandable, but also without singing or the tolling of bells.[5] Hymns and psalms are sung at the Liturgy of the Hours but oddly not at a funeral.

2. Communion may be distributed to the faithful only during the celebration of the Lord's passion. There may be no separate Communion service. However, those who are sick and unable to participate in the main liturgy may receive Communion at any time. This

permission has loosened the practice in effect all the way up to 1966, when the reception of Communion apart from the main liturgy was restricted to those in danger of death.[6]

3. No cross, candles, or cloth should adorn the altar. It is left completely bare. This instruction continues the traditional practice without any change.

THE CELEBRATION OF THE PASSION OF THE LORD

4. The main liturgical observance today is called the Celebration of the Passion of the Lord. It is not a Mass. The entire liturgy unfolds in three parts: the Liturgy of the Word, the adoration of the cross, and Holy Communion. The earliest record of a liturgical observance of Good Friday comes from Egeria.[7]

Ideally, the service begins at 3:00 p.m., the hour when Jesus died on the cross, according to the gospels.[8] The rubrics permit a later celebration, but they do not envision anything earlier, and they offer no latest possible time. This seems to update the time given in the Circular Letter, which explicitly permitted the celebration after midday or in the evening, though no later than 9:00 p.m.[9] Three o'clock was the starting time throughout the tradition of the Gelasian Sacramentary, though there are examples among the *Ordines Romani* and Pontificals for this service beginning at 2:00 p.m. or even at 11:00 a.m.[10]

As late as 1954 the service began after the liturgical hour of None, or probably about 3:00 p.m., but in 1956 the time was noted simply as "afternoon."[11] However, as early as 1952, requests for an evening celebration had come to the Pontifical Commission for the Reform of the Sacred Liturgy.[12] In 1956 the Commission responded favorably to the request for a starting time of 7:00 p.m. when it was put forth at the insistence of Msgr. Giovanni Battista Montini, the future Pope Paul VI, speaking on behalf of the Lombard bishops.[13] The window of time for starting the liturgy expanded from midday to 9:00 p.m. later that year.[14] Today there is no latest possible starting time.

In the United States, a bishop may permit parishes to repeat the service. This usually pertains to the size of the parish, the number of people wishing to attend, or the administration of more than one parish by a single priest.

Also in the United States, the rubrics now disallow the possibility of a deacon or lay minister presiding for the Good Friday service. In June 1994 the Bishops' Committee on the Liturgy had discussed the question of having a deacon preside and had reached a different conclusion: "It was the unanimous opinion of the Committee that although the Sacramentary makes no specific provision for such a practice, it is within the competence of the bishop in particular cases to permit such a practice."[15] Now, however, the bishops have clearly stated that only a priest may lead the service. In his absence, this celebration may not take place. Perhaps the community could observe a devotion, such as the Stations of the Cross.

5. The priest and the deacon, if one is available, wear red Mass vestments. In silence they go to the altar, reverence it, prostrate or kneel, and pray in silence. All others kneel.

Up until the postconciliar Missal, the vesture for this celebration was black.[16] The wearing of red vesture was not completely revolutionary; it had been in use in the Sarum Rite.[17] An explanation of the change in color was given in one of the drafts of the postconciliar liturgy:

> The color red is chosen in the same sense [that the character of this day has been changed somewhat into triumph, although the renewal of lamentations should not be abolished] and in the celebration of martyrdom: because of the blood poured out. Perhaps also because of the Holy Spirit, through whom Christ offered himself without blemish for God (cf. Heb 9:14), who was at work in the martyrs according to the opinion of the Fathers. It signifies more than the triumph of the cross.[18]

When a bishop presides, he does not wear his ring.[19] When the bishop receives the ring at his ordination, the ordaining bishop says to him, "Receive this ring, the seal of fidelity: adorned with undefiled faith, preserve unblemished the bride of God, the holy Church."[20] The removal of the ring probably indicates that these days fulfill Jesus' own prediction that he, the bridegroom, would one day be taken away from his disciples.[21]

A deacon may assist. The previous postconciliar editions of the Missal implied that a deacon was expected to be on hand; the third edition realizes that a community may not have one.

If any announcements need to be made to the people, they should be made before the ministers enter.[22] However, making no announcements beforehand will heighten the sense of silence that the entrance rite is striving to achieve.

The rubric does not say where the priest and the deacon begin their approach to the altar. Presumably, this could be from a sacristy on the side of the sanctuary or up the main aisle of the church. In the Gelasian Sacramentary, the ministers entered from the sacristy.[23] The 1956 revised liturgy had the ministers process through the church,[24] and the 1966 version retained this instruction.[25] However, the rubric today has removed the words "through the church" and simply states that the ministers "go to the altar." A long procession engages the participation of the people, but a shorter procession diminishes its importance and moves the liturgy more immediately toward its more significant parts. When a bishop presides, he does not carry his pastoral staff.[26] He usually carries it in procession; its elimination here minimizes the nature of this particular procession, which serves a more perfunctory purpose of just getting the ministers to the sanctuary. No music accompanies the procession.

The priest and deacon reverence the altar. The rubric does not explain how they do this; not even the 1956 liturgy explained this any further, though the 1954 liturgy had him kiss the altar.[27] Today a profound bow would be expected, but it would also be appropriate to kiss the altar. Both actions are described as reverencing the altar in the GIRM.[28] The tabernacle is empty, so even if it is located in the sanctuary, the rubrics indicate no reverence toward it. Incense is not used throughout the Good Friday liturgy, so reverencing the altar should not include incense.

The priest and deacon prostrate or kneel. Prostration is the first option and hence is preferred. A draft of the revised postconciliar liturgy made this observation in response to a proposal to eliminate it:

> But for the people this rite is a sign of most profound devotion. Friday of the Passion of the Lord is truly a unique day in the liturgical year. On this day should there not also be such a most profound reverence by a visible sign in front of the altar of God? Throughout the entire liturgy the number of genuflections and bows has been lessened. . . . In this sense, once a year, the customary form of prostration may also be granted as a most intense sign of devotion.[29]

The Circular Letter further states, "This act of prostration, which is proper to the rite of the day, should be strictly observed for it signifies both the abasement of 'earthly man' [alternative opening prayer] and also the grief and sorrow of the church."[30]

The Latin words for this kneeling were changed in the third edition of the Missal, and they are not the same as the usual verb that appears in the GIRM.[31] The words now are *in genua se prosternunt*, which are similar to the words for prostration (*se prosternunt*) as they appear in the earliest record of this posture in the Good Friday liturgy, *Ordo Romanus* 23.[32] There, however, they describe the posture the bishop takes before venerating the relic of the true cross, which was placed on the altar to open the liturgy. This particular verb has as much to do with the humble attitude one assumes as it does with the position of the body.

The third edition of the Missal makes it clear that everyone should kneel. This may have been understood in the past, but it was never explicitly stated.

6. The priest stands and goes to the chair. The ministers accompany him. The people stand. The priest faces them and says one of the two alternative prayers with his hands extended. He does not say, "Let us pray."

When the priest stands, the people do as well. However, they were to remain kneeling in the preconciliar liturgy.[33]

The priest turns to face the people before saying this prayer. This was new to the postconciliar liturgy. The Order of Mass has the priest face the people when he starts the sign of the cross to open the liturgy.[34] The instruction probably appears here in the Good Friday liturgy because this is the first opportunity the priest has to face the people. It implies that at a typical Mass the priest keeps facing the people from the sign of the cross through the collect. A draft of the postconciliar liturgy expressed concern that people would not be able to hear or understand this prayer if it was to be offered on the step in front of the altar, as had been the custom.[35] "In its place before the first reading, it will hardly be understood by the faithful, especially because there is no microphone there. At least it should be said at the chair."[36]

The priest does not say, "Let us pray." In previous editions of the postconciliar Missal, this was noted at the heading of the prayer. Now it has been moved more logically to a rubric. The reason he does not say the invitation is that silent prayer has already been happening. The rubrics expect the ministers to be praying silently. In past editions of the postconciliar Missal, the rubric said, "all pray in silence," but the third edition makes this expectation of the ministers. All will naturally join them in praying silently when they kneel, but the rubric seems oblivious to this. The omission of the words "Let us pray," on the other hand, seems to imply that everyone is already doing that.

The priest says this prayer with hands extended. This is new to the third edition of the Missal. Even in the preconciliar liturgy, he joined his hands for this prayer. No explanation is given for either gesture. Perhaps in the preconciliar liturgy, his oration was intended to look different from the ones that begin the eucharistic liturgy. Perhaps the change is meant to relate this prayer more closely with others with which it shares a structural genre. Note that it is not called a "collect," the specific prayer that concludes the introductory rites of the Mass. It is simply called a "prayer."

Two options are given for the prayer. The first prays for the sanctification of God's servants for whom Christ established the paschal mystery by shedding his blood. The second prays that those who by nature bear the image of the man of earth (Adam) may by grace bear the image of the Man of heaven (Christ). The second has the longest history at the beginning of the Good Friday liturgy, since it appeared in the Gelasian Sacramentary.[37] The Gelasian is the source for the first option as well, though it appears there as the collect for Monday of Holy Week.[38] In 1956 it became the last of three prayers after Communion. In the draft of the postconciliar liturgy, it was proposed as the prayer that opens the Good Friday liturgy "because it is easier to understand."[39] This is clear to see from the revised translation of the two texts.

Both prayers end with a shortened conclusion, the one typically used for the prayer over the offerings and the prayer after Communion, rather than the one for the collect. It serves to simplify the opening rites and heightens the sense of fasting.

First Part: The Liturgy of the Word
7. All sit for the first reading. Isaiah 52:13–53:12 is proclaimed, and the responsorial follows (Ps 31 [30]:2, 6, 12-13, 15-16, 17, 25). Both texts were new to the postconciliar liturgy.

Prior to the council, it was customary to hear Hosea 6:1-6,[40] which has been moved to Saturday of the Third Week of Lent. In its place is the fourth oracle of the servant of the Lord, the one that most dramatically describes the suffering servant. The other three oracles have been proclaimed earlier in Holy Week; they reach their climax on this day. A passage from Isaiah is noted in the Gelasian Augiense,[41] but otherwise the Roman tradition has held to Hosea's prophecy, "It is love that I desire, not sacrifice." However, the Mozarabic tradition did use Isaiah 52:13–53:12 as early as the seventh century.[42] In the drafts preparing the postconciliar liturgy, Hosea was first replaced by Isaiah[43] and then offered as an alternative.[44] It was not retained in the final postconciliar Lectionary for Good Friday.

For the responsorial, the study group preparing the postconciliar liturgy was immediately drawn to Psalm 22 (21). They found it "incomparably appropriate," for "it appears twice in the Passion according to John."[45] But this was assigned for Palm Sunday instead. As Jesus dies on the cross in Luke's gospel (23:46), he references Psalm 31 (30):14-15 instead of 22 (21):1.

8. The second reading is Hebrews 4:14-16; 5:7-9. The gospel acclamation follows.

This passage was newly added to the Good Friday liturgy after the council. Formerly, the second reading was Exodus 12:1-11,[46] essentially the reading that has been transferred to the first position on Holy Thursday. In the post–Vatican II Lectionary, the second reading routinely comes from the New Testament. The revisers of the Good Friday service suggested Hebrews 9:11-15 or another passage proposed by the study group responsible for the Lectionary.[47] The passage from chapter 9 tells of Christ entering the Holy Place not with the blood of goats and calves but with his own blood, obtaining eternal redemption. The passage from chapters 4 and 5, which was accepted for the revised Lectionary, addresses the suffering of Christ the High Priest.

The versicle preceding the gospel is the traditional passage from Philippians: "Christ became obedient."[48] As is clear from the next paragraph, the procession that this text accompanies will be executed as on Palm Sunday, with diminished solemnity. The exclusion of incense and candles has antecedents at least as far back as the eleventh century.[49]

9. The passion according to John (18:1–19:42) is proclaimed in the same way that the passion from one of the other evangelists was proclaimed on Palm Sunday (see above, p. 14).

The history for hearing John's passion on this day is quite deep. Egeria says the passions were read at the place where Jesus died, but John's—especially the part about Jesus handing over his spirit—was proclaimed at three o'clock.[50] One of the earliest listings of Lectionary texts, probably from the seventh century, cites exactly the verses in use today: John 18:1–19:42.[51]

As revisions to this liturgy were underway in 1953, it was proposed that the passion according to John be proclaimed in the vernacular languages.

> Father [Anselmo] Albareda opposed the insertion in the text that the Passion could be sung or said in the vernacular for the same reasons

already advanced in other circumstances; i.e., the unity of language in the liturgy is so great a treasure for the Church that no advantage could compensate for its demise. If the vernacular were to be introduced for the *Passio*, it would also have to be introduced for the other readings. Msgr. [Enrico] Dante agreed. The other members of the Commission were also of the same mind, more or less. The insertion was deleted.[52]

In 1956 the passion was proclaimed from unadorned lecterns, and the location had moved from the epistle side of the altar, which had been traditional, to the gospel side.[53] Those who proclaimed the passion had to possess at least the order of deacon.[54] There was a custom in the eighth century that he read or sang the passion having removed his shoes.[55] The custom of having several cantors sing the passion was established by the seventeenth century.[56] Lay readers received permission to take part in the passion in 1965.[57]

When a bishop presides, all rise as the deacons approach him for a blessing. Then he rises, putting aside his miter as usual. The Ceremonial of Bishops never explicitly states that the bishop proclaims any part of the passion.[58]

During the proclamation of the passion, the Lectionary for Mass instructs all present to kneel and pause for a short time at the words of Jesus' death. The practice appears in the fourteenth-century *Ordo Romanus 14*:

> It must be noted that in the beginning of the passion the pope rises from the cathedra, and his miter being removed, stands his heels against the altar near the middle. He steadies himself on it behind his shoulders, looking at the one who reads the Passion, hands joined in front of his breast. He stands that way continuously until it comes to the place in the Passion where it is said, "And bowing his head, etc." And then the pope kneels in the same place, face towards the altar, and remains kneeling for as much time as it takes to say the Lord's Prayer once. Then he stands up as before. All others do something similar.[59]

10. The priest gives a brief homily, and people may be invited to silent prayer afterward. Previous editions of the postconciliar Missal said, "there may be a brief homily," but the third edition expects that one will be given. It also explicitly assigns the homily to the priest. In some parishes the task has been handed to a deacon, but the third edition presumes the priest will preach. It is not clear if this excludes the deacon, because the priest may ordinarily invite him to preach.

The rubric says that people "may be invited" to silent prayer, but it does not say who issues this invitation. When the bishop presides, he or a deacon gives it.[60] The invitation could even be nonverbal.

In 1953 when the revised liturgy was under discussion, there had been no practice of a Good Friday sermon. When it was suggested, "Father Albareda opposed [the proposal], because after all the Lenten preaching it did not seem appropriate, especially on such a day when the sacred action spoke eloquently for itself."[61] The 1969 draft of the reformed postconciliar liturgy allowed a homily: "After the reading of the Passion a brief homily may be given, at the end of which the priest invites the people to spend time in prayer (if possible on their knees)."[62] The proposed posture for the faithful never carried into the revised rite.

THE SOLEMN INTERCESSIONS

11. The solemn intercessions conclude the Liturgy of the Word, just as the prayer of the faithful does in a typical celebration of the Eucharist. If a deacon is present, he stands at the ambo; otherwise, a lay minister does so. This person sings or says each of the ten invitations that introduce the intention of the prayer. All pray in silence, and then the priest sings or says the prayer. He stands at the chair or the altar and extends his hands in the posture he usually assumes for prayer. The faithful remain kneeling or standing throughout the prayers, but other options are proposed in paragraph 12.

The third edition of the Missal adds the phrase, "if a Deacon is present." It was probably assumed in the previous postconciliar editions, but it is made explicit here.

Prior to the postconciliar Missal, the priest stood at the altar for this prayer, vested in a black cope, and covered the altar with a cloth.[63] If he stood at the chair, the altar cloth was added near the end of the veneration. The Missal had been ambivalent about when the communion rite began. In the 1969 draft of the postconciliar Missal, the priest offered both the invitation and the prayer and did so at the chair, the ambo, or the altar. The people were permitted to kneel or stand throughout.[64] If the priest led the prayer from the altar, the same draft called for a cloth to cover the altar from the beginning of the celebration.[65] The present liturgy keeps the cloth off the altar at this point, even if the priest leads the prayers from there, because these intercessions are still part of the Liturgy of the Word.

12. Between each announcement of the intention and the prayer of the priest, the deacon's invitations, "Let us kneel" and "Let us stand,"

may be retained. Musical notation is provided for singing these texts. The conference of bishops may provide other invitations before the prayer of the priest.

The third edition of the Missal makes a change here. The postconciliar Missal used to permit the conferences to supply an acclamation between the invitation and the prayer. That acclamation is no longer mentioned; instead, the conference may compose a new introduction to the prayer. This honors the tradition that the intentions for the prayer of the faithful be locally composed (if one can consider the conference local), while preserving the traditional text of the orations.

Before the council, the priest used to sing or say both the invitation and the prayer. He proclaimed the first part with hands joined, the second with hands extended. The deacon sang in between these two parts the commands to kneel and stand.[66] The commands from the deacon can be found at least in the seventh-century *Ordo Romanus* 16, which reports people "kneeling on the ground with tears and a contrite heart."[67] In Latin, the deacon uses two different command forms, probably for stylistic purposes. The first is hortatory: "Let us kneel." The second is imperative: "Stand!" In one of the drafts for the postconciliar liturgy, instead of a change in posture, the people were given a dialogue: the priest said the invitation in the usual form, all prayed in silence, and then the deacon would sing, "Through your cross and passion," and all would respond, "Christ, have mercy on us." Then the priest would conclude with a prayer. Territorial authorities were permitted to compose other acclamations.[68] It was thought that the genuflection actually disturbed the quiet of prayer and an acclamation of the people directed to Christ could profitably be added.[69] In the third edition of the Missal, this acclamation has been suppressed, and the kneeling and standing of the faithful has become optional.

13. In addition to the prayers that follow, the diocesan bishop may permit or order a special intention for a situation of grave public need. The third edition of the Missal assigns this to "the diocesan bishop," where previous editions allowed "the Ordinary" to do so.[70] The third edition eliminates the postconciliar permission for the priest to select from the list of intentions, just as the Ceremonial of Bishops permitted the bishop to reduce the list to the "most relevant" intentions.[71] The presider is now expected to pray them all.

If the prayers are sung, the notes appear on the page for the invitation but not for the prayer itself. Instead, one finds (new to the third edition) a note that the simple tone is used, unless the invitations to kneel and stand are included, and then the solemn tone is sung. Examples of the simple and solemn tones are found in the first appendix of the Missal. The solemn tone fits the modality of the invitations to kneel and pray and makes a better complement. Ironically, the priest, who probably is following his text from the Missal, sees the notes for the invitation, and the deacon or layperson delivering the invitation from the ambo cannot physically see the musical notation in the Missal being used by the priest.

A list including prayers for catechumens, heretics, the Jewish people, and idolators can be found in a letter of Pope Celestine I (+432) to the bishops of Gaul.[72] Although this list was not offered on Good Friday, his collection of intentions may have diversified into the modern list. The intentions have varied over the years. For example, the Gelasian Sacramentary included nine prayers: for the church; for the pope and the local bishop; for all bishops, priests, deacons, subdeacons, acolytes, exorcists, lectors, porters, confessors, virgins, widows, and all the people of God; for the Christian emperor and the king; for catechumens; for the removal of errors, the taking away of illness, the dispelling of hunger, the opening of jails, the freeing of bonds, the return of wanderers, the health of the sick, and the safety of sailors; for heretics and schismatics; for faithless Jews; and for pagans.[73] In the mid-eighth century, there is evidence that the entire sequence of solemn prayers was offered first on the morning of Wednesday of Holy Week and then again on Good Friday.[74] In 1953[75] the commission working on the revised rite changed one word in the intention for civil authorities to indicate prayer for "the rights of peoples" instead of "the rights of kingdoms." The commission reinstated the practice of kneeling during the silent prayer for the Jews; this had been eliminated for centuries. The Gelasian Sacramentary had called for kneeling during the prayer for the Jews,[76] but *Ordo Romanus* 31 forbade it.[77] Even the "Amen" at the end of the prayer for the Jews had been eliminated from the preconciliar rite.[78] By 1966 this list had been amended to the following nine intentions: for the holy church; for the supreme pontiff; for all orders and ranks of the faithful; for civil authorities; for catechumens; for the needs of the faithful; for the unity of Christians; for the Jews; and for those who do not yet believe in Christ.[79]

The postconciliar liturgy reformed this list as well as its contents into ten intentions. Most famously it changed the prayer for the Jews, but that was not the only intervention to the traditional list. Prayers for heretics, schismatics, and pagans were redrawn as well. Overall, the sequence of prayers was redone so that they move from the church, the pope, the faithful, and the catechumens; to the unity of Christians, the Jewish people, those who do not believe in Christ, and those who do not believe in God; and finally to those in public office and for various needs. The sequence presents a more logical arrangement of the traditional intentions for this day.

The first prayer is for the holy church, for its peace, protection, and unity, and that it may glorify the Father in tranquility. The priest prays that the church throughout the world may confess God's name. This is still the same invitation and prayer that appeared in the Gelasian Sacramentary, except that the original hoped that principalities and powers would be subject to the church. Those forces were removed out of an ecumenical concern that the phrase "would not be pleasing to separated brethren, and justifiably, for Christ is the one to whom principalities and powers are subject (cf. 1 Cor 15:24) and in whom they were made (Col 1:16)."[80]

The second prayer is for the pope, that he may be safe and unharmed to govern the people of God. The priest prays that God will protect the pope so that the Christian people may grow in merit by reason of their faith. This prayer also comes from the Gelasian Sacramentary, where it also occupies the second position, but there it also prayed for the local bishop. The current practice gives the pope his own prayer.

The third prayer is for all orders and degrees of the faithful: namely, bishops, priests, deacons, and all the faithful people. The priest prays that all may serve God faithfully. He mentions the bishop by name; this was new to the postconciliar Missal. Those who prepared it thought it was necessary to pray expressly for him, and they added his name here rather than increase the number of prayers.[81] A footnote indicates that mention may be made of the coadjutor or auxiliary bishops. The third edition at first included "another bishop" among those who could be mentioned, but this was eliminated in the 2008 republication of the third edition in order to conform with the practice established for eucharistic prayers.[82] As noted above, the original Gelasian prayer named quite a few categories of ministers, but these have been simplified to the three major orders and the lay faithful in general. In the drafts of the postconciliar liturgy, a proposal to join the first three intentions into one was rejected.[83] This proposal was probably brought forth under the inspiration of the Second Vatican Council's vision of the church as the people of God.

The fourth prayer used to be for civil rulers, but they have been moved later in the list in order to group religious categories first. After praying for all the baptized in the church, the next prayer concerns catechumens, those who are associated with the church by their desire for baptism, and most of whom will probably be baptized the following night. The petition asks that God will open wide the ears of their inmost hearts and mercifully forgive their sins that they may be one with Christ through baptism. The priest prays that catechumens may grow in faith and understanding and be added to God's adopted children through baptism. The prayer for catechumens has remained virtually unchanged since it appeared in the Gelasian Sacramentary. It now puts the word "our" in parentheses, to accommodate those parishes that have no catechumens. This was done to allow "a greater correspondence to truthful liturgy."[84]

The fifth prayer is for the unity of Christians, that God may gather them together and keep them in one church. The priest prays that all baptized Christians may be joined together in integrity of faith and the bond of charity. This prayer was newly composed for the postconciliar Missal; it has no precedent in the Gelasian Sacramentary. It replaces the prayer for heretics and schismatics, which used to carry the title, "For the unity of the Church."[85] The invitation to that prayer asked that they be rescued from all their errors and that God would be pleased to call them back to the holy, catholic, and apostolic mother church. The priest's prayer asked that God, who saves all and wants no one to perish, would look upon those souls deceived by diabolic fraud and that, leaving behind the depravity of heresy, their hearts would come to sense their errors, and they would return to the unity of God's truth.[86] The change in tone between these two prayers speaks volumes about the impact of the ecumenical movement at the time of the Second Vatican Council.[87] The new prayer, incidentally, reappears in the Missal among those for the votive Mass for the Unity of Christians.

The sixth prayer is for the Jewish people, that they may advance in love of God's name and faithfulness to the covenant. This invitation went through several drafts; one asked that the Jewish people would grow in knowledge and love of God's word and made no reference yet to the covenant.[88] The priest prays that the Jewish people may attain the fullness of redemption. The new text replaces a prayer for the conversion of Jews: "Let us pray for the faithless Jews: that our God and Lord may remove the veil from their hearts; and that they may recognize Jesus Christ as our Lord. . . . Almighty, everlasting God, who do not reject even Jewish perfidy from your mercy: hear our prayers, which we bring on behalf of the blindness of this people; that recognizing Christ, the light of your truth, they may be rescued from their darkness."[89] That prayer had remained unchanged from the seventh-century Gelasian Sacramentary until the late twentieth century. References to the veil and blindness were removed before the 1966 revision was published,[90] but the complete prayer was redrafted for the postconciliar Missal.

The seventh prayer is for those who do not believe in Christ, that with the Holy Spirit they may enter the way of salvation. The priest prays that they may find the truth and that the faithful may be more perfect witnesses to God's love. This prayer was newly composed for the postconciliar Missal. In the spirit of the council, it reaches out to non-Christian believers. It replaces the one for those "not *yet* believing in Christ."[91] That prayer, which appeared shortly before the council, went like this: "Almighty, everlasting God, who handed over all nations to your most beloved Son, gather the families of all peoples to your Church; so that, seeking the light of truth, they may arrive at you, the true and only God."[92] The final prayer is more evangelistic, praying that the faithful may bear witness to their belief.

The eighth prayer is for those who do not believe in God, that they may find the way to God by following what is right. The priest prays that all may recognize the signs of God's love and may witness the good works of believers so that they may confess the one true God and Father of the human race. This was added because the group preparing the revised liturgy thought that there should be a prayer not just for those who are atheists. Both this and the previous prayer replace the preconciliar one for the conversion of infidels: "Let us pray for pagans: that the almighty God may remove iniquity from their hearts; that, leaving behind their idols, they may turn to the living and true God, and his only Son, Jesus Christ, our God and Lord. . . . Almighty, everlasting God, who seek not the death of sinners but always their life: kindly receive our prayer, and free them from the false worship of idols; and gather them to your holy Church, to the praise and glory of your name."[93] A draft of the revised prayer went like this: "Let us pray for those who do not believe in God, that, living in the sincerity of conscience, they may please the Creator and Savior. Almighty and merciful God, who fashioned humanity in your image and who reveal your invisible powers through your creations in the world: grant that all people contemplating your works may recognize you, their Creator, and having taken delight in the diversity of things, let them sense how much more spectacular are you, their Lord."[94]

The ninth prayer is for those in public office, that God will direct them for the true peace and freedom of all. The priest prays for the prosperity of peoples, the assurance of peace, and freedom of religion. This prayer was moved later in the series from its historical placement in order to group the prayers more coherently. It has been lightly retouched from its original version in the Gelasian Sacramentary, underscoring the theme of religious freedom and broadening the scope and style of governance.[95]

The final prayer is for those in tribulation; it asks God to cleanse the world of errors, disease, and hunger, to unlock prisons, loosen fetters, grant safety to travelers, a return to pilgrims, health to the sick, and salvation to the dying. The priest prays that God will show mercy to mourners, laborers, and those who cry out in any tribulation. It is basically the same prayer from the Gelasian Sacramentary, moved to a new position at the end to gather various intentions into one. The petition for the safety of sailors was removed "because it no longer corresponds to our times. Prayer should rather be made for all pedestrians because of automobiles. Therefore sailors may be subsumed among travelers."[96]

Second Part: The Adoration of the Holy Cross

14. The solemn adoration of the cross takes place after the intercessions. Two forms are given; neither is preferred over the other. Pastoral needs decide which is more appropriate.

The earliest record of the practice comes from Egeria. According to tradition, the relics of the true cross had been discovered in Jerusalem shortly before this time,[97] so the veneration of its wood had become an intense part of the Good Friday observance.[98] Egeria says the community gathered at Golgotha, where the relics of the cross and the superscription for it were displayed in an ornate gold and silver box. People filed past, including the catechumens, touching the wood with their forehead or eyes, and then kissing it. In her record, this took place in the morning before the readings from Scripture, but she attests to the practice of venerating the cross early in church history.[99]

Relics of the cross spread to other centers, and the superscription was transferred to Rome, where it was housed in what is still known as the Church of the Holy Cross in Jerusalem. With it came the customs of veneration, and the Church of the Holy Cross became the traditional location for the pope's stational liturgy on Good Friday. That is where the kissing and adoration took place, according to the earliest Roman liturgical records of it in the eighth-century *Ordo Romanus* 23 and 24. As in Egeria's diary, this was done at the beginning of the service before the Scripture readings.[100] Eventually churches without a relic began the custom of adoring the cross as well.[101] As Amalarius wrote, "There were some people who wanted to say that they wanted the same cross to be venerated on which the Lord was crucified. If only it were present in all churches! It is indeed venerated within other ones. Although not every church can possess it, nevertheless the power of the holy cross is not absent in those crosses that were made in the likeness of the Lord's cross."[102] In the preconciliar liturgy the cross was unveiled in the sanctuary and adoration followed.[103]

As the postconciliar liturgy was being developed, two alternative forms for showing the cross were offered, one in which its branches were unveiled, the other in which the cross was processed up the aisle. The first is more traditional; the first option that appears anyplace in the Missal usually carries a slight preference. But the rubric clearly states that the choice of forms is based on pastoral need. This could pertain to visibility for the participants, the physical abilities of the one carrying the cross, or other practical matters that could weight the decision toward one of the forms.

Regarding the sequence of events, those preparing the revised liturgy were aware of the early tradition that the adoration of the cross preceded the Liturgy of the Word and that it switched positions when a communion rite was added to the celebration: "Although in the soul of the people the adoration of the cross was psychologically of greater importance, nevertheless theologically the reading of the Scriptures exceeded it."[104] It is more in keeping with the logic of Roman liturgy to have an action follow the Liturgy of the Word, so this may have influenced the switch once the procession migrated to Rome from its Eastern origins.[105]

The same study group preparing the postconciliar liturgy noted that the character of the celebration had changed. In the earliest records of Egeria, Pope Innocent I, and the Apostolic Constitutions, it felt like lamentation. However, through the adoration of the cross, this changed into a celebration of its glorious triumph. This could be seen in the arts, such as the ornate decoration of containers holding the relics and the poems written for chanting. "Certainly the Passion of Christ in itself also held a moment of triumph, though a hidden one. . . . The paschal mystery, i.e., the mystery of the Passion and resurrection, is not established in the Passion alone, nor in the resurrection alone, but in both intimately and inseparably conjoined."[106]

Furthermore, the postconciliar study group foresaw difficulties translating the traditional Latin word *adoratio* for this part of the service.[107] "The term '*Adoratio*,' which is important, presents no difficulties in the Latin language. In popular languages, interpretations may appear. For example, in German, it would never be possible to translate it '*Anbetung*' ['adoration/worship']. There it is certainly preferable to say '*Verehrung*' ['veneration/reverence'], and similarly in other languages. It is a good example for practice in translation!"[108] In 1965 the study group working on the postconciliar reform recommended changing the very title of this part of the service from *Adoratio crucis* to *Veneratio crucis*,[109] but it remained *Adoratio* in the published text. The first English translation rendered the word *adoratio* as "veneration," but the revised translation rules now call for a closer cognate of the Latin that has been there for hundreds of years; hence, "adoration" appears in the third edition of the Missal.

The perseverance of the word "adoration" in the history of this liturgy can be understood from St. Thomas Aquinas. He argued that Christians worship that in which they place their hope of salvation. In this case that is not only Christ but his cross. Thomas says that Christians venerate the cross insofar as it represents the figure of Christ, but also from its contact with the limbs of Christ and its saturation with his blood. Consequently, Thomas says that the cross is "worshiped with the same adoration as Christ."[110] This is probably why the Vatican's Congregation for Divine Worship and the Discipline of the Sacraments, which establishes rules for punctuation and capitalization in vernacular languages, decided to capitalize the word "cross" in the rubrics for Good Friday.

The word "adore" was also discussed in regard to the dialogue that accompanies the showing of the cross (see the forthcoming paragraphs). The 1968 draft for the postconciliar liturgy expanded the response of the people from "Come, let us adore" to "Come, let us adore the Lord."[111] The commentary on it made these points:

> It is true that the original sense of the rite evolved almost into something else. For it no longer seems to concern the veneration of the relic, although the text "Behold the wood" still speaks of it. Rather it concerns the adoration of the crucified one. It was not arbitrary without

reasonable cause that the slowly evolving rubric prescribed a cross with the crucified as in the [1956] O[rdo] H[ebdomadae] S[anctae instauratus]. It is true that the elements of the rite contradict themselves a bit: On the one hand, the chant is of the "wood of the cross"; on the other hand, adoration intends the crucified one.

For this reason the question must be pondered whether the whole rite ought to revert to the veneration of the relic, or become a true adoration of the crucified Lord before his image.

As to the first possibility, it must be said: The high point of the Liturgy of the Word is the Lord himself in his death, but not the holy cross, although it must be venerated as a relic. For this reason this place of celebration is not fitting for the worship of the relic, but for the adoration of the crucified Lord.

If such is the case, the chant accompanying the unveiling ought to be corrected, even though it has only one tradition; for example, this way: "Behold the wood of the cross, on which hung. . . . Come let us adore *the Lord*." This would also be for an ecumenical sense. [With respect to] R. D. Thurian, who proposed: "In your cross we adore you, Lord," it is proposed that "Lord" be added to the rite.

Even in this case the possibility would be open to using also a jeweled cross, as not a few recommend.

The proposal to change the people's response was not approved for the postconciliar Missal. Today, the word "adoration" is being used in the English translation for the first time, and it needs careful explanation that the faithful adore Christ, not the wood of a cross. The adoration of the cross in the Good Friday liturgy should not be interpreted as idolatry, though some will misunderstand the intent. The community does not adore the cross as if it were God; the community adores the risen Christ, of whom the cross is a most sacred symbol.

The Showing of the Holy Cross

First Form

15. The deacon or another suitable minister goes to the sacristy, accompanied by other ministers. He takes up the cross, which is covered with a violet veil, and processes with it, two ministers holding lighted candles on either side. The minister walks through the church to the middle of the sanctuary. The priest, standing before the altar and facing the people, receives the cross, uncovers the upper part, lifts it, and sings, "Behold, the wood of the cross." The deacon or the choir, if necessary, assists him in singing. All respond, "Come, let us adore." Then all kneel in silence as the priest remains standing, holding up the

cross. He uncovers the right arm of the cross; the sung dialogue takes place, all kneel, and he lifts the cross again. Finally, he uncovers the cross entirely for the third singing, kneeling, and lifting.

The third edition of the Missal gives much more detail here. New is the instruction to go to the sacristy and to process through the church, as well as the implication that the lighted candles do not accompany the walk to the sacristy but the procession with the cross on the way to the sanctuary. New also is the instruction that the veil should be violet. In the past, some have used red because it is the color of the day's vesture. New is the instruction that the priest should stand before the altar facing the people. New also is the inclusion of the notes for the chant, both in the Latin and English editions of the Missal. The minister's chant is not easy, and it will require some rehearsing, but the people's response is quite learnable. The third edition no longer calls the minister's chant an "invitation." In the past it was called an antiphon,[112] but now it is simply called "Behold the wood of the Cross."

The deacon is the preferred minister for this, but anyone may carry the cross from the sacristy to the sanctuary. The deacon held this responsibility in the preconciliar liturgy,[113] and his role has carried over wherever possible. The sacristy was also mentioned in the 1956 revision,[114] but the starting place for the procession was not so designated in the first editions of the postconciliar Missal. The same is true of the two ministers with lighted candles who participated in the procession from the sacristy to the sanctuary in the 1956 revision.[115] The 1969 draft of the postconciliar liturgy said, "The veiled cross is carried in a simple way to the altar,"[116] making no mention of candles or other ministers at all. The violet color of the veil was explicitly mentioned in the 1956 revised liturgy.[117] No color was mentioned in the first editions of the postconciliar liturgy, and the newly designated red vesture for the ministers influenced the choice of veil color in many places. That the priest stands before the altar facing the people can be traced back even before the 1956 revision of the Good Friday liturgy.[118]

"Behold the wood" and its response, "Come let us adore," can be found in antiphonals dating to the eighth and ninth centuries, first as the communion antiphon[119] and then for adoration of the cross;[120] however, the Gelasian Sacramentary had combined these two events into one procession: "When all these things have been completed, all adore the holy cross and receive Communion."[121] Both parts of the antiphon also appear in *Ordo Romanus* 24, one of the first witnesses to the practice of adoring the cross in Rome.[122] It seems based on a seventh-century antiphon from the Mozarabic tradition.[123] In the preconciliar liturgy, the priest was instructed to raise the musical pitch of the antiphon each time he repeated it, and only in 1956 was the response given to all the people to sing, not just to the choir.[124] The rubrics no longer request a change in pitch. The earliest reference for covering and uncovering the cross at this time is in the ninth-century *Ordo Romanus* 31.[125]

The Good Friday rubrics most commonly presume the use of a cross without the image of Christ. Even the antiphon has always invited people to regard the wood on which hung (past tense) the salvation (or Savior) of the world. The dialogue is another way that the theme of the liturgy balances lamentation and triumph. The earliest explicit reference to a crucifix is in the eleventh-century *Monastic Constitutions of Lanfranc*, where the Archbishop of Canterbury says the abbot and vested ministers prostrate briefly and then "each one shall kiss the feet of the crucifix and return to choir."[126] The 1886 edition of the Ceremonial of Bishops speaks of unveiling "the head of the figure of the Crucified";[127] however, the Roman Missal for centuries simply used the word "cross."[128] In 1956, the rubric for the removal of the second part of the veils changed to say that that action revealed "the right arm of the Crucified,"[129] and it says later that the faithful kiss the feet "of the Crucified."[130] However, both these descriptions were eliminated in the postconciliar Missal in favor of the more traditional word "cross." Still, some churches use a crucifix. The advantage of a cross is that it keeps the two themes of the day in balance—lamentation over the suffering of Christ, and rejoicing in his triumph. The crucifix emphasizes the former, whereas a bare cross captures both.

Second Form

16. The priest, the deacon, or another minister goes to the door of the church and picks up the unveiled cross. Ministers take lighted candles there. The procession moves through the church to the sanctuary. Three times—near the door, in the middle of the church, and at the entrance of the sanctuary—the person carrying the cross elevates it and sings "Behold the wood of the Cross," and all make the response and kneel for a brief moment of silence, as in paragraph 15.

When a bishop presides, the deacon—not the bishop—carries the cross.[131] In the 1968 draft of the postconciliar liturgy, the person with the cross was to be a deacon or another minister, or even a layperson dressed in an alb—the priest was not listed among the candidates for this role.[132]

Once again, the first part of the dialogue, which was formerly called an antiphon and in the previous editions of the postconciliar Missal was called an invitation, now carries neither descriptor. It is simply called "Behold the wood of the Cross."

In some respects, this second form resembles the papal procession of the Middle Ages from the basilica of St. John Lateran to the Church of the Holy Cross in Jerusalem.[133] However, the pope was walking to the place where the relics of the cross were kept; he was not walking with a cross as this form has in mind.

The near antecedent for the second form was the Ambrosian Rite. According to those preparing the 1969 draft for the postconciliar liturgy, "In the second form the priest [sic] now carries the cross in the manner of support and according to the Ambrosian custom."[134]

This second form, which was entirely new to the postconciliar liturgy, was proposed with some second thoughts:

> The second form is less pleasing because of the procession with the cross. It does not make a persuasive analogy with the entrance of the light in the paschal vigil. For if the candle/column of the paschal vigil is a sign of the rising Christ, it makes good sense that it represents his entrance into the church through the procession. But how can the crucified Christ enter into the church, even if only in a symbol?
>
> For these reasons, the difficulty already recalled remains, that the worship of the relic is alien from this place of celebration between the Liturgy of the Word and the Communion.
>
> For this reason it seems that the first form must be recommended.[135]

However, this recommendation did not survive. Instead, the two forms are presented as equal options.

The Adoration of the Holy Cross
17. The priest or the deacon carries the cross to the entrance of the sanctuary or another suitable place. Two ministers with lighted candles accompany this movement. The priest or deacon sets the cross down or hands it to two ministers who hold it. The candles are set on either side of the cross. The point is to set the cross in a place where people may come to adore it. It should be set down or held in a spot where the faithful will have access to it, including those using wheelchairs.

These instructions are very similar to those in previous editions of the postconciliar Missal, but the third edition moves them to this place from their former position at the end of the description of the first form of showing the cross (paragraph 15 above). This is a more logical placement for these instructions because they pertain to the adoration of the cross, no matter which form the showing takes. In the 1956 revision, the priest adored the cross in the sanctuary. Then the cross was moved to a position where the people could approach it.[136] Now everyone adores the cross at the same location.

The third edition specifies that a priest or deacon is to set the cross in place. This was the case in the preconciliar rite.[137] The two candles, absent from the first postconciliar editions of the Missal, returned in the third edition. They had been present in the 1956 revision.[138]

18. The priest goes to adore the cross before anyone else. His chasuble and shoes may be removed if this seems appropriate. The clergy, lay ministers, and faithful approach as in a procession. Upon reaching the cross they may genuflect, kiss it, or use some other gesture appropriate to their region.

New to the third edition is that the priest alone goes first. This was the custom in the preconciliar liturgy,[139] but this may seem like an odd time to emphasize the hierarchical structure of the church. All will be well if the priest approaches the cross as the first among penitents.

New also to the third edition is the suggestion that the priest approach without his shoes. This too was in the preconciliar liturgy[140] and also in the Ceremonial of Bishops.[141] In all these cases, the verb does not say who removes the priest's shoes. There is a custom that other ministers remove the shoes of the bishop or the priest before he goes to adore. Although this rubric would tolerate that interpretation, one should be careful lest people misperceive what is to be stressed: humble adoration of the suffering Jesus, not an inappropriate obeisance to a cleric. For the first time in hundreds of years, the 1956 revised liturgy permitted the faithful to adore the cross, first the men and then the women.[142] The rubrics have never suggested that the faithful remove their shoes at this time, but there is nothing to forbid them if they would find this appropriate.

Kissing the cross is the most historically repeated action of adoration. As mentioned above, Egeria tells of the reverence shown the cross on this day in Jerusalem. The kissing of the cross appears in *Ordo Romanus* 23 and 24,[143] showing that in time the practice migrated to Rome, probably along with relics of the cross. Today, other actions may be done. People may touch the cross, bow before it, or stand for a few moments of contemplation.

19. Only one cross should be used for adoration. If the crowd is too large, the priest offers the cross for some clergy and faithful to adore, then stops the procession. He stands in the middle of the sanctuary before the altar, invites the people to adore, lifts the cross higher for a brief time, and everyone adores in silence. In the 1985 Sacramentary, this paragraph carried a note that a second or third cross could be used in the United States "if pastoral reasons suggest." This permission is not repeated in the revised Missal.

The third edition has added the "clergy" to the group of the few who may adore before the priest lifts up the cross for all to see.

In cases where crowds were large, the commission discussing the revised liturgy in 1957 approved a version of the solution that appears in the liturgy today: "Following the adoration of the cross by the clergy, the cross should be shown to the people from the altar, on the pulpit, or the altar rails, while the celebrant would invite the faithful to recollect themselves in adoration, during a minute's silence."[144] An early discussion of the postconciliar Good Friday liturgy suggested, "if the number of the faithful is such that the veneration would be extended for a long time, the veneration may take place by means of a blessing of all with the cross, given by the celebrant."[145] This was not approved.

Although no reason is given for the use of a single cross, the presence of more than one diminishes the impact of the cross serving as a symbol of Christ. If three crosses were used, people might imagine Calvary and find themselves processing toward a cross symbolizing a thief!

20. Chants are sung during the adoration of the cross. Those recommended are "We adore your cross, O Lord," the reproaches, and the hymn "Faithful Cross." After people adore the cross, they are seated. The chasuble and shoes of the priest would logically be put back on after he finishes his adoration, and he also would be seated.

The third edition moves these instructions from their former position two paragraphs earlier because they more naturally describe the sequence of events here. The notes for the Latin chants have never appeared in the Missal, but they are all in the *Graduale Romanum*.

The antiphon "We adore your cross" has roots in a ninth-century antiphonary and the Roman-Germanic Pontifical.[146] It is thought to have a Byzantine origin.[147] The third edition has removed the indications for the two halves of the choir, "1 and 2," from "We adore your cross" and from "Faithful Cross," probably because they have never appeared in the *Graduale Romanum*. It has also added line breaks and given only the beginning words rather than the complete text when the antiphon is repeated.

The reproaches are sung by two separate choirs, and some verses may be alternated between two different cantors. The division of this text into choirs is noted in the thirteenth-century Pontifical of William Durandus.[148] The third edition moves this rubric from its former place in front of the antiphon "We adore your cross" to this position because it actually belongs with the reproaches. Permission for two cantors to sing some verses is new to the Missal. In the second half of the reproaches, the third edition abbreviates some of the responses.

The beginning of the reproaches includes several lines in Greek. The Latin Missal interleaves these with the Latin translation, so the English edition leaves the Greek lines in place and supplies the English translation after each phrase. The Greek text, called the *Trisagion*, probably dates to the first half of the fifth century.[149] It first appeared in the ninth-century *Ordo Romanus* 31 during the adoration of the cross, and it is thought that the *Trisagion* was added to the Roman liturgy by way of Gallican texts.[150] Together with the *Kyrie* in the Order of Mass, these are the only Greek words that survived in the Roman Rite.

The earliest record of the first part of the reproaches comes from a ninth-century antiphonary and the Roman-Germanic Pontifical.[151] It is based on the following Scripture passages: Micah 6:3-4; Deuteronomy 8:2, 3, 7; Isaiah 5:4; Jeremiah 2:21; and Psalm 68:22. The second part of the reproaches probably dates to the eleventh century,[152] and it is inspired by passages such as Judith 5 and 2 Esdras 9, as well as the apocryphal 4 Esdras. Acts 13 and 1 Corinthians 10:1-13 may also have stimulated the composition of these lines.[153]

The reproaches have been criticized for their anti-Jewish implications. They appear to blame all Jews for not responding to God's call and instead provoking the death of the Son of God. Furthermore, they put these accusations on the lips of Jesus. The reproaches are optional, and many churches choose not to use them to avoid any semblance of disrespect. The 1968 draft of the postconciliar Missal eliminated the reproaches altogether.[154] Nonetheless, they were retained when the Missal was published.

Near the end of the reproaches is the line, "you hung me on the scaffold of the Cross." ICEL's translation had used the word "gibbet" for the Latin word *patibulo*.[155] This became one of the most derided words in the translation and a symbol of the opposition to the vocabulary of the revised translation. The Latin word means the crossbeam upon which Jesus' hands were affixed, but translating the phrase as "crossbeam of the cross" would have been redundant. ICEL chose a less frequently used word, "gibbet," but the Congregation for Divine Worship and the Discipline of the Sacraments changed it here to "scaffold."

The hymn "Faithful Cross" now carries a refrain for all to sing. In previous editions of the Missal, this hymn was assigned to the halves of the choir. Now the cantors sing *Pange, lingua*, "Sing my Tongue," while all sing the refrain about the cross. Even though some congregations have been singing along, this is the first time the rubric explicitly assigns the antiphon to them. The English-language edition of the Missal now offers a metered translation for ease of singing this to a known hymn tune. This hymn may be shortened if the adoration of the cross has concluded, but its final stanza must always be sung.

As noted above in the Holy Thursday liturgy, the *Pange, lingua* was composed by Fortunatus, bishop of Poitier, on the occasion of the gift of relics of the holy cross. The antiphon *Crux fidelis* ("Faithful Cross") is found in the Mozarabic tradition as a hymn for Good Friday.[156] It appears in the Roman liturgy in *Ordo Romanus* 31 during Communion, which could also have been during the salutation (adoration) of the cross.[157]

At the conclusion of these traditional texts is a new rubric in the third edition. It now suggests a chant in memory of the compassion of the Blessed Virgin Mary. It proposes *Stabat mater*, the traditional hymn for Stations of the Cross, but permits any other hymn in accordance with local circumstances, popular traditions, and pastoral appropriateness.

21. After adoration, the cross is carried to its place at the altar. Lighted candles are placed around it, or on or near the altar. The idea is to make a kind of tableau that will last after the conclusion of the service. Most logically, the cross has been situated in a place that also serves as a communion station because that is where the faithful can have access to it. The communion station needs to be opened up, so the cross is moved toward the altar.

This instruction had appeared *before* the texts for adoration in the postconciliar Missal, but the third edition moves it here where the information is more easily discovered. The 1956 revised text suggested that the cross be placed upon the altar up high so that people could see it. This language no longer appears. The altar should probably remain clear for the communion rite, but the cross belongs "at" it—wherever one interprets that to be.

Third Part: Holy Communion

22. Upon the altar is placed a cloth, the corporal, and the Missal. All stand as a deacon—or the priest in his absence—puts on a humeral veil and brings the Blessed Sacrament to the altar. Two ministers with lighted candles accompany the Blessed Sacrament and place their candles around or on the altar. If a deacon has carried the ciborium, he uncovers it, and then the priest approaches the altar and genuflects.

The third edition of the Missal specifies that the "Missal" is placed on the altar. This should have been clear, but in truth previous editions simply called it the "book." The 1969 draft of the postconciliar Missal said only the altar cloth and book were placed on the altar, not the corporal,[158] but this was added in the final publication. The rubric does not say who places these items on the altar. Normally, servers or sacristans would set the table.

The third edition has added the instruction for the deacon or priest to wear a humeral veil. The veil was used here in the preconciliar liturgy,[159] but it was omitted from the postconciliar revision. It has been restored.

The third edition says the Blessed Sacrament is brought to the altar "by a shorter route." Previous editions said "by a short route." The new Latin words *breviore via* can mean "by a rather short route." This is not to be a major procession. The focuses of this day are on the passion, the cross, and Communion, not on the reserved sacrament. Still, some simple reverences are to be in place: the humeral veil and the candles. The Ceremonial of Bishops underscores this point when it says that the Blessed Sacrament is brought to the altar "without any procession."[160] The point had to be made because the preconciliar liturgy called for the Blessed Sacrament to be carried beneath a baldachin at this time.[161] This has been firmly removed from the rubrics. This commentary appears among the drafts for the postconciliar liturgy: "The most Blessed Sacrament is brought back in silence. This is proposed lest the procession of the previous evening be duplicated. Besides, all solemnization seems to contrast poorly with the character of this day. As was said above, the former *sacramentum* on this day was not pleasing because of lamentation. Certainly it cannot now be abolished. But excessive solemnization may be avoided. Let all things be done with dignity, but in a rather simple way."[162]

The possible absence of a deacon is noted twice—at the beginning and end of this paragraph. It was noted only once at the beginning in previous editions of the postconciliar Missal. The third edition takes an extra step to show what is expected with or without a deacon.

Communion has not always been part of the Good Friday liturgy. Pope Innocent I (+417) said that the sacraments were not celebrated at all on Good Friday and Holy Saturday, largely due to the fast, which apparently included a fast from Communion.[163] The eighth-century *Ordo Romanus* 23 explicitly stated that the pope and deacons did not receive Communion at this service, though others could from the reserved sacrament there or in the parish churches.[164] However, in time, a communion rite appeared in the Roman liturgical books, including the Gelasian Sacramentary, where it was combined with the procession to the cross.[165] Eventually this found its way into the preconciliar liturgy where it was commonly called "the Mass of the presanctified." The word "Mass" was already in use to describe the two halves of a typical celebration of the Eucharist: the Mass of the catechumens and the Mass of the faithful. This was another way of specifying the nature of the liturgy at hand. In this case, the Communion had been consecrated at the previous day's Mass, and hence was "presanctified." The resulting ritual included some elements of the Mass not part of today's Good Friday service, such as an incensation of the altar and the dialogue *Orate, Fratres* ("Pray, brethren [brothers and sisters], that my sacrifice and yours . . .).[166]

There never had been a tradition behind reserving any of the consecrated wine, probably for practical reasons. But there had been a practice of placing some of the consecrated bread into unconsecrated wine before distributing it in the Good Friday communion service.[167] In time, though, this part came to resemble a communion service involving whatever had been reserved as usual in the tabernacle. However, in 1622 during the years when very few people were receiving Communion regularly, Communion was officially removed from the faithful on Good Friday and was received only by the ministers.[168]

Still, the question of a communion rite on Good Friday came up in 1953. One concern for introducing Communion to the people was that the Eastern Rites had neither Mass nor Communion on this day.[169] Ferdinando Antonelli observed, "Holy Communion on Good Friday has a profound theological significance: there is no Eucharistic sacrifice, but all share in the fruits of the redemption by Communion with the Divine Victim, having commemorated the bloody sacrifice of

Christ in the adoration of the cross."[170] The decision to restore Communion to the faithful was made in 1955: "everyone will be able to render more copiously, in his soul, the fruits of the sacrifice of Calvary by sacramentally sharing in the Divine Victim."[171]

23. The priest introduces the Lord's Prayer as usual, with hands joined. The location for the musical chant is now noted on the page. Once again, the third edition promotes singing such parts of the service.

The Lord's Prayer has been a consistent part of the tradition for Good Friday in the Roman Rite at least since the seventh century.[172] Nearly all the liturgical documents attest that the introduction, the prayer, and its embolism introduced the reception of Communion.

Even though Catholics take it for granted that the Lord's Prayer precedes Communion, efforts were made to distinguish this particular recitation of the prayer. The 1956 revision said that all present should recite the text in Latin "solemnly, gravely, and distinctly." It was to be recited, not sung.[173] That opinion has changed now that the third edition of the postconciliar Missal actually directs the reader to the place where the chant notation can be found. The 1969 draft of the postconciliar rite had the priest recite the prayer with hands joined,[174] but this did not appear in the final publication of the Missal.

24. The priest prays the embolism, and the people sing the acclamation as usual. The 1969 draft instructed the priest to sing it with the people.[175] However, the published Missal has always said that the people sing this acclamation without the priest. In practice, many priests have sung along. However, this was designed as a dialogue, introduced by the priest with his prayer to Father, and concluded by the people with their acclamation.

The third edition of the Missal introduces new line breaks in the text and refers the priest to the page where the musical notes for these words can be found and chanted.

The Lamb of God is not included in this liturgy. This was true even before the council.[176] However, up until 1956 the priest broke the host into three parts,[177] an action associated today with the Lamb of God. That action was removed from the Good Friday liturgy. The Circular Letter points out that the sign of peace is not included in this celebration either.[178] Some have associated this as an avoidance of the sign by which Judas betrayed Jesus, but it can also be understood as a sign that belongs during the Eucharist, not during a communion service.

25. The priest recites a private prayer before receiving Communion. He is given only one choice: the second of the two options he has at a typical celebration of the Eucharist. Prior to the council, the priest offered three private prayers at every Mass before receiving communion. One of them has been made a public prayer and put into the plural ("Lord Jesus Christ, you said to your apostles . . ."), and the other two have become alternatives. However, on Good Friday, the preconciliar liturgy instructed the priest to recite just one of the three prayers of preparation. That is still the one given here because it is the one prayer the priest has said for hundreds of years before receiving Communion on Good Friday.

26. The priest genuflects, lifts a particle and holds it above the ciborium, and addresses the people while facing them. He gives the invitation to Communion, and he joins the people in making the response.

This is very similar to what happens at a typical Mass. Normally, the priest has a choice of holding the particle above the paten or the chalice. In this case, neither of those vessels is on the altar. He holds it slightly above the ciborium for the same reason in all cases—to collect any particle that might fall.

It may seem unusual for the rubric to say "facing the people" because this is what the priest naturally does at a freestanding altar. The same rubric appears in the Order of Mass in this place. The Order of Mass covers circumstances when the priest is presiding at an altar placed against a wall; for example, in the side chapels of some historic church buildings. In circumstances such as this, the priest needs to be facing the people.

The invitation to Communion did not exist in the preconciliar liturgy because the people did not receive Communion at this service at the time.[179] However, the priest did say, "Lord, I am not worthy . . ." as part of his preparation for Communion. The invitation was inserted in the postconciliar service, but not without some discussion. The 1969 draft of the postconciliar liturgy had the priest say only the first half of the invitation: "Behold the Lamb of God, behold him who takes away the sins of the world." The rest ("Blessed are those who are called to the supper of the Lamb") was omitted "because it is not appropriate on this day when the bridegroom has been taken away. In session IX a more appropriate embolism for this celebration was desired by the Fathers."[180] This idea did not advance beyond the 1969 draft.

The rubric still says that everyone gives the response "once." Prior to the council, everyone recited it three times at every celebration, so the point had to be made clear. It is less necessary now, but the word has remained in place.

27. Facing the altar, the priest reverently consumes the Body of Christ, saying quietly, "The Body of Christ."

Again, the rubric concerning the direction he faces is taken directly from the Order of Mass. If the priest is celebrating Mass at an altar against a wall, he has turned to face the people for the preceding dialogue. To consume Communion, he should do so over the altar, so he turns back at this point. In most circumstances, however, the priest is celebrating facing the people across the altar, and he does not need to turn before or after the dialogue.

28. The priest distributes Communion to the faithful. Psalm 22 (21) or another chant may be sung. New to the third edition is the specific recommendation of this psalm, which served as the responsorial on Palm Sunday and appears in the passion accounts. This had been the practice in the 1956 revision.[181] It had also been recommended in the Circular Letter[182] and is now appearing in the Missal for the first time.

However, what has always been there is the verb "may be sung." The postconciliar liturgy has never required singing during this Communion, and in fact there is a long tradition behind receiving this Communion in silence. For example, Ordo Romanus 24 said explicitly, "All receive this Communion in silence, and that brings the service to a close."[183] The Roman-Germanic Pontifical said the same.[184] Of course, in instances when Communion took place at the same time as the adoration of the cross, the traditional music for the adoration prevailed.[185] Drafts for the postconciliar liturgy considered permitting the singing of an antiphon[186] but ended up stating strongly, "Then [the priest] proceeds to the distribution, and all receive Communion in the usual way, but in silence, singing nothing."[187]

Today an antiphon is permitted, as was the case in the 1956 revision, but communities may consider the impact of receiving Communion in silence on this day.

29. After Communion, the deacon or another minister takes the ciborium to a place outside the church. If necessary, the tabernacle may be used.

The priest does not have to do this, and if the movement requires leaving the sanctuary, it is probably best if another minister performs this action. The third edition of the Missal mentions the deacon as its first preference. No procession with lighted candles, no humeral veil is expected. This is a simple, practical action of putting away the remaining consecrated breads. Because they need to be properly reserved, the tabernacle may be used, but it is more in keeping with the character of this day if the Blessed Sacrament is reserved outside the main body of the church. The tabernacle will need to be empty for the start of the Easter Vigil.

Even in the preconciliar liturgy, the Blessed Sacrament was carried to a place of reposition where a candle was lighted, but no ceremony accompanied this, and the rubrics did not call for any kind of adoration. The Blessed Sacrament was reserved primarily for the sick who might need to receive Viaticum.[188] As will be seen, the Circular Letter envisions that the place used for adoration of the Blessed Sacrament on Thursday night might also be used on Friday for the cross.[189] This suggests a different location for the Blessed Sacrament tonight than what was used on Thursday. A simple place in the sacristy may be sufficient. As in the past, the Blessed Sacrament is reserved today only for those who may need it as Viaticum.[190]

30. The priest invites the people to pray. He may observe a moment of sacred silence. Then he recites the prayer after Communion.

This is the way that the Communion prayer normally happens at the Eucharist. The silence is generally recommended if none has preceded it. Here, especially if the entire distribution of Communion took place in silence, it may not be necessary. The description "sacred silence" is not part of the Order of Mass and occurs only here. It was here in previous editions of the postconciliar Missal as well.

In the preconciliar rite there was no prayer after Communion at all, but the 1956 revision added three of them.[191] The second of these has been lightly retouched and now serves as the prayer after Communion. The first, as will be seen, reappears now as a prayer over the people to conclude the liturgy. The third, as noted above, has become the first option for the prayer that opens the Good Friday service.

In the prayer that remains, the community prays that the work of God's mercy may be preserved in them. They have been restored to life by the death and resurrection of Christ. They hope to live unceasingly devoted to God. The prayer focuses on the effects of the entire paschal mystery, not specifically of this Communion. In a sense, it draws the entire liturgy to a close since it has little to do with the communion rite itself.

In the 1969 draft of the postconciliar liturgy, the priest was instructed to say this prayer with hands joined.[192] That had been the custom for all three of the post-Communion prayers in the 1956 revision.[193] The suggestion did not survive. The priest recites this prayer as he does every other prayer after Communion: with hands extended. To conclude, all answer, "Amen."

31. The deacon, or in his absence the priest, invites people to bow down for the blessing. The priest prays for them, facing them and extending his hands over them. The text of the prayer asks for God's blessing to descend on those who have honored the Son's death in hopes of the resurrection.

The third edition has added the role of the deacon here, as well as the text inviting people to bow down. These clarifications make this similar to the other prayers over the people throughout the Missal. A prayer over the people is now recommended for each day of Lent. This one feels as if it culminates the entire series. Daily Lenten prayers over the people can be found in the Gelasian and Gregorian sacramentaries. The Missal has never included a rubric for the people, but the intent is that they obey the deacon's command. The English translation of the third edition implies that the people make a low bow for these blessings, not a bow of the head.

This prayer over the people, however, does not conclude with the traditional trinitarian blessing. In 1953 the preparatory commission working on the revised liturgy for Good Friday entertained a suggestion to conclude the service by blessing people with a cross. This was a frequent practice in the Eastern Rites in ceremonies commemorating the mystery of the cross. However, since it was unknown in the Roman Rite, it was decided not to create something new for this liturgy.[194]

When a bishop is presiding, he removes his miter for this prayer. It is a prayer over the people, not a solemn blessing. It addresses God, not the people.[195]

32. After genuflecting to the cross in silence, all leave. This gesture is new to the third edition of the Missal. The 1956 rite called for the ministers to make a genuflection before returning to the sacristy, but it did not indicate anything further. The first editions of the postconciliar Missal did not include a genuflection at the end of the liturgy, but it has been restored with the third edition, and now for the first time it is to be made "to the Cross." This is logical because of the adoration that has been made to the cross earlier in the liturgy.

This is the only incident in a liturgical text where a genuflection is made to anything other than the consecrated elements on the altar during Mass or to the Blessed Sacrament in the tabernacle. The holy cross carries that kind of reverence during the period after the liturgy of Good Friday until the beginning of the Easter Vigil.[196]

33. The altar is stripped after the celebration, but the cross remains surrounded by two or four candlesticks. Earlier editions of the post-conciliar Missal said to do this at a convenient time, but the third edition now clarifies that this should take place after the service. This is similar to the rubric in the preconciliar rite, in which the action comes at the very end of the service. On Holy Thursday in the preconciliar rite, this was an elaborate part of the celebration, during which part of Psalm 22 (21) was recited and the ministers carried on the stripping of the altar while still vested. All this has been put completely outside the liturgical action.

The Circular Letter suggests that the location for the cross might be the same place where the Blessed Sacrament was placed after the Thursday night liturgy: "An appropriate place (for example, the chapel of repose used for reservation of the Eucharist on Maundy Thursday) can be prepared within the church, and there the Lord's cross is placed so that the faithful may venerate and kiss it, and spend some time in meditation."[197]

34. Those who have participated in this service do not celebrate Evening Prayer from the Liturgy of the Hours on Good Friday.

Earlier in the Missal, on the Fifth Sunday of Lent, a rubric says that crosses veiled from that day forward were to remain veiled until after the service on Good Friday. As the meaning of this day intensifies, and as preparations for the Easter Vigil get underway, the veils of any other crosses are lifted.

Holy Saturday

1. The church waits at the Lord's tomb with prayer and fasting. Today calls for meditation on the suffering and death of Jesus, as well as his descent into hell. The church awaits the resurrection with hungry anticipation.

New to the third edition is the mention of the descent into hell and the anticipation of the resurrection. Both these elements show influence from the Eastern Rites, which honor the descent intensely on this day.

The Circular Letter suggests that churches set up an image for veneration. The subject may be Christ crucified or lying in the tomb, his descent into hell, or an image of the sorrowful Virgin Mary.[1]

2. The altar table is bare, and the community abstains from the sacrifice of the Mass. Paschal joys lasting fifty days begin after the solemn vigil, the anticipation by night of the resurrection of Christ.

Although the Eucharist is not celebrated during the day today, the Circular Letter strongly suggests that communities gather to pray the Office of Readings and Morning Prayer. Absent that, they conduct some celebration of the Word of God or another act of devotion suited to the day.[2] Many communities add these services, but where the practice is uncommon, it can add an extra burden to those preparing several complicated and important liturgies this week. Besides, the Rite of Christian Initiation of Adults calls for the celebration of the Preparation Rites sometime during the day on Holy Saturday for those who are to be baptized that evening.[3] This celebration may be opened to the entire community.

The Circular Letter says that penance and anointing of the sick may be celebrated today, but not marriage.[4] This will interest catechumens and their spouses in irregular marriage situations who have completed their annulments. The convalidation of those marriages should have taken place as soon as the annulments were completed, not reserved for the last minute before baptism. The last day to convalidate a marriage is Holy Thursday.

Funerals may take place on Holy Saturday, but only according to the rite without Mass. The restrictions forbidding singing and the tolling of bells on Good Friday do not carry over to Holy Saturday.[5]

3. Holy Communion is given only as Viaticum on this day. This, of course, means prior to the Easter Vigil, which usually concludes before midnight. Communion is not brought to the sick unless they are dying, and communion services are not permitted to the faithful.

Easter Time:
Easter Sunday of the Resurrection of the Lord

THE EASTER VIGIL IN THE HOLY NIGHT

1. On this night the faithful await the return of the Lord with lighted lamps in their hands, recalling the gospel parable in Luke 12:35-37, which tells of servants awaiting their master's return from a wedding banquet. This night also recalls the exodus of Israel from Egypt, which was kept for the Lord as a vigil, and which succeeding generations were also to keep.[1] Citing St. Augustine, the Circular Letter says, "The full meaning of vigil is a waiting for the coming of the Lord."[2]

The Easter Eucharist is the most ancient of all the Holy Week liturgies. It was probably celebrated as early as the second century, but without the observance of Palm Sunday, Holy Thursday, and Good Friday.[3] It was a unitive celebration, embracing the entire paschal mystery of the suffering, death, and rising of Jesus Christ.

The Easter Vigil went through many evolutions over time, but a significant turning point happened in 1951 when the Vatican made optional a revised liturgy for the vigil, just four weeks before Easter of that year. Even with the brief time for implementation, the liturgy was received with much anticipation, and in spite of some difficulties, it virtually launched the liturgical renewal, especially with regard to the active participation of the people.[4] This was the first liturgical rite in hundreds of years to assign specific responsibilities to the faithful. Participants in the revised rites reported to the Vatican: "Thus far, 125 official reports had been received; 63 were Italian, 24 were French, and the remainder coming from elsewhere. The five continents were represented, and none of the reports was contrary. The success was most consoling since the experiment had been a complete success."[5]

The liturgy for the vigil is complex, and there are temptations to shorten it. However, the Circular Letter cautions, "Great care should be taken that this eucharistic liturgy is not celebrated in haste; indeed, all the rites and words must be given their full force."[6]

2. This is the greatest and noblest of all solemnities, and there should be only one celebration of it in each church. It begins with the lucernarium and Easter proclamation, then in the Liturgy of the Word the church meditates on the wonders God has done. As day approaches, new members are born in baptism, and the church gathers at the table of the Eucharist for the memorial of the Lord's death and resurrection. Thus, the vigil unfolds in four parts.

New to the third edition is that this is the "greatest and most noble of all solemnities." This description had been introduced in the Ceremonial of Bishops.[7] St. Augustine calls it "the mother of all vigils,"[8] as will be seen in the introduction to the second part of the vigil, the Liturgy of the Word.

The third edition is the first to restrict the celebration to one per church. It also expands the description of the first part: no longer a mere ceremony of light, it includes the paschal proclamation, popularly known as the *Exsultet*. In the 1985 Sacramentary, this paragraph said that new members are reborn as the "day of resurrection" approaches; the third edition says that the Eucharist is celebrated with newborn members "as day approaches." Perhaps this was done because the celebration of the "day of resurrection" is already beginning in the night. It could also imply that the vigil begins later than people think it should, placing its culmination closer to dawn. But this is probably a vestige of a preconciliar concern about when the Mass begins.

The third edition also expands the description of the Eucharist, the fourth part of the vigil. It now says that the Eucharist is a "memorial" of the Lord "until he comes again." These ideas can be found in 1 Corinthians 11:25-26.

The Circular Letter encourages people to attend the vigil in its entirety[9] and not to miss it even if on vacation.[10] The so-called Second Synod of St. Patrick, which probably dates to the eighth century,[11] said, "Whoever does not receive Communion at the Easter Vigil is no longer among the faithful."[12] Nothing so strong is stated today, but this is the first celebration of the resurrection of Jesus Christ, the first proclamation of the gospel of the resurrection, the occasion for baptizing new members into life in Jesus Christ, and the first celebration of the paschal Eucharist in which Christians share the Body and Blood of the risen Lord. In practice, most of the faithful skip the Easter Vigil and participate in the Eucharist on Sunday morning, but they are missing the theological and liturgical center of their Catholic lives.

3. The Easter Vigil begins after nightfall and ends before daybreak. The entire celebration should take place at night.

Celebrating this liturgy at night is "an ancient tradition," as the first paragraph asserts. Egeria maddeningly says, "The paschal vigils take place as they do with us."[13] She says virtually nothing more about them, figuring that her audience at home knew the local customs, but today's readers do not know what she did. Tertullian (+220) wrote of the nocturnal character of the day.[14] Ambrose died on the night of the Easter Vigil, according to Paulinus.[15] Augustine calls it the "mother of all vigils."[16] Among the *Ordines Romani* and the early sacramentaries, there are witnesses to a variety of starting times: 3:00 p.m., 2:00 p.m., and 1:00 p.m.[17] "The trend toward an earlier hour for the Vigil began in the seventh century and went on until by the twelfth century it was being celebrated in the morning. With the Missal of 1570 this was made a matter of law, and so we arrived at the absurd situation of celebrating a night service on the morning of the wrong day."[18]

When the revised Easter Vigil came under discussion in the 1950s, the liturgy had migrated to the morning, which caused difficulties for its symbols of the fire and the night.[19] A proposal in 1950 would have started the vigil at such an hour that the Mass within it would begin at midnight, making it parallel to the Christmas celebration.[20] The experimental liturgy became available in 1951, and later that year some bishops preferred starting the celebration in the late evening, whereas a smaller number favored the early morning on Easter.[21] In 1952, realizing that "in some places grave reasons would not recommend the celebration of the Vigil at midnight," it was permitted to start it earlier in the evening, but not before 8:00 p.m.[22] This marked a great departure from the custom of celebrating the entire vigil in the morning of Holy Saturday. However, in 1953 when some of the German-speaking bishops asked to start the vigil at 7:00 or 8:00 p.m., or at 3:00 or 4:00 a.m., the commission believed it had to be done during the middle of the night. "Father Albareda pointed out that existing usage had to be accommodated to the new rite and not *vice versa*. The Easter Vigil is the only liturgical celebration to commemorate the mystery of the 'proper' time. This was historically certain."[23] This line of thinking prevailed but softened. In 1957 it was still preferred that the Mass would begin at midnight, but for serious reasons and under the judgment of the local ordinary, the vigil could be anticipated. Still, it had to begin after sunset and end before dawn.[24] This is the language that has endured in the rubrics to this day.

Those preparing the postconciliar vigil said, "The Vigil is per se a nocturnal office."[25] The Circular Letter finds reprehensible the practice of celebrating "at the time of day that it is customary to celebrate anticipated Sunday Masses."[26]

4. Even if the Mass is celebrated before midnight, it is the paschal Mass of Easter Sunday. This may seem obvious today because of the frequent occurrence of anticipated Saturday evening Masses throughout the liturgical year. But in the years before that practice began, no Mass for Easter could begin before midnight; the same was true of Christmas. The Gelasian Sacramentary instructed the priest not to progress from the vigil to the Mass until "a star appeared in the sky."[27] The rubric in the third edition of the postconciliar Missal clarifies the current practice of the church.

Prior to the council, there was a stronger distinction between the vigil and its Mass, which began at a certain point. Today these parts form one celebration. In the past, certain elements could begin before midnight, but the Mass would have to begin later. In 1967, the study group wrote, "In this celebration, there are not many independent parts standing on their own, but a single theme: redemption through the Lord's death and resurrection."[28] A commentary on the 1968 draft of the postconciliar liturgy presumed this point: "Indeed this first part is the introduction to the whole. But this whole is joyful. For the way is toward the Light of Christ, the Passover from darkness to light, from Egypt to the Promised Land, which foreshadows eschatological time and the coming of the Lord, and which Passover again and again is set before the eyes of the faithful in the readings. Insofar as there is 'penitence,' it is 'metanoia' in the Greek sense; i.e., a person's conversion from darkness to light."[29]

5. Those who receive Communion at this Mass may receive again the next day. Priests who celebrate or concelebrate may do so again on Easter Day. Those who participate in the Easter Vigil do not also pray the Office of Readings from the Liturgy of the Hours. The vigil replaces it.

The third edition made a few minor changes to this paragraph. The notice about Communion had been part of the previous paragraph, and it was moved here where it fits more logically with the content concerning priests. It also referred to the "second Mass of Easter," which only existed before the council; that has been changed to "Mass during the day."

Also new to the third edition is that the vigil replaces the Office of Readings. A draft of the postconciliar liturgy had said that the vigil would replace Vespers and Compline,[30] but this did not carry through. In fact, the Liturgy of the Hours offers Evening Prayer for Holy Saturday. It is the only Saturday in the entire liturgical year that has its own evening prayer instead of Evening Prayer I of Sunday.

6. A deacon normally assists, but if there is none, the celebrant or a concelebrant may fulfill his duties. The priest and deacon wear white Mass vestments.

The reference to the deacon is new to the third edition. As in other places, the Missal is clarifying the procedures and encouraging the participation of deacons. Assigning diaconal roles to concelebrants in the absence of a deacon is common to any Mass.[31]

It was necessary to specify the color and kind of vestments because, in the preconciliar liturgy, the vigil began in violet vesture, the priest wearing a cope,[32] and the ministers changed vestments several times. This fit the idea that the "vigil" was different from the "Mass." After midnight, the priest would change to a white chasuble. Now he wears it from the beginning, unifying by his vesture the elements of the celebration, and treating all of it like Mass. A draft of the postconciliar liturgy still permitted the celebrant to put on the chasuble only after performing the baptisms, but the vesture was still to be white.[33]

If images in the church have been veiled since the Fifth Sunday of Lent, these should be uncovered before the start of the vigil, as indicated in the Missal on that Sunday.

7. All who participate should have candles. The church lights should be put out.

It is sometimes hard to keep the lights out because of many last minute details, but an effort should be made. There are no rubrics governing the lighting of votive candles in the church, but it is more in keeping with the spirit of the day if these candles are not available until after the vigil. The third edition has moved the rubric about the darkened church from the next paragraph to this one, where it more reasonably pertains to conditions before the liturgy begins. The preconciliar vigil began with some candles already lit; these had to be extinguished after the Easter candle was lighted so that they could be relighted with blessed fire.[34]

There is no rubric forbidding catechumens from holding candles, but logically they would not. The candles are ultimately a sign of the risen Christ dwelling in the baptized, and these individuals will receive candles right after they are baptized.

First Part: The Solemn Beginning of the Vigil or Lucernarium

THE BLESSING OF THE FIRE AND PREPARATION OF THE CANDLE

8. Outside the church a burning fire is prepared. The people gather and the priest and ministers approach. One minister holds the paschal candle. The processional cross and candles are not carried. If a fire cannot be lighted outside the church, see paragraph 13 below. In accordance with paragraph 15 below, charcoal should be included with the fuel.

There is no rubric that says how the fire is to be lighted, but prior to the council it was struck with flint.[35] Some were using cigarette lighters because they complied with this rule, but the fire today may be ignited in any feasible way.

The third edition adds the Latin word *ardens* to its description of the fire and it is translated here as "blazing." Perhaps more significant is the word for the fire that remains the same: *rogus*, not *ignis*. It means a sizeable fire, a bonfire. The adjective "blazing" may seem redundant, but it indicates a large fire. It also means that the fire is already aflame while the people are gathering. The prayers that are forthcoming concern the blessing of the fire, not the lighting of the fire. One of the drafts for this postconciliar liturgy did call for the striking of the fire after the introduction to the service and just before the prayer of blessing the fire.[36] This idea did not prevail.

Fire has been part of this rite for centuries, but in different ways. In the fourth century, Eusebius says that Constantine had the whole city illuminated during the night of the vigil, and Cyril of Jerusalem speaks of "that night whose darkness is like day."[37] There is a tradition that the custom was begun by St. Patrick in the fifth century, whose seventh-century biographers say that he lit a fire on the hill of Slane the night before Easter, before appearing before King Laoghaire at Tara.[38] The Gelasian Sacramentary instructed the ministers to go to the church, enter the sacristy, vest, and then sing a litany. Meanwhile, fire that had been hidden since Good Friday was brought forth.[39] Pope Zachariah (+752) wrote that large fires were ignited on Holy Thursday on the occasion when the chrism was consecrated, and these were kept lit in order to light the candles for Holy Saturday.[40] *Ordo Romanus* 26 from a little later in that century ordered that the new fire be struck from a rock.[41] The ritual has prevailed through all the revisions of the twentieth century, even though the group preparing the postconciliar reforms heard from some sources that the rite was "theatrical and vulgar,"[42] and they actually omitted it from one of the first drafts, which started immediately with the lighting of the candle and its procession into the church.[43] In the end, the fire ceremony was retained because it was loved by many of the faithful.

New to the third edition is the clarification that the processional cross and candles are not carried. The paschal candle replaces them. The preconciliar vigil did call for the cross to be in this procession,[44] but this is no longer the case. Although this clarification is new to the Missal, it had already appeared in the Ceremonial of Bishops.[45]

Today, the word "people" is barely noticeable in this rubric: "When the people are gathered there . . ." Catholics have become accustomed to seeing the role of the people spelled out in the liturgy. However, prior to the liturgical reform this was not the case. The rubrics consistently told the bishop, the priest, the deacon, and other ministers what to do, but the full, conscious, active participation of the people was a later development. It came as a result of the liturgical renewal, as evidenced in the revised vigil of 1951. In the parallel paragraph of that revision, paragraph 3, are found these words telling the ministers where to stand once the fire had been lighted and they were properly vested: *ubi scilicet populus ritum sacrum melius sequi possit*, or "namely, where the people can better follow the sacred rite." That is the first mention of the word "people" in the liturgical renewal. It appeared in the opening of the Easter Vigil, and it served to notify the ministers that the people had a role that could not be ignored.

9. The service opens with the sign of the cross, just as happens in any celebration of the Eucharist. The priest says the greeting in the usual way and then instructs the people about the vigil. A sample text is provided, offering a catechesis on the Christian Passover.

The sign of the cross is new to the third edition. In previous editions the liturgy began with the greeting. This provided a subtle connection to the other liturgies of the Triduum. Holy Thursday ended without a dismissal, and Good Friday began without a greeting and ended without a dismissal, so the Easter Vigil logically began without the sign of the cross to show its unbroken unity with the other services, reaching back to the evening Mass of the Lord's Supper. Even in 1950, Antonelli had written, "The great Vigil concluded in an atmosphere of joy for the Lord's resurrection. This joy continues throughout Easter, a day that is considered the end of the great solemnity, begun on Holy Thursday and continued through Good Friday. The resurrection is inseparable from Christ's death. The fathers often and rightly speak of a twofold Pasch: the Pasch of the Cross (*Pascha staurosimon*), and the Pasch of the Resurrection (*Pascha anastasimon*)."[46]

There never has been a sign of the cross in the rubrics for the Easter Vigil, so its insertion probably forms another way to signal that the entire vigil is a celebration of the Eucharist. The Mass does not begin midway through. It is underway from the first words of the liturgy.

As sometimes happens with new rubrics, this one seems incomplete. It does not indicate that the people answer, "Amen," nor that they respond to the priest's greeting, but that surely is the intent.

The priest delivers the introduction, but when a bishop presides, a deacon or concelebrant may say these or similar words.[47] The sample text, which was new to the postconciliar Missal, imagines the scattered church coming together to watch and pray. In John's Gospel, Caiaphas said it was better for one to die for the many, and John comments that this was a prophecy that Jesus would gather into one the scattered children of God.[48]

10. The priest extends his hands and blesses the fire. He prays that the faithful may be inflamed with heavenly desires and attain festivities of unending splendor. This prayer is based on one that has been part of the Roman Rite since the first edition of the Missal in 1474.

The third edition explicitly states that the priest says this prayer. There was little doubt about this, but earlier editions of the postconciliar Missal said, "the fire is blessed," without indicating who does it. New also is the instruction for him to pray with his hands extended, though this has appeared in the Ceremonial of Bishops.[49] The previous editions said nothing about the position of his hands. Prior to the revisions of this liturgy in the 1950s, the priest recited three prayers to bless the fire. It was reduced to one in 1951, and that prayer is still the one in use.[50]

The previous editions of the postconciliar Missal followed the prayer with this rubric: "The paschal candle is lighted from the new fire." This was most peculiar because the same rubric appeared two paragraphs later. That sentence has been removed from the third edition. One of the last drafts of the postconciliar Missal had the rubric in place right after the blessing of the fire, but it had streamlined the rest of the ritual, moving immediately from this point to the procession into the church.[51] Apparently, when that draft was expanded with more of the intervening rituals for publication, the rubric mistakenly remained in place after the prayer for blessing the fire.

The revisions of the vigil in the 1950s all called for the priest to sprinkle the new fire with holy water and to incense it with the thurible.[52] This has been eliminated; holy water is to be blessed later in the service, so its introduction here probably seemed inappropriate. Similarly, the charcoal for the incense has just been blessed with the rest of the fire, so there was little point in using blessed fire further to bless the fire.

11. After the new fire has been blessed, a minister carries the paschal candle to the priest, who cuts a cross into it with a stylus. He draws the Greek letter alpha above the cross and the letter omega below it, and then the four numerals of the current year, while reciting the traditional text. This rite had been optional in the previous editions of the postconciliar Missal. Now it has become obligatory.

The third edition says the candle is brought forward by one of the ministers; previous editions of the postconciliar Missal said an acolyte or minister performed this function. Today anyone may do it.

Clear references to the paschal candle come from the Middle Ages. Earlier testimony is scant, sometimes unreliable, yet provocative nonetheless. Still, when the Gelasian Sacramentary has the archdeacon stand before the altar, receive the fire that had been hidden since Good Friday, cut a cross into the candle, light it, and sing a blessing about it, the tradition for the candle ceremony in the Roman Rite has begun.[53] The Roman Pontifical of the twelfth century had the archdeacon cut the cross, alpha and omega, and the year since the incarnation.[54] In time, the paschal candle became so large that it could no longer be carried in procession. Candles arranged in a small triangle eventually replaced it.[55] During the reforms of the 1950s, the words "paschal candle" returned to the Roman Rite.[56] With it came the cutting of the cross, the Greek letters, and the numbers of the year.[57] The text and actions for this ritual have remained virtually unchanged since 1951. They blend the mysteries of the cross and resurrection of Jesus Christ.

The Greek letters alpha and omega are not translated. As mentioned earlier, the only usage of Greek in the Roman Rite is the *Kyrie* and the *Trisagion* of the Good Friday reproaches. However, these two letters have also remained, and their existence shows the connection to the biblical tradition where Jesus calls himself the Alpha and Omega.[58] They also point to the unity of the church East and West.

The drafts of the postconciliar rite omitted this incision altogether.[59] A commentary said, "The incisions introduced in the O[rdo] S[anctae] H[ebdomadae] are also omitted. For the excellent intrinsic sense of this rite almost always loses its meaning because the signs and words for the required incisions are already present in the candle before the whole rite."[60] Still, the rite that was once criticized became optional after the council and now has become obligatory again.

The Circular Letter has some preferences about the candle: "The paschal candle should be prepared, which for effective symbolism must be made of wax, never be artificial, be renewed each year, be only one in number, and be of sufficiently large size so that it may evoke the truth that Christ is the light of the world."[61] Some are tempted to light reusable candles or to change the numbers on the same candle each year. However, the symbolism of new life demands a new candle each and every Easter.

This is one of the rare places where the rubric is accompanied by a diagram. Ever since the 1950s, a diagram has appeared in the book to show what the instructions have in mind. This tradition continues.

12. The priest may insert five grains of incense into the candle in the form of a cross, reciting a text about the wounds of Christ. This was made optional after the council and it still is. Another diagram accompanies the text in the Missal.

A tenth-century publication of the English Pontifical of Egbert included two alternative prayers for blessing incense under this fragmented heading: "The blessing of incense on Holy Saturday before you bless the candle, and you should have it put into the candle in the very place where 'Receive the incense' is said [in the proclamation (*Exsultet*)]."[62] The practice derived from a misunderstanding of the procedures in the Gelasian Sacramentary. That source included no blessing or insertion of incense grains into the candle, but its proclamation concluded with a prayer called *Benedictio super incensum*.[63] From the context, the heading means "Blessing on the lighted candle," but it was misunderstood to mean "Blessing on the incense." Consequently, medieval Pontificals added a blessing of incense before the proclamation, and the insertion of grains during this final part of the same prayer.[64] The practice continued this way all the way up to 1951.[65] After that time, the insertion of the grains was moved up earlier in the ceremony to the place where they were blessed.[66] They were removed from the drafts of the postconciliar liturgy[67] with this explanation: "These grains signify the sacrifice of the candle, which is also commemorated in the text of the proclamation. But it is of ecumenical importance that this idea disappear, lest our separated brethren think that in the Catholic

Church there is another sacrifice besides the sacrifice of Christ. Besides, all these matters will also serve the shortening of the entire liturgy of this night."[68] Today the blessing of the incense has been omitted and the insertion of the grains has become optional. After the council, the word that caused the confusion, *incensum*, was replaced with the word *laudis* (praise)—God is asked to receive not the evening sacrifice of the lighted candle, but the evening sacrifice of praise.

There is no mention of the wax nails for Easter candles. In many parishes, instead of incense grains, these nails are inserted. At the very least, the nails could be used to drive the grains into the candle, but the only rubrical reference is to the grains.

13. Wherever a large fire cannot be lighted outdoors, the fire blessing is to be adapted. People gather in church as on other occasions; the priest and ministers carrying the candle go to the door. The people turn toward the priest as they are able. The greeting and address take place as in paragraph 9 above, then the fire is blessed and the candle is prepared as in paragraphs 10–12.

It is hard to see from the English translation, but the Latin text is describing two types of fire: *rogus* and *ignis*. Where difficulties prevent the lighting of a *rogus* (something like a campfire), an *ignis* (a much smaller fire) is lighted.

One of the drafts for the postconciliar liturgy had a different solution: "Where because of present difficulties a large fire is not lighted, the blessing of a fire may be omitted. In this case, the paschal candle is lighted at the door of the church and the procession takes place as [noted above]."[69] The circumstances that had been submitted for consideration were "storms, wind, rain, cold, snow, limited space, insufficient lighting to read the text, etc."[70] Now the fire is not to be omitted but replaced with something smaller.

When the people are invited to turn toward the priest, they are performing the first action assigned to them in the liturgical renewal that began in 1951 (see above, p. 119).

The sign of the cross is not mentioned here. This is probably an oversight; it was inserted at the start of the liturgy only in the third edition of the Missal, and the revisers probably neglected to mention it again here. The third edition simply copied this paragraph from the second edition, though it was brought forward ahead of the priest's text, which now appears in the next paragraph to make the instructions flow more smoothly.

14. The priest lights the paschal candle from the new fire, singing a prayer that the light of Christ will dispel the darkness of minds and hearts.

The local conference of bishops may adapt the preceding elements. This is more restrictive in the third edition; formerly, pastoral circumstances determined how many of the preceding rites to do.

This short prayer was new to the 1951 revision of Holy Saturday.[71] It has retained its place through the postconciliar revisions. The priest has always said this prayer as he lighted the paschal candle, and it now appears with chant notation in the Missal for the first time. A 1968 draft of the postconciliar liturgy had the people light their candles as soon as the paschal candle was lit.[72] This did not carry over into the final text, and the Circular Letter explains that the people should be led by the light of the paschal candle alone: "Just as the children of Israel were guided at night by a pillar of fire, so similarly Christians follow the risen Christ."[73] The 1969 draft omitted this short text in its streamlined ceremony of the light.[74] At this point of the liturgy, prior to the council, the priest blessed the grains of incense, and then the lights of the church were extinguished in order that they might be relighted with the blessed fire.[75] Today, the text expresses the meaning of the light of Christ as soon as the candle is set ablaze.

PROCESSION

15. A minister takes a burning charcoal from the fire and places it in the thurible. The priest adds incense to it. The deacon, or another minister in his absence, takes the candle in procession, preceded by the thurifer. The priest, ministers, and people, all holding unlighted candles, follow. At the door of the church, the deacon pauses, lifts the candle, and sings, "The Light of Christ." All answer, "Thanks be to God."

Most of this is new to the third edition of the Missal. The pre-1951 liturgy had an acolyte take blessed charcoal and place it in the thurible while the priest said the prayer of blessing over the incense. This was removed from all the revisions of the liturgy from 1951 until the third edition of the Missal, which instructs "one of the ministers" to do the deed. The purpose is to have blessed fire inside the thurible before the incense is added, especially since the blessing of the incense is no longer part of the liturgy. However, there are practical difficulties. The fire has to be lit well in advance, and charcoal should be part of the fuel from the very beginning. Otherwise, adding incense to recently ignited charcoal will not accomplish very much. In practice, someone will have to use tongs or some other device to move the hot coal from one location to another. The third edition updates the rubric from the Ceremonial of Bishops, which said, "The censerbearer lights the charcoal in the censer from the new fire."[76] The problem remains: the charcoal will not be hot enough to create smoke when incense is added next.

The description of the order of the procession was in the previous editions of the postconciliar Missal, but after singing the first acclamation in the procession. It appears now where it can more easily be found. A similar description of the procession had occurred in the preconciliar liturgy of 1951.[77]

The deacon sings at the door, "The Light of Christ." The rubric does not say what to do if there is no deacon, but presumably the chant is sung by whoever is holding the candle. In 1951 it was proposed to have an acolyte assist the deacon, but the pontifical commission for the revised Holy Week liturgy struck the suggestion.[78]

The revised translation changes the text from "Christ our Light" to "The Light of Christ." The word *Lumen* could also be translated "brightness" instead of "light." *Lumen* is not the same word as *lux*. The third edition of the Missal provides musical notation for this dialogue for the first time.

In the preconciliar liturgy the deacon sang this text once he entered the church.[79] In the first postconciliar editions of the Missal, he sang this at the fire. The third edition now has the deacon go to the door of the church as he did before the council. The difference is that he is now "at the door of the church," not inside it, because the people have gathered outside.

The preconciliar editions all asked the deacon to raise the pitch each time he sang, "The Light of Christ."[80] This is no longer the case.

The first editions of the postconciliar Missal allowed the conferences of bishops freedom to devise another acclamation, and the Circular Letter reinforced the idea,[81] but this has been removed from the third edition. As an example of what might have happened, the 1968 draft of the postconciliar liturgy considered this: "According to the vote of the Fathers of the council, the participation of the people may be rendered a little more intensely with a broader acclamation: 'Light shines in the darkness. Thanks be to God.' It does not seem necessary to multiply the acclamation."[82]

New to the third edition is the instruction that the priest lights his candle outside before the procession enters the church. He did this in the preconciliar liturgy ever since 1951.[83] However, in the postconciliar liturgy, no other candle was lighted until after the second singing of "The Light of Christ."

A procession existed in *Ordo Romanus* 16, though it took place in silence.[84] In the twelfth century Roman Pontifical is found this instruction for the deacon who has just prepared the candle with the cross, alpha, omega, and year: "After this, humbly bowing, coming to the priest, he receives a blessing from him, and then rising and turned toward the choir he says three times, lifting up his voice: 'The Light of Christ.'"[85] No response was yet indicated, but it became part of the Missal tradition after the Council of Trent and was sung by the choir.[86] In 1951, that response was explicitly given to the people for the first time.[87]

When a bishop presides, another minister carries his pastoral staff because he is carrying a candle.[88] Normally, the bishop carries the staff in processions, but his hands are not free at this time.

16. The deacon or the minister carrying the candle moves to the center of the church, raises the candle, and sings the acclamation a second time. All respond. After this, all light their candles from the paschal candle and continue in procession.

The second dialogue was carried out at the door of the church in previous editions of the postconciliar Missal, even though the 1969 draft still had it inside.[89] It has now been moved back inside, where it was in the preconciliar liturgy.[90] Before the council, the candles of the clergy were lit at this point, not those of the people, but the third edition retains the postconciliar practice of lighting everyone's candle after the second intonation.

Logistically, this is often the most difficult part of the ceremony. Some people are impatient and want their candle lighted sooner. The 1968 draft of this liturgy envisioned it this way: "Some of those who attended the blessing of the fire enter before the ministers; the second half follows. Those who precede light the candles of those inside the church who await the procession with the paschal candle."[91] However, today's liturgy tries to preserve the symbolism of the paschal candle as the light of the risen Christ, leading the entire church on pilgrimage.

17. The deacon or minister carrying the candle arrives at the altar, faces the people, lifts the candle, and starts the dialogue for the third time. Then the deacon or minister places the candle in a large stand near the ambo or in the center of the sanctuary. All lights in the church are lit, except for the altar candles.

The third edition of the Missal clarifies that the minister holding the candle lifts it for this third dialogue. This should have been understood, but the previous postconciliar editions neglected to mention it. The third edition has also moved up the instruction for placing the candle in the sanctuary. It used to be in the next paragraph, but it more logically belongs here.

In 1951 the candles of the people were lighted at this point;[92] this has been moved up in the postconciliar Missal. Prior to 1951, the people did not hold candles, so the only candles lit were the three fixed on a single stand. The paschal candle was lit near the end of the proclamation.

The third edition clarifies that the altar candles are not yet lighted. This should have been deduced from the instructions concerning the Gloria (see below, p. 140), but it is made explicit now. The rest of the candles should be lit, and the electrical lights in the building should all come on.

This is probably the most ignored rubric in Holy Week. Many communities leave the electrical lights off until after the proclamation, or even until the readings have concluded. In 1971 the ecumenical British Joint Group issued a ceremony that began with the readings and then moved to the light service, a pattern that can be detected in some Eastern rites.[93] However, the rubric in the postconciliar Roman Missal has remained unchanged. It seems to signify that the light of the paschal candle spreads to every light in the building, not just to the candles in the hands of the faithful; in a sense, the paschal candle illumines the electrical lighting as well. Some communities prefer the effect of experiencing the proclamation by candlelight, switching on the electrical lights afterward. However, this creates an additional symbol not foreseen in the rubrics, a further illumination not directly connected with the light of the candle as it is progressively heralded on its journey to the sanctuary.

THE EASTER PROCLAMATION (EXSULTET)

18. The priest goes to his chair, hands his candle to a minister, adds incense to the thurible, and blesses it as usual. If a deacon is to sing the proclamation, he requests a blessing from the priest as he does before the gospel. The priest gives the blessing; it is identical to the text before the gospel, except it replaces the words "that you may proclaim his gospel" with the words "that you may proclaim his paschal praise." Although the translation says, "his paschal praise," the Latin

words are identical to the heading of this section, which appears as "The Easter Proclamation." The priest is not praying that the deacon may proclaim just any praise of the Lord but specifically the Easter Proclamation that soon follows. This text has remained unchanged from the preconciliar Missal.[94]

The deacon answers, "Amen." Before the gospel at a typical Mass, the deacon signs himself with the cross as he receives and responds to the blessing. The deacon's gesture is not mentioned here, but it is probably an oversight because the priest's gesture is indicated.

If the person singing the proclamation is not a deacon, the request and blessing are omitted.

19. The deacon incenses the book and the candle and sings the proclamation at the ambo or a lectern. Everyone else stands holding a lighted candle. If there is no deacon, the priest or a concelebrant may sing the proclamation. If necessary, a lay cantor may do it, omitting the section that refers to the singer as a deacon as well as the greeting, "The Lord be with you." The proclamation has a shorter form that may be used. It may be recited, but it is more effective when sung.

New to the third edition is the suggestion that a concelebrating priest sing the proclamation if there is no deacon. Also new is the stipulation that a lay cantor would sing the text "because of necessity." Presumably this refers to a situation in which the priest does not possess the skills to sing it. However, any different singer here can help avoid unduly wearying the ears of the people or the voice of the priest, who has much more to sing and say before the night is over.

In 1951 the deacon was instructed to incense the candle by walking around it. This was discontinued in the postconciliar Missal. He simply gives the candle three swings of the thurible.[95] The 1969 draft implied that the deacon, priest, or cantor who sang the proclamation would also incense it.[96] This is still the sense of the postconciliar Missal, even though the English translation of the third edition says, "The Deacon, after incensing the book and the candle, proclaims . . ." A more literal translation of the Latin reads, "The Deacon, once the book and the candle have been incensed, proclaims . . ."[97] There is no obstacle to having a priest, cantor, or thurifer incense the book and the candle.

The possibility of singing at the ambo was introduced just before the postconciliar revision.[98] The ambo is now listed as the first option for the location of this proclamation. Formerly, the deacon stood sideways in the sanctuary, facing the candle with the altar on his right and the assembly of the faithful on his left.[99] If the candle has been situated some distance from the ambo, a case could be made for singing from a lectern adjacent to it.

The third edition omits the reference to acclamations during the proclamation. Earlier postconciliar editions of the Missal noted that a conference of bishops could adapt the text by inserting acclamations for the people. This is no longer the case.

The third edition lavishly provides the chant notation for both the long and the short versions of the text. This adds to the pagination, but makes it much easier on the singer.

All hold lighted candles. This should have been understood, but it was made explicit just before the council.[100] The idea was affirmed in 1952 by the commission working on the first revisions to Holy Week.[101]

The text of the proclamation has undergone some modifications over the years. There are early references to a praise of a candle sung by a deacon in sources such as Ambrose, Augustine, and Jerome,[102] but no examples of the words. The earliest text of the proclamation is in the seventh-century Gothic Missal,[103] which has remained largely unchanged except for the abbreviation of its one lengthy section about bees and the elimination of its concluding prayers for the clergy and people of the church.[104]

The opening phrase calls upon the hosts of heaven, the angel ministers, to exult. The Latin word *mysteria* is well translated as "ministers," under the assumption that it is a misreading of *ministeria*. When a deacon sings the text, he asks those standing in the awesome glory of this holy light to pray that God will pour light on him who, though unworthy, is numbered among the Levites. Deacons were called "Levites" because of the Old Testament sons of Levi who assisted the priests at the temple.[105]

The proclamation includes a dialogue that resembles the opening of a preface. Although the Gothic Missal did not completely spell it out, it can be inferred from the following lines, which begin, "It is truly right and just." The proclamation thus shares resonances with the gospel in the way that the deacon prepares to proclaim it, in the place where he sings it, and with its message of resurrection. It resembles the eucharistic prayer in the dialogue that introduces it, in the way that it gives thanks to God and in the way that the candle is offered to God.

After thanking God for the forgiveness of sins won by the death of Christ, the proclamation recounts the feasts of Passover that this night celebrates. It speaks of this being the night of both the Jewish and the Christian Passovers, the night when Israel was set free from slavery in Egypt to cross the waters of the Red Sea, and the night when Christ rose from the underworld to set the faithful free from sin. The phrase, "Our birth would have been no gain, had we not been redeemed," is nearly a direct quote from 2.41–42 in *The Exposition on Luke* by St. Ambrose.[106] The line "to ransom a slave you gave away your Son" is derived from Romans 8:32. The justly famous oxymoron "happy fault" (*felix culpa*) is based on the words *felix ruina* from a commentary on Psalm 40 (39):9 by Ambrose.[107] Where the text says, "This is the night of which it is written: The night shall be as bright as day," it refers to Psalm 138:12.[108]

The next section briefly praises the sanctifying power of this night. After the words "brings down the mighty" is the point where the preconciliar proclamation was interrupted for the insertion of the grains of incense into the unlighted candle. This took place because the next line was misinterpreted to mean the sacrifice of incense instead of the sacrifice of the candle (see above, p. 122). The next line now has "sacrifice of praise," which eliminates the confusion. The preparation of the candle has been moved forward with the optional blessing of incense, and the entire text of the proclamation is now sung without interruption.

The deacon asks God to accept the candle, a solemn offering, the work of bees and of the hands of God's servants. The candle is a sacrifice of praise, a gift of the church. The Gothic Missal had the rather lengthy excursus on the bees here, inspired by the Georgics of Virgil.[109]

Calling the candle a "sacrifice" was considered to be problematic in 1968 because of misunderstandings among both Protestants and Catholics,[110] but the text remained in place. The candle is called "a fire into many flames divided," and this was questioned in the 1968 draft. Scholars believed it originally referred to the practice of people taking fire home with them, and this was no longer being practiced.[111] A second reference to the paschal insect says that mother bees had drawn out the wax now melting. This was composed at a time of the erroneous perceptions that the queen produced the wax and that bees symbolized purity because they reproduced asexually.

Where the deacon sings, "O truly blessed night, when things of heaven are wed to those of earth," another cut was made in the postconciliar Missal. It used to say, "O truly blessed night, which destroyed the Egyptians and enriched the Hebrews. Night when things of heaven . . ."[112] The removal of these words was proposed in 1968 "because it is quasi-politically intolerable today."[113] These words were eliminated in the 1969 draft.[114]

Finally, the deacon asks that the flame of the candle may mingle with the lights of heaven and be found still burning by Christ, the morning star, probably a reference to 2 Peter 1:19, Revelation 2:28, and especially Revelation 22:16.[115]

The very end of the proclamation used to pray for the pope, the bishop, and the Roman Emperor. In 1951 Father Agostino Bea requested that the last of these be changed, and Father Joseph Löw was asked to draft a rewrite.[116] The naming of the emperor was changed to "those who rule over us in power," and the petition was expanded that God might "direct their thoughts toward justice and peace, that by their earthly labors, they may reach the heavenly fatherland with all your people."[117] All these final petitions were struck from the proclamation in the postconciliar Missal.

In a 1965 draft of the revised postconciliar liturgy, the Gloria was to be sung immediately after the proclamation. Bells would ring and the organ would play. The Gloria ended up in a very different place.

Second Part: The Liturgy of the Word

20. Nine readings are provided for this, the mother of all vigils. Seven come from the Old Testament and two from the New. All should be read whenever possible, that the character of the vigil may be preserved. The length of the service is one of its primary symbols.

As indicated above in the commentary on the second introductory paragraph for this liturgy, St. Augustine is the source for calling the Easter Vigil "the mother of all vigils."[118] The Circular Letter also cites him,[119] as do the General Norms for the Liturgical Year and the Calendar.[120]

New to the third edition is the rubric that all nine readings should be read whenever possible. This has been imported into the Missal from the Circular Letter.[121]

21. Where more serious pastoral circumstances demand it, the number of Old Testament readings may be reduced. At least three readings come from the Old Testament, and they must be drawn from both the Law (or the Historical Books) and the Prophets. Their psalms should also be sung. The third reading in the list, the story of the exodus from Egypt, should never be omitted, nor should the canticle that follows it.

New to the third edition is the criterion that "serious pastoral circumstances" permit a reduction in the number of readings. Prior to this time, "pastoral circumstances" governed the choice. In addition, previous editions of the postconciliar Missal permitted a minimum of two readings from the Old Testament; this was the minimum required in the 1968 draft, one of which had to be the story of the exodus.[122] That number has now been raised to three. Combined with the previous paragraph, this liturgy intends to resemble an extended vigil.

Also new to the third edition is that the two parts of the Old Testament must each contribute readings. A community cannot proclaim, for example, only the first three readings in the list; they need to add something from the prophets as well. The entire Old Testament leads to a deeper understanding of the New.

The third edition also now requires that the responsorials follow each reading, and it especially mentions the canticle that follows the third reading in the list—both the reading and the responsory are obligatory. However, as will be seen, paragraph 23 still permits replacing the responsorial psalm with a period of silence.

22. All set aside their candles and sit. The priest instructs the people about the Liturgy of the Word. A sample text is provided, but he may use his own words. The sample text invites people to listen, meditate, and pray over the paschal mystery.

It should be obvious, but the candles of the faithful should be extinguished when they sit down, not merely "set aside." Perhaps the verb was chosen because in the preconciliar liturgy the ministers "set aside" their white vestments and put on violet ones at this point.[123] They no longer do so, but the people do set aside their candles.

When a bishop presides, he may permit a deacon or concelebrant to give this instruction.[124] When a priest presides, the Circular Letter permits him to pass this introduction to the deacon.[125] The closest event to this in the preconciliar liturgy was this instruction to the priest before the readings began: "Before or during the time when the prophecies are read, priests catechize the catechumens expecting to be baptized, and they prepare for baptism."[126] That instruction, together with the readings that followed, formed the final preparation of those to be baptized. However, in reality, baptism at the Easter Vigil was rare in those days. The instruction is more related to a practice that may now take place at any Mass. Before the readings begin, the priest may give a brief introduction to them.[127] The Lectionary for Mass explicitly allows a deacon or layperson to do so at a typical celebration of the

Eucharist.[128] As the General Instruction of the Roman Missal was being developed, the 1968 draft did not include this suggestion, but the 1969 draft did.[129] Similarly, the 1968 draft of the Easter Vigil liturgy did not include an introduction to the Liturgy of the Word,[130] but one did appear in 1969.[131] The text is identical to the one that still appears in the Missal today.

23. The readings follow as usual. A lector goes to the ambo and proclaims the first reading. A psalmist or cantor leads the people in the psalm. All rise. The priest invites them to prayer. All pray in silence. Then the priest says the prayer that corresponds to the reading. The responsorial may be replaced by a period of silence, in which case the priest does not pause after he says, "Let us pray."

The Circular Letter says, "Great care is to be taken that trivial songs do not take the place of the psalms."[132] It would be interesting to know what provoked that concern.

Previous editions of the postconciliar Missal in Latin called these prayers "collects," though the English translation called them prayers. Now even in Latin they are called "prayers." There is one collect at this Mass, and it comes after the Gloria. Although the rubrics in 23 do not indicate that the people are seated after each prayer, logically they are.

The number of readings for the Easter Vigil has fluctuated throughout the centuries and locations where Christians gathered. Egeria says the gospel of the resurrection was proclaimed twice, once in each of the principal services,[133] but she gives no other details. A fifth-century Armenian Lectionary may reflect the early Jerusalem experience. It had twelve readings: Genesis 1:1–3:24 (the story of creation); Genesis 22:1-18 (the binding of Isaac); Exodus 12:1-24 (the Passover charter narrative); Jonah 1:1–4:11 (the story of Jonah); Exodus 14:24–15:21 (the passage through the sea); Isaiah 60:1-13 (the promise to Jerusalem); Job 38:2-28 (the Lord's answer to Job); 2 Kings 2:1-22 (the assumption of Elijah); Jeremiah 31:31-34 (the new covenant); Joshua 1:1-9 (the command to possess the land); Ezekiel 37:1-14 (the valley of dry bones); and Daniel 3:1-90 (the story of the three children).[134] In Rome, Gregory the Great reduced the number of readings from twelve to four, perhaps to keep the people from getting too tired.[135] An early seventh-century Roman list of gospel readings assigned Matthew 28:1-7, the story of the resurrection, to the Holy Saturday celebration.[136]

The list of readings from the Gelasian Sacramentary, from about the same period, greatly influenced the Roman Rite: Genesis 1:1-31, 2:1-2 (the story of creation), Genesis 5–8 (the story of Noah), Genesis 22:1-19 (Abraham and Isaac), Exodus 14:24-31, 15:1 (the exodus from Egypt), Isaiah 54:17, 55:1-11 (the invitation to the waters), Ezekiel 37:1-14 (the valley of dry bones), Isaiah 4:1-6 (with the canticle on the Lord's vineyard from Isa 5:1-2), Exodus 12:1-11 (the Passover charter narrative), Deuteronomy 31:22-30 (with its canticle: Deut 32:1-4, Moses' song of the covenant), Daniel 3:1-24 (the three young men), and Psalm 42 (41) (as the deer yearns for running streams). In time, the Roman Missal added Baruch 3:9-38 (the wisdom of God's commandments)and Jonah 3:1-10 (the repentance of Nineveh).[137] These readings were proclaimed without introducing their title and without the response, "Thanks be to God."[138] All of them came to be called "prophecies."

The pontifical commission planning the revision in 1951 agreed to reduce the number of prophecies from twelve to four, similar to the decision made centuries ago by Gregory the Great. Bea recommended the creation (Gen 1:1-31, 2:1-2), the fulfillment of the Messianic kingdom (Exod 14:24-31, 15:1—a symbol of baptism), the happiness of the Messianic kingdom (Isa 4:1-6—with the canticle of the vine), and the exhortation of Moses to the people of God (Deut 31:22-30—an admonition of fidelity to baptism).[139] A proposal came forward later that year to proclaim these four readings in the vernacular languages, but this was not approved.[140] Still, the priest was instructed to sit and listen while a lector proclaimed them. In 1951, moving the action from the priest to a lector was a novelty because in the Mass of the day, if a lector read the lessons aloud, the priest would still have to read them at the altar.[141]

When the postconciliar revision was underway, several different schemas were considered. In 1965 it was decided that four Old Testament readings should be proclaimed, two from the Law and two from the Prophets. Here is the pool of readings from the Law, from which two choices would be made: "Genesis 1:1-31 and 2:1-2 (= first prophecy of the old Order): the story of the first creation; or Genesis 5–8 (= second prophecy): the flood; or Genesis 22 (= third prophecy): the sacrifice of Abraham; or Exodus 12:1-11 (= ninth prophecy): concerning the Passover of the Lord; or Exodus 14:19-31 and 15:1 (= fourth prophecy); or Deuteronomy 31, 22-30 (= eleventh prophecy)."[142] All the suggestions were already in the Roman Missal, but they were sequenced according to their appearance in the Bible.

The selections from the prophets were these: "Daniel [sic][143] 37:1-4 (= seventh prophecy): bones coming back to life; or Isaiah 54:17 and

55:1-11 (= fifth prophecy); or Baruch 3:9-38 (= sixth prophecy); or Isaiah 4:2-6 (= eighth prophecy); or Jonah 3:1-10 (= tenth prophecy); or Daniel 3:1-24 (= twelfth prophecy). Afterwards the canticle Isaiah 5:1-2 ('the vineyard . . .' = canticle after eighth prophecy); or Psalm 135 with the antiphon sung by the people, 'For his mercy is eternal.'"[144] By 1968 the readings had changed to Genesis 1:1–2:2; Genesis 22:1-8 (both these first two readings came with shorter forms); Exodus 14:15–15:1; Isaiah 4:2-6; Isaiah 55:1-11; and Daniel 3:49-51.[145]

This same draft included a prayer that preceded the readings,[146] which eventually moved to become an alternative for the prayer following the seventh Old Testament reading. Its purpose was explained in a commentary: "The prayer is introductory and exceedingly appropriate to demonstrate the purpose of the readings that follow. The instruction is for the understanding of the mercy of God and for stirring up hope of the future."[147]

As can be seen, the postconciliar Easter Vigil Liturgy of the Word chose a different sequence of readings than the one inherited from the Gelasian Sacramentary. In the tradition, Christians were fasting up until the Easter Eucharist. Consequently, some believed that the readings of the preconciliar service were influenced by the fast and sorrow over the death of Christ. "Many authors think that even the readings of this night participate in this character and are of a penitential nature. For this reason they sense a great difficulty because of the joy of the liturgy of light, thinking that the liturgy will descend the participants from joy into sadness and from there lift them up again to joy. Indeed the color of the vestments once encouraged this impression."[148] But the commentators disagreed. "These texts intend to show the history of salvation in the Old Testament. They are filled with messianic and eschatological hope, and are never sad. Even though the Old Testament is only a shadow compared to the New Testament, in these readings a certain joyous quality appears, for the Old Testament is the hope of the new."[149] Consequently, they proposed a distillation of the twelve readings into six.

Regarding the prayers that conclude the readings, those preparing the postconciliar revision were aware that some of these would pose a challenge to understand. A 1968 commentary made them optional: "Nothing prevents having the responsorial psalm or prayer done 'if it seems appropriate.'"[150] In 1969 the draft noted, "Other orations are being prepared, easier to understand and shorter, to be chosen *ad libitum*."[151]

The choice of readings was revised in 1968. "Concerning the readings, an eventual revision must be expected. Perhaps in place of the sixth reading, Ezekiel 36 could be assigned. But it is not necessary that the brief song of the [three] young men proposed in the Order be seen to conflict with the song 'Gloria in excelsis,' which according to the present proposal follows it before the readings of the New Testament are taken up."[152] The study group on the Lectionary proposed Isaiah 54:5-14 in place of Isaiah 4:2-6, and Baruch 3:9-15, 32–4:4 and Ezekiel 36:24-28 in place of Daniel 3:52-56.[153] The double Liturgy of the Word, straddling the Gloria, had precedents in Ember Days and in the Pentecost Vigil.[154] The revised schema of readings, then, aimed to highlight themes of conversion as it related to baptism, but all in the joy of the resurrection.

Some traditional readings found other places in the liturgical year. Isaiah 4:2-6 moved to Monday of the First Week of Advent, where it is proclaimed only in Year A. And the passage from Daniel appears in abbreviated form on Wednesday of the Fifth Week of Lent.

PRAYERS AFTER THE READINGS

24. The first reading on creation is Genesis 1:1–2:2, but a shorter form may be chosen: 1:1, 26-31a. The psalm may be 104 (103) or 33 (32). The passage can be traced at least to the fifth-century Armenian Lectionary, one of the earliest lists of vigil readings on record. The abbreviated version is offered out of a pastoral concern for the length of the vigil. The two psalms both deal with the theme of creation. Just as God created the world in the beginning, so God recreates the world through the resurrection of Jesus Christ.

The third edition of the Missal clarifies the rubric, which formerly said the prayer followed the reading but now says it follows the reading and the psalm. This clarification is now made for all seven Old Testament readings.

There are two options for the prayer. The first asks for understanding that the marvels of creation are surpassed by the sacrifice of Christ at the end of the ages. This text draws its final image, "Christ our Passover has been sacrificed," from 1 Corinthians 5:7. The original version of this prayer came from the Gelasian Sacramentary, where it followed the reading about Noah. It makes a better fit here because of its reference to the creation of the world.

The alternative prayer, called "On the creation of man," asks God who created and redeemed human nature to set the minds of the faithful free from sin, that they may attain eternal joys. The Gregorian Sacramentary included this prayer after the reading about creation. It was the choice of the preconciliar Missal[155] and is retained now as the second option.

25. The second reading tells of Abraham's sacrifice (Gen 22:1-18). It has an abbreviated form for pastoral reasons (vv. 1-2, 9a, 10-13, 15-18). This reading also appeared in the fifth-century list for the vigil. Psalm 16 (15) follows because of its belief that God's faithful one will not undergo corruption.

The prayer appeared in the Gelasian Sacramentary, where it followed this very reading. The two have formed a unit ever since this prayer was composed. It recalls God's promise that Abraham would be the father of nations and sees the fulfillment of that promise in baptism.

26. The third reading concerns the passage through the Red Sea. It has been part of the vigil at least since the Gelasian Sacramentary, and it is the only one of the seven Old Testament readings that must be proclaimed every year because it so clearly foreshadows the mystery of the resurrection.

There are two choices for the prayer, the second of which was added only in the 1969 draft of the vigil.[156] The first praises God, who freed people from Pharaoh's persecution and now brings salvation through baptism, and prays that the whole world may become Abraham's children. This prayer appeared in the Gelasian Sacramentary after this reading, so the two share a common history on this night. The only difference is that the postconciliar liturgy changes the words "Egypt's persecution" to "Pharaoh's persecution." The only explanation is that it seemed "appropriate."[157]

The second option appears in the Pentecost Vigil of the Gelasian Sacramentary, where it follows the reading of the song of Exodus. It compares the Red Sea to the baptismal font, and the nation delivered from slavery to the Christian people. It similarly prays that all nations may be reborn by the Spirit. It was added to the Easter Vigil texts for the first time in the postconciliar Missal.

These first few prayers have been strongly linked to the readings they follow, but that is not so true of the remaining prayers in this series.

27. The fourth reading concerns the New Jerusalem (Isa 54:5-14) and is followed by Psalm 30 (29). It is new to the postconciliar Easter

Vigil. It mentions the days of Noah, so the reading hearkens back to the tradition of hearing about Noah's flood at this liturgy. This passage tells of the faithfulness of God and the conversion of Israel. Psalm 30, which praises God for a rescue, says, "you brought me up from the netherworld."

The prayer that accompanies this reading comes from the Gelasian Sacramentary, where it follows the passage from Isaiah 55. That reading survives as the next in the postconciliar Missal, but the prayer that originally followed it has been assigned here. The change occurred rather late in the 1969 draft.[158] However, as the rubric indicates, a different prayer from the series may be offered in place of this one if the corresponding reading is to be omitted. The third edition clarified this rubric, which previously could have been understood to mean that some readings would definitely be omitted. The problem existed in the Latin original, not in the English translation. This is a small change but another indicator of the Missal's preference to proclaim all the readings on this night.

28. The fifth reading dates to the Gelasian list: Isaiah 55:1-11. Its theme is salvation freely offered to all. The canticle of Isaiah 12 follows it; it sings of the source of salvation as a fountain of water, hence foreshadowing baptism. In place of the Gelasian's prayer that originally followed this reading, the one that now follows the fourth reading, the postconciliar Missal offers the Gelasian's prayer that followed the passage from Daniel.[159]

The prayer, which calls God the "sole hope of the world," asks for an increase in longing, for only with God's grace do the faithful progress in virtue. In the 1968 draft, this prayer followed the reading from Isaiah 4, even though the passage from Daniel still appeared in the list.[160] In 1969, the readings from Isaiah 4 and Daniel were omitted from the list, and this prayer moved to its current position after Isaiah 55.[161]

29. The sixth reading is Baruch 3:9-15, 32–4:4, on the fountain of wisdom. It is followed by verses from Psalm 19 (18). This is a slightly different reading from the one that was added fairly late in the development of the Roman Missal and remained in use up to 1951. It was removed with the revisions of the 1950s but restored in the postconciliar Missal. The psalm draws its refrain from John 6:68, "Lord, you have the words of everlasting life," and meditates on the precepts of God. Since Baruch refers to God as the "fountain of wisdom," its

conjunction with this psalm blends the themes of baptism and enlightenment. Those to be baptized are truly wise, the ones who follow God's precepts.

The prayer asks for God's unfailing protection upon those to be baptized. It comes from the Gregorian Sacramentary, where it followed what is now the fifth reading from Isaiah 55. It was brought into the Roman Missal for the first time after Vatican II.

30. The seventh reading is Ezekiel 36:16-28, about a new heart and a new spirit. Verses from Psalms 42 (41) and 43 (42) follow, unless baptism is not celebrated, and then one chooses from two different options: the canticle from Isaiah 12, which is used after the fifth reading, or verses from Psalm 51 (50). In truth, the third edition of the Missal, which is the first to give the references to the psalms in all seven places here, does not mention the option of using anything except Psalms 42 (41) and 43 (42). However, the other options still appear in the Lectionary. Psalm 42 (41) used to be proclaimed as a final reading in the list of the Gelasian Sacramentary,[162] and it now occupies a similar position as the response to the last of the seven Old Testament readings for the vigil.

This reading from Ezekiel 36 was added to the postconciliar Missal in place of the traditional excerpt from Ezekiel 37 on the dry bones. Chapter 36 perhaps underscores the theme of conversion of heart more than chapter 37 does. It was proposed as an alternative to the Daniel reading: "Some of our companions nevertheless propose that in place of the sixth reading concerning the three young men in the furnace (Dan 3) be read Ezekiel 36:24-29, concerning the new spirit and the purification in clean water, especially for this reason: The canticle of the three young men has to follow the reading of Daniel 3; since, however, after the canticle of the children, the hymn 'Gloria in excelsis' must be sung [see below, p. 141], two [similar] chants would immediately follow each other."[163]

The prayer asks God to accomplish the work of salvation, raising up what was cast down, making new what was old, and restoring all things through Christ. This prayer used to follow the first reading in the Gelasian Sacramentary.[164] It has been moved here and amplified with lines from an April (Easter?) preface in the Verona Sacramentary.[165]

Another option for this prayer may be used. It asks that the God who instructs and prepares the community through both the Old and New Testaments will help them comprehend his mercy. This prayer came in this position in the Gelasian Sacramentary, right after its passage from Ezekiel.

The 1969 draft included a third option for this prayer, the one that followed the Litany of the Saints in the preconciliar Missal.[166] That prayer still follows the litany in the postconciliar Missal. The 1969 draft offered it as an option to conclude the Old Testament readings if there were candidates for baptism present. It is still used only if there are candidates for baptism, but later the service (see below, p. 149).

31. After the last set of a reading, psalm and prayer, the altar candles are lit, and the priest intones the hymn "Glory to God in the highest." All sing along, and bells ring according to the local custom. The third edition of the Missal now gives the musical notation for the first line of the Gloria in Latin so that the priest may sing it directly from the altar book. The rest of the Latin hymn is found in a completely different book, the *Graduale Romanum*. However, any vernacular setting of the hymn may be sung.

The third edition also makes a slight change in the description of when this all takes place. The previous postconciliar editions said it takes place after "the responsorial," but the third edition says after "the responsorial psalm." It may be a simple clarification, or it could be another indication that the Missal aims to eliminate the Lectionary's options for the responsorial after the seventh reading, one of which is a canticle, not a psalm.

In the Gelasian Sacramentary, the Gloria concluded the baptismal ceremony at the vigil,[167] and it seems to have been there as a baptismal hymn of praise.[168] However, later witnesses imply that the Gloria rather began the Easter Mass, because the *Kyrie* had been absorbed into the baptismal litany. *Ordo Romanus* 24 called for the lighting of altar candles after the baptisms,[169] signaling the start of the Mass, and then the Gloria was sung. This practice endured in the preconciliar Roman Missal.[170]

This sequence remained the custom throughout the preconciliar period.[171] However, the council reconceived the structure of ceremonies at which sacraments were celebrated, putting them after the homily, as was seen above in the options for the chrism Mass. As a result, the baptismal ceremony at the vigil was moved from its location after the Old Testament prophecies to its new position after the homily. That drew together the two parts of the Liturgy of the Word. However, the Gloria and the collect for the Mass remained between the Old and New Testament readings as a bridge from one to the other. With the lighting of the altar candles, this arrangement still seems to imply that Mass begins with the Gloria, but the revisers of the liturgy conceived the entire liturgy as a whole, albeit with certain moments of emphasis.

Deciding on a place for the Gloria proved especially difficult for the postconciliar revisers. "The *Gloria* is a paschal hymn par excellence. Up to the eleventh century priests were permitted to sing the 'Gloria' only at the Easter Vigil (see Gregorian Sacramentary, 1: 'Again the Gloria in excelsis Deo is said if the bishop is present, only on the Lord's Day or on feast days, but when priests preside it cannot be said except only at Easter'). Therefore it absolutely must be retained."[172] But when?

> Concerning the place, different people feel differently. Many proposals have been made:
>
> a) after the Exultet: for in the opinions of many, that a song or acclamation may be made as a response of the faithful to the Easter Proclamation, and there are those who think the Gloria is an exceptionally appropriate hymn.
>
> b) before the prayer and the epistle of the Liturgy of the Word, as in the traditional order.
>
> c) after the gospel, as the response of the people to the announcement of the resurrection.
>
> d) after baptism; in the Gelasian Sacramentary, the Gloria is placed under the heading of Baptism in the order of Mass. Besides, there are authors who think that the Gloria was a baptismal hymn (cf. P. H. Schmidt, *Hebdomada Sancta*, p. 867).
>
> e) at the end of the Mass before the postcommunion as a hymn of praise and thanksgiving, according to the intent of the recent instruction, "Tres abhinc annos," n. 15.
>
> The study group, for now and without a better idea, agrees that the *Gloria* should be sung between the readings of the Old and New Testament.[173]

A comment on the 1968 draft reads as follows:

> The place of the "Gloria" was again discussed, and the proposal was affirmed again. The completely new arrangement of the Liturgy of the Word of God tends toward it, so that the readings of the Vigil may be united with the readings of the Mass, and so that a double Liturgy of the Word may be avoided. . . . In the history of salvation, the "Gloria"

occupies exactly the place between the preparatory history of Redemption and the beginning of the Redemption itself. "Gloria" is a kind of sign of the new and messianic Age, a sign of passing over from shadow to truth. And the song "Gloria" is so appropriate for this moment of joy that the prophets foretold as much with jubilation.[174]

A comment on the 1969 draft of the postconciliar liturgy reaffirmed this: "In session X it pleased the Fathers that the hymn *Gloria* be sung in its place in salvation history, that is between the readings of the Old and New Testament."[175] Thus, it had less to do with baptism or the sweep of the Mass than with the trajectory of salvation history narrated in the nine readings.

The ringing of bells during the Gloria has been a custom throughout the four hundred years of the preconciliar Roman Missal,[176] and the practice has been retained. The bells, silenced since this point of the Holy Thursday evening Mass, return with joy to announce another high point in the evening celebration. Anyone may ring the bells. Some parishes invite people to bring their own.

32. The priest prays the collect as usual when the hymn is concluded. All the faithful pray that God will stir up in the church a spirit of adoption, so that they may render undivided service. This is essentially the same prayer that has existed in this place ever since the Gelasian Sacramentary.[177] The only difference is that the prayer used to ask God to "preserve" the spirit of adoption. The postconciliar Missal asks God to stir it up. The preconciliar liturgy positioned this prayer after the baptisms had been celebrated. Since it was now to be proclaimed before the baptisms, God was asked to stir up that spirit in anticipation of the baptisms to come.

This is clear from the bumpy journey that this particular oration took. Once it was decided to move the baptismal liturgy after the homily, it was difficult to know what to do with the collect. The 1965 draft of the postconciliar liturgy moved it after the gospel acclamation and before the gospel.[178] This design envisioned two Old Testament readings, one epistle, the gospel acclamation, the collect, and then the gospel. This draft proposed that the collect be the one from Easter Day, not from the vigil, which presumed that baptisms had already taken place. This sequence of events, though, apparently proved unsatisfactory, because in the 1968 draft, the collect had disappeared from this place, and the traditional collect from the Easter Vigil had now been moved as the suggestion to conclude the prayer of the faithful—after the baptisms. A different unspecified prayer could be used in its place.[179] In 1969 it had moved again, this time as the second of two options for a prayer to conclude the renewal of baptismal promises.[180] In the end, it was restored as the collect for the vigil, with a change in the verb, allowing it to serve the liturgy before the baptisms take place.

33. The lector reads the epistle. The rubric says it is "from the Apostle," which refers to St. Paul. Today the reading is Romans 6:3-11, which was new to the postconciliar Missal. The preconciliar Missal used Colossians 3:1-4 ("If you have risen with Christ").[181] That has now become the first of two options for the Mass on Easter Day. The Romans reading is found in tenth-century Constantinople and is used in the present-day Byzantine liturgy.[182] It appealed to the postconciliar renewal because of the way it relates baptism to resurrection, linking the ceremonies and the meaning of this holy night.

In the 1965 draft of the postconciliar liturgy, the community was expected to choose one from among four options for the epistle: Colossians 3:1-4 (the reading for the vigil at that time); 1 Corinthians 15:1-10 (the epistle from the eleventh Sunday after Pentecost); Romans 6:3-10 (the epistle of the sixth Sunday after Pentecost); and Acts of the Apostles 10:37-43 (from Monday in the Octave of Easter).[183] By 1968, the choice had been made: Romans 6:3-11,[184] which has remained ever since. The reading from Acts ultimately became the first reading for the Mass on Easter Day.

34. After the epistle, all rise. The priest intones the Alleluia three times, raising his voice a step on each repetition. All repeat after him. If necessary (presumably if the priest cannot sing well), the psalmist intones the Alleluia. The chant notation for the Alleluia now appears in the third edition of the Missal. After the third time, the psalmist or cantor sings the verses of Psalm 118 (117) assigned for this day.

Throughout the season of Lent, the church has abstained from singing Alleluia and has replaced the word of the gospel acclamation with a sentence of praise. Now the Alleluia returns with much solemnity, becoming the song of the church rejoicing in the resurrection. Evidence for omitting the Alleluia during the weeks before Easter dates to the turn of the seventh century.[185]

When a bishop presides, an additional step may take place here. "After [the epistle], as occasion suggests and if it is in keeping with local custom, one of the deacons or the reader goes to the bishop and says to him, 'Most Reverend Father, I bring you a message of great joy, the message of Alleluia.' After this greeting or, if it does not take place, immediately after the reading, all rise."[186] No parallel for this is noted in the Missal for a parish celebration.

New to the third edition is singing the Alleluia three times and raising the pitch. However, these instructions already appeared in the Ceremonial of Bishops.[187] The order of these rubrics has been rearranged in the third edition so that they flow more logically. As it did for the responsories following the Old Testament readings, the third edition names which of the psalms contributes the verses for the Alleluia.

Psalm 118 is one of the psalms that include the word "alleluia" in their body. It is perfect for Easter because it proclaims the mercy of God, the power of God's right hand, and the repositioning of a rejected stone as the cornerstone. It is cited many times in the New Testament, including the gospel parable of the wicked tenants,[188] the post-Pentecost sermon of Peter in Acts,[189] and what may be a baptismal homily in 1 Peter 2:7. The connection between the Alleluia and Psalm 118 dates at least to the ninth-century antiphonaries.[190] For a while, verses from Psalm 117 (116) were added to the Alleluia,[191] but the postconciliar Lectionary favored the additional verses of Psalm 118.

35. As usual, the priest puts incense in the thurible and blesses the deacon. Those instructions are new to the third edition, but they were implied previously. Candles are not carried in the gospel procession, but incense is. The prohibition of candles in this procession dates at least to *Ordo Romanus* 24.[192] No other flame should conflict with the paschal candle, which has been set near the ambo.

Previous editions of the postconciliar Missal said of the incense in Latin, "if it is used," but those words have been struck from the third edition. It seems to expect incense will be used here, as it was for the fire ceremony in the first part of the vigil.

The gospel for this Mass changes with the lectionary year. It always proclaims the account of the resurrection: Matthew 28:1-10 in Year A; Mark 16:1-7 in Year B; and Luke 24:1-12 in Year C. John's account (20:1-9) is proclaimed on Easter Day, but it may be replaced with one of these or with the story of the journey to Emmaus (Luke 24:13-35). The traditional reading for this day is Matthew's version, though slightly shorter (vv. 1-7). As noted above, it has appeared in the Roman Rite at least since the mid-seventh century.[193] It was the only option for the gospel at the vigil throughout the life of the preconciliar Missal.[194] The expanded lectionary cycle allows the faithful to achieve a greater familiarity with the variety of testimonies to the resurrection.

36. A homily is never to be omitted, even if it is brief. In Latin, the previous postconciliar editions said it takes place "immediately" after the gospel. The adverb had appeared in the 1969 draft,[195] but the third edition has removed it. It was probably superfluous.

The language requiring a homily is unusually strong, especially when one considers that the preconciliar liturgy never indicated a homily after the gospel.[196] Even in 1969 the language was much weaker. A footnote explained, "A homily is not excluded, but frequently the address that takes place before the renewal of baptismal promises will be enough."[197] The role of the homily has grown in importance since then. On this night, above all others, a homily should be given.

Third Part: Baptismal Liturgy

37. If the baptismal font can be seen by the faithful, the priest and the ministers go there. Otherwise a vessel with water is placed in the sanctuary.

The third edition has moved this note from the end of the second part to the beginning of the third part. Because it indicates that the liturgy of baptism follows the homily, it belongs more appropriately here.

The history of celebrating baptism at the Easter Vigil is quite ancient. Even Egeria mentions it.[198] It was probably not much practiced in the preconciliar era, but its popularity has grown with the revised Rite of Christian Initiation of Adults. The opening rubric has a very practical concern: make sure people can see what is going on.

38. If there are catechumens, they are called forth and their godparents present them to the church. If those to be baptized are small children, parents and godparents carry them.

The word "catechumens" causes some puzzlement here because the Rite of Christian Initiation of Adults consistently calls those to be baptized "the elect" after the Rite of Election has taken place. Even the description of their baptism will call them "those to be baptized," not "catechumens." Furthermore, children young enough to be held by their parents and godparents never become "catechumens." They are infants, and they are baptized according to the Rite of Baptism for Children, without entering a catechumenate. The Missal, however, is a different book. It is aware of the "oil of catechumens," and perhaps it is holding on to an older name because it was developed apart from the RCIA.

39. If there is to be a procession to the font, it forms. A minister with the paschal candle leads the way. Those to be baptized follow with their godparents, then the ministers, the deacon, and the priest. The litany is sung, and at its conclusion the priest gives an address.

All this is new to the third edition. Previous editions described a different situation, which is covered below in paragraph 41.

40. There is no procession if the baptismal liturgy takes place in the sanctuary. The priest makes an introductory statement, asking the people to pray that God will give merciful help to those to be baptized. The priest may use the words supplied, which are based on a similar text from the Gothic Missal,[199] or he may improvise his own. The Missal now provides chant notation for this address, so if the priest is making up his own text and wishes to sing it, he will have to make up his own melody as well.

He gives a different address if the font is to be blessed but no one is to be baptized during the vigil. He invites people to pray for the grace of God upon the font, that those baptized there may be numbered among the children of adoption in Christ. The priest may use other words than those in the Missal, but if he does and he wishes to sing, again, he will have to improvise. The suggested words now appear with notes in the third edition.

The 1969 draft did not supply a text: "If there are no candidates for baptism, the invitation should be adapted to circumstances."[200] A sample invitation appeared in the published postconciliar Missal.

41. All stand and respond as two cantors lead the litany. Standing is the appropriate posture when a litany is sung during the Easter season, or, for that matter, on a Sunday.[201] If the procession to the baptistery is of some length, the litany is sung during it. First those to be baptized are called, and then the procession moves as described above. The priest gives the address before the blessing of water.

The thirteenth-century Pontifical of Durandus called for two cantors to lead the litany.[202] It probably served a practical purpose, doubling the volume so the voices could be heard, or perhaps providing alteration so that neither one's voice gave out.

Tertullian considered it unlawful to kneel for prayer on the Lord's Day. For him, standing was a sign of the resurrection. "We regard fasting or kneeling to adore unlawful on the Lord's Day. We enjoy the same privilege from Easter up to Pentecost."[203]

The order of the procession is clearer in the third edition than in previous ones. The deacon is mentioned again. His presence is more thoroughly acknowledged throughout the revised rubrics for Holy Week.

In Latin, the first sentence of paragraph 41 begins with the word *Et*: "And the litany is sung by two cantors." It was also there in the previous Latin editions of the postconciliar Missal. The sentence was lifted from the 1969 draft of this liturgy, where it followed the rubric telling the priest to adapt the address if there was no one to be baptized. It was the second sentence of that paragraph. Even there, the word "And" was not absolutely necessary, but it made a little more sense. When the instruction to the priest was cut and an adapted text inserted for him, the next sentence, which began with the word "And," became the first sentence of the new paragraph. The extraneous first word remains there in Latin, but the English translation has removed it.

42. If no one is to be baptized and the font is not to be blessed, the blessing of water does take place, but not the Litany of the Saints. This condition fits the circumstance where a community of the faithful gathers regularly where no baptisms take place, such as the chapel for a religious order or a nursing home.

This rubric existed in previous editions of the postconciliar Missal, but it is now set apart from the rest of this section with solid lines before and after the paragraph. The circumstance is so rare that the editors wish not to confuse those planning and executing the vigil.

Even though communities with this circumstance may feel that they have less of a vigil to celebrate than those where baptism takes place, the Circular Letter notes that if no one is to be baptized, the blessing of water and the sprinkling become significant elements of the ceremony.[204] These are important for the renewal of the commitment the faithful make in their celebration of Easter. Incidentally, the Circular Letter does not say, "If no one is to be baptized, the reception of baptized Christians into the full communion of the Catholic Church becomes significant." As will be seen, the Missal does not envision such a ritual taking place during the Easter Vigil.

43. The litany is sung. Names may be added, especially the titular saint of the church or the patrons of the locale and of those to be baptized. This suggestion existed in the 1968 draft, which also permitted inserting those names in proper places into the series.[205] The litany begins with a *Kyrie*. It then evokes biblical figures in a hierarchy of

importance, followed by early martyrs, both men and women. The early fathers of the church come next, followed by saints who founded religious communities, all in chronological order. Some later women saints complete the list. The litany then makes a generic plea for deliverance before specifically asking for the new birth of those to be baptized. It concludes with brief intercessions to Christ. The priest then offers a prayer if there are candidates for baptism.

There are some minor changes in the third edition. The opening invocations to Christ are lined out more clearly on the page. The Latin words for "Xavier," "Vianney," and "Siena" are placed in parentheses; saints are generally known by their first names, but the added descriptor may clarify just who is being invoked. The names appear that way in the *Graduale Romanum*. Theresa's title has changed from "of Avila" to "of Jesus."

The oration that concludes the litany is not found in the Rite of Christian Initiation of Adults. This will require the juggling of some books as the liturgy of baptism gets underway, or the preparing of a special collection of texts to help the events flow more smoothly. This is a small point, but the rubric introducing the prayer used to call for the priest to say "the following prayer"; the third edition says "this prayer."

Those familiar with the previous English translation are used to seeing the chant notation here for the Litany of the Saints. It was never in the Latin postconciliar Missal, probably because the music pertains to the cantors, who find it in the *Graduale Romanum*, and not to the priest, who sings the responses with everyone else.

The litany found a place in this part of the celebration partly as processional music to move the ministers from one place to another and partly to give the people something to do as the order of baptism got underway.[206] There are references to several litanies during this service in the Sacramentaries and *Ordines Romani* of the seventh to ninth centuries: litanies before the blessing of the candle, litanies before the readings, litanies at the font, and litanies in place of the entrance chant of the Mass. However, none of these is clearly a litany of the saints.[207] The Pontifical of Durandus split the litany into two parts.[208] Names of saints appeared in the 1474 Roman Missal, and this tradition has been carried down to the present day. That litany maintained the two-part structure, one accompanying the procession to the font,[209] and the other, culminating in the *Kyrie*, accompanying the procession to the altar, which effectively began the Mass after the vigil.[210] In reordering the parts of the vigil, the postconciliar liturgy combined the litanies into one, placing it as the processional music to the font. The saints are invoked on behalf of those who will be baptized here, whether during the vigil or in the future. The people participate in the litany, which was not the case prior to the revisions of the 1950s.

The postconciliar revision of the litany passed through several phases. The 1965 draft envisioned it as the processional music from the fire to the altar before the Liturgy of the Word, and it envisioned Psalm 42 (41), which had been the final reading and is now the final responsorial psalm, as the processional music to the font.[211] The 1967 draft omitted the Litany of the Saints but said, "In order that some elements from the traditional Litany of the Saints be preserved, mention of the communion of saints may be made in the [introduction to the prayer of the faithful]; intentions may be chosen from those which are had in this litany."[212] The 1968 draft started the litany with an invocation of the Trinity, then followed with the "holy mother of God, St. Michael and all angels, St. Abraham, St. Moses, St. Elijah, and all holy patriarchs and prophets," before listing the names of Christian saints. These were arranged in groups, and each group concluded with a summary petition: "all holy disciples of the Lord," "all holy martyrs," and "all men and women saints."[213] The final petitions had been eliminated. In 1969 the list of the saints had become abbreviated, eliminating the angels and most of the martyrs, conserving representative names from the various groups.[214] When the first postconciliar editions were published, many of these names had been restored, but the concluding formula calling upon Christ had been eliminated. The third edition brings it back: "Christ, hear us. Christ, graciously hear us."

The prayer that concludes the litany was in this place in the preconciliar liturgy, following the litany and before the blessing of the water.[215] It did not appear in the drafts for the postconciliar liturgy (see above, p. 140), but it was reinserted in the published Missal and has remained there, now as a more natural conclusion to the entire litany.

Blessing of Baptismal Water

44. The priest prays the blessing over the water, extending his hands. The prayer invokes God who accomplishes wonderful effects through the sacraments and prepared water to show forth the grace of baptism through many events in the Old and New Testaments. It asks God to unseal the fountain of baptism for the sake of the church and to send the Holy Spirit upon the water, so that human nature may be

washed clean through baptism and rise to the life of newborn children. The priest may lower the paschal candle once or three times into the water as he prays for the power of the Spirit to come upon the font, so that those who are buried with Christ in baptism may rise to life with him. At the end, the people answer, "Amen."

The overall structure imitates elements of a eucharistic prayer: it recalls the institution of baptism (anamnesis), and it asks God to send the Holy Spirit on the water of the font (epiclesis).[216] The preconciliar version prefaced the text with the same dialogue used at the beginning of a eucharistic prayer.[217]

The chant notation appears for the first time in the third edition of the Missal in Latin. It had already appeared in the English translation of the previous edition. The final line of the text has been emended in the third edition. It used to say, "through Christ our Lord," and now, because Christ is mentioned in the previous sentence, it says, "who lives and reigns with you . . ."

Cyprian (+258) and the *Apostolic Tradition* both say that the water for baptism had to be blessed first,[218] but there is little other evidence of the practice and no existent text until the Gelasian Sacramentary.[219] That is the original source for the prayer in use today, which has undergone some abbreviations and fewer additions.

The practice of dipping the candle into the water can be traced at least to the eighth century in some derivatives of the Gelasian Sacramentary.[220] Some of those working on the postconciliar revision thought that the immersion of the candle should be omitted, but it remained as an option.[221] Although it is tempting to attach the sexual imagery of an impregnation of the font with the candle, it is more naturally an extension of the epiclesis, invoking the Spirit of the risen Christ, symbolized by the candle, upon the water. The 1968 draft made this point by saying that this blessing would also appear in the Rite of Baptism for Children:

> The immersion of the candle into the water greatly displeases not a few people if it happens three times. But it must be noted that this rite best expresses the sense of the complete epiclesis, namely that the Holy Spirit sanctifies the water. Although in the sacramental reality this does not happen before the act of baptism itself, nevertheless it is of the greatest importance for understanding the grace of the Holy Spirit, that a person is reborn from water and the Holy Spirit. With all the other gestures being suppressed, this at least should remain and indeed as a triple immersion, as threefold is the immersion of the ones

being baptized: "In the name of the Father and of the Son and of the Holy Spirit."[222]

As the revisions were underway in the 1950s, the location of the blessing was moved into the view of the people so that they might better participate.[223] Even so, the blessing of that time included some features that are no longer in the rite: the priest touched the water with his hand, he spoke exorcisms, he made multiple signs of the cross over the water, he altered the tone of his singing voice for the second half of the prayer, he breathed three times upon the water in the form of a cross, he breathed three more times in the form of the Greek letter psi (Ψ, the first letter of the word for soul or breath), he added the oil of catechumens and the oil of chrism to the water, and he incensed the font.[224] Many of these were being added as early as the eighth century, but they were not included in the postconciliar rite.

The water retains a purpose after the ceremony: "The water blessed at the Easter Vigil should, if possible, be kept and used throughout the Easter season to signify more clearly the relationship between the sacrament of baptism and the paschal mystery. Outside the Easter season, it is desirable that the water be blessed for each occasion, in order that the words of blessing may explicitly express the mystery of salvation that the Church remembers and proclaims."[225]

45. Having just answered "Amen," the people continue singing an acclamation inviting springs of water to praise and exalt the Lord forever. If the candle has been lowered into the water, it is now withdrawn. Previous postconciliar editions allowed the people to sing a different acclamation, but that permission is no longer stated in the third edition.

There had been no acclamation here in the preconciliar Missal. The idea was proposed in 1967 as a way of facilitating the active participation of the people.[226] A specific text appeared in the 1968 draft, citing Daniel 3:78 and 77: "Springs of water, bless the Lord; praise and exalt him above all forever. Seas and rivers, bless the Lord; praise and exalt him above all forever."[227] By the 1969 draft, this was reduced to the first half,[228] which is how it appears in the Missal today. It recovers lines from one of the traditional canticles for the vigil that the postconciliar Missal suppressed.

The third edition of the Missal in Latin provided musical notation for this acclamation. It had already existed in the English translation.

46. For the priest who will recite the blessing instead of sing it, the complete text appears a second time without musical notation.

47. The text for the people's acclamation also appears without musical notation for ease of reading when it is not sung.

48. The priest poses questions of renunciation to the adult catechumens and to the parents and godparents of the infants. They make the responses as indicated in the Rite of Christian Initiation of Adults and the Rite of Baptism for Children.[229] Adults may be anointed with the oil of catechumens if this has not already taken place in the preparatory rites. This is new to the third edition of the Missal, but it had appeared already in the Ceremonial of Bishops.[230] Evidence for anointing catechumens with the oil of exorcism on Holy Saturday can be found in the mystagogical catechesis of Cyril, or possibly of his successor John.[231]

In the United States, the National Conference of Catholic Bishops approved the omission of the anointing with the oil of catechumens both in the preparatory rites of Holy Saturday and in the rites of baptism at the Easter Vigil.[232] This probably followed the discussions about whether or not to retain usage of the oil of catechumens at all. See the summary above in the section on the chrism Mass. With the new rubric in the Roman Missal, the practice in the United States needs a clarification.

The postconciliar Missal says the priest does this standing. It is not clear why this has to be stated. In the preconciliar Missal, a rubric says he stands before inviting the renewal of baptismal promises.[233] Perhaps the posture was copied from there in the postconciliar drafts.

49. The priest poses questions about faith to the adult individuals and to the parents and godparents of the infants. They respond as indicated in the ritual books.[234] If the number of baptisms is large, the celebrant may immediately ask for the renewal of promises from the rest of the assembly at this time. This saves a little time.

All this is new to the third edition. These questions of faith can be found in the Gelasian Sacramentary,[235] but even Tertullian described the questioning of those to be baptized.[236]

50. After the questions, the priest baptizes the adult elect and children. This is a new rubric to the third edition of the Missal, and it calls those to be baptized "elect," the term used in the Rite of Christian Initiation of Adults after the Rite of Election. It shows the influence of the initiation rites on the third edition of the Missal.

The Missal traditionally does not include the details of the rite of baptism. They are found in the pertinent ritual books, the Rite of

Christian Initiation of Adults and the Rite of Baptism for Children. Previous editions of the postconciliar Missal did not even say explicitly that the baptisms were done. It said that the questions were given before baptism, and it described the ceremonies that followed baptism. The third edition now clarifies that baptisms do happen and at this time.

51. Several ceremonies follow baptism. The priest anoints the infants with chrism.[237] He anoints the crown of the head, not the forehead of the infants. He does not anoint the adults on the crown of the head. These distinctions are meant to eliminate potential confusion with the sacrament of confirmation. Adults and infants all receive a white garment. The priest or deacon receives the paschal candle, and the candles of the newly baptized are lighted. Anyone may actually light the candles, but this is often assigned to the godparents. The *Ephphetha*, which comes after baptism in the rite of infants,[238] is omitted. Adults may have received the *Ephphetha* in the preparatory rites of Holy Saturday.[239]

The option for the deacon playing a role here is new to the third edition. In fact, this entire paragraph is new. It clarifies the procedures that should have been understood from following the rite of baptism in the other books. This paragraph does not duplicate material already in the other books, but it clarifies the points that might need attention because of the context of the vigil.

The vigil rubrics also make a few different points than the Ceremonial of Bishops did:

> After their baptism, infants are anointed with chrism by presbyters or by deacons, particularly when a large number have been baptized; and over all the infants as a group, the bishop says the formulary of anointing, "The God of power." All those baptized, both adults and children, receive the baptismal garment, as the bishop says, "N. and N., you have become a new creation." Next the bishop or a deacon receives the Easter candle from an acolyte and says the invitation, "Godparents, please come forward," and the candles of the newly baptized are lighted as the bishop says, "You have been enlightened by Christ." In the case of infants the presentation of a lighted candle and the *Ephphetha* rite are omitted at the Easter Vigil, as indicated in the Rite of Baptism for Children.[240]

Here too, if a bishop were to anoint an infant with chrism, people may confuse it with confirmation. Having other ministers anoint while the bishop says the text is the solution. However, even in the other ceremonies, the bishop says the words while other ministers perform the actions. This is unusual in the Roman Rite, which generally has both words and actions performed at the same time by the same minister. However, it does establish a paradigm for situations where the priest cannot physically anoint all the children, hand them garments, and light their candles without unduly prolonging the ceremony. He perhaps could say the text while other ministers assist.

52. A procession forms as the ministers and the baptismal party return to the sanctuary—unless, of course, the baptism took place there. This time the newly baptized or the godparents or parents of the infants carry the candles. Music may accompany this procession, and the baptism canticle *Vidi aquam* ("I saw water") is suggested.

Once again, all of this is new to the third edition of the Missal, which is trying to clarify some parts from the rites of baptism that may not otherwise be obvious to see. The Missal exercises restraint by not saying too much here.

In the development of this section of the vigil, the commission working on the revised rite in 1951 did not favor a suggestion that the hymn *Christus vincit* be sung after the baptisms.[241] The 1965 draft of the postconciliar liturgy suggested Psalm 23 (22) for the same occasion: "The Lord is my shepherd."[242] The third edition recommends *Vidi aquam*. This hymn has always been part of the blessing and sprinkling of water during the Easter season, and the third edition still recommends it in the appendix. In fact, the rubrics for the Easter Vigil recommend *Vidi aquam* during the sprinkling in paragraph 56 below. The same edition now suggests it may be sung during the procession from the font to the sanctuary.

The Missal has never included the Rite of Reception of Baptized Christians into the Full Communion of the Catholic Church. It may be done because the American edition of the Rite of Christian Initiation of Adults permits it in the combined rite, but it has never been part of the official vision for this ceremony.[243]

53. The bishop, or in his absence the priest who baptized, administers confirmation to the newly baptized adults. This information is all new to the third edition of the Missal. In practice, priests confirmed during the life of the other postconciliar Missals because the Code of Canon Law[244] and the Rite of Christian Initiation of Adults[245] instructed them to do so. Little understood and often not practiced is the

canonical ruling that this applies to children of catechetical age as well as to adults: the priest who baptizes children should confirm them. Any child catechumen of First Communion age and older should be admitted to baptism and confirmation at the same vigil ceremony, regardless of the diocesan age of confirmation. Permissions for a priest to confer confirmation in these circumstances came with the Second Vatican Council.[246]

The rubrics now say that confirmation should take place in the sanctuary. This was so stated in the Ceremonial of Bishops,[247] which cited the Rite of Christian Initiation of Adults 231–35. However, 231 says, "The place for the celebration of confirmation is either at the baptismal font or in the sanctuary, depending on the place where, according to local conditions, baptism has been celebrated." In the Middle Ages, confirmation took place in the sanctuary[248] because the font was located somewhere else and the ministers went there only to baptize. If baptisms today take place at the font because they are fully visible there, confirmation could logically take place there at the same time, thus uniting the two sacraments.[249] However, celebrating confirmation in the sanctuary perhaps unites it better with the Eucharist. The procession and music described in the previous paragraph depend greatly upon the location of these two ceremonies.

It may seem odd that every copy of the Missal, even one in the most remote parish, says "the Bishop, or in his absence, the Priest" confirms. After all, the bishop celebrates one Easter Vigil, and there are many more where he is absent and confirmation has to take place. However, even the Rite of Christian Initiation of Adults says something similar when it describes the initiation rites.[250] The sacrament of confirmation is still tied theologically to the bishop, so even though he is not likely to be present in a typical celebration of the parish Easter Vigil, his role is still noted as the ordinary minister of confirmation.

THE BLESSING OF WATER

54. If no one is to be baptized and there is no font to be blessed, the Litany of the Saints is omitted, and water is blessed for the sake of this gathering of the faithful. The invitation and water blessing are entirely different from those pronounced when water is blessed for a font. The 1969 draft of the postconciliar liturgy foresaw this possibility and simply noted, "But where there is no baptismal font nor anyone to be baptized, the common blessing of water is said."[251] The text did not appear until the published editions of the postconciliar Missal. It

used texts from the preconciliar Missal for the blessing of water at the beginning of a high Mass. That prayer appeared in the appendix of the postconciliar Missal, where the options for the blessing and sprinkling of holy water were found.

The introduction at the vigil today is virtually the same as the generic one that appears in the appendix. One verb differs in the Latin text (*deprecemur* in the appendix and *exoremus* in the vigil texts), but the two are synonymous. The blessing at the vigil is virtually the same as the one recommended for the Easter season at the beginning of Mass. The opening of the blessing at the vigil differs by making an explicit reference to the day. There are two further differences. First, when the priest says this prayer at a typical Sunday Mass, he does so with hands joined, which had been the instruction in the previous editions of the postconciliar Missal. Now he says it with hands extended only at the vigil. Second, the blessing prayer at Mass calls for the priest to make the sign of the cross over the water at the words "graciously bless this water." That gesture is missing from the text at the vigil. It is hard to discern why. In the longer text for the blessing of water when there is someone to be baptized, the water is blessed by the immersion of the candle. But this text calls for neither immersion of the candle nor a sign of the cross from the priest. It is possible that this was an oversight and that the priest is expected to bless the water in some way besides reciting the words.

The introductory rubric has been slightly emended in the third edition. In the previous postconciliar editions, the rubric stated that the priest blessed the water with the prayer, but the text that followed the rubric was addressed to the people and was not the blessing of water. The previous English translation had apparently seen the difficulty and corrected it. Now the Latin has been revised. The third edition also provides chant notation for both the introduction and the blessing for the first time.

The Renewal of Baptismal Promises

55. All stand, holding lighted candles to renew their promise of baptismal faith, unless this has already been done together with those to be baptized (see paragraph 49 above). Actually, paragraph 49 says that all may renew their promises "immediately after" those to be baptized, not "together with" them, as paragraph 55 states. Either way, the option of renewing baptismal promises at that earlier point in the Vigil is new to the third edition.[252] The priest addresses the faithful,

notes that Lent has concluded, and asks them to renew their baptismal promises. They respond. At the end, the priest offers a prayer, and all answer, "Amen."

The reference to Lent is spiritually significant. The faithful have been observing penance throughout the season of Lent. Ever since Ash Wednesday, they have been trying to overcome sin and be faithful to the Gospel. Now they seal their recommitment to Christ; they bring their observance of Lent to a close by turning away from sin and toward Jesus Christ.

Two alternatives are given for the questions of renunciation, and the conference of bishops may adapt the second of these, which is not as ancient as the first formula.

In the revision of the vigil liturgy in the early 1950s, it was believed that the renewal of baptismal promises was an "ancient liturgical tradition."[253] When the proposal came forward to the commission at work on the project, it "was favorably accepted and its implementation will be accelerated by drawing up a fixed Latin formula based on the exhortations given at Ordinations. Subsequently, each nation would be asked to produce an official translation for use in the rite."[254] The practice was restored to the liturgy in 1951.[255] It was the only part of the liturgy of that era put into the vernacular. "In view of the particular concession that had been made and of the fact that the renewal of baptismal promises was completely new, but corresponded to those parts of the bilingual rituals that could be administered in the vernacular, Father Bea asked that the rubric should state explicitly that the renewal of baptismal promises could be done in the language of the proper rituals."[256] After further discussion of using the vernacular not only for the renewal of baptismal promises but also for the readings, "The conclusion was that the vernacular might be conceded only for the renewal of baptismal promises."[257] The translation had to be approved by the ordinary; that is, by the bishop of the local diocese.[258] Today such a translation has to be approved by the Congregation for Divine Worship and the Discipline of the Sacraments.

Shortly before the council, the rubric expanded to invite all the clergy and the faithful to hold lighted candles for the renewal of baptismal promises.[259] This had not been part of the ceremony when it was introduced in 1951.[260] In the 1965 draft, the Lord's Prayer concluded the renewal of promises, but this idea did not survive.[261] The 1968 draft questioned the address that had introduced the preconciliar revision of the rite.[262] It cited Romans 6:3-11 rather generously: "And because, as the Apostle teaches, we have been buried with Christ through a baptism into his death, as Christ has risen from the dead, so also we should walk in newness of life; knowing that our old self has been crucified with Christ, that we might no longer serve sin. Therefore let us consider ourselves dead to sin, but alive for God in Christ Jesus our Lord."[263] This was thought unnecessary because the same passage was now assigned as the epistle for this Mass. The 1968 draft had a completely different introduction: "We renounce Satan and his works and also the world, which is an enemy of God, and we promise to serve God faithfully in the holy catholic church."[264] The final version of the introductory address, which is nearly identical to the one in the 1969 draft,[265] has simplified the one that appeared in 1951 and builds on its connection between Lent and the vigil. It also permits the priest to use "these or similar words."

A further change was introduced in the 1967 draft. Prior to this time, the questions for the renewal were made in the plural and the responses were given in the plural: "Do you [plural] renounce Satan?" "We do." ". . . Do you [plural] believe in God the Father almighty, Creator of heaven and earth?" "We do."[266] But the question of changing the response to the singular arose in the 1967 discussion.[267] No reason is given, but the result resembles more nearly the formula of the Creed in Latin: *Credo*, or "I believe." Since the Creed was omitted in this liturgy,[268] this perhaps gave more reason to use the singular formula. The remaining drafts of the renewal of baptismal promises all kept the priests' questions in the plural[269] but put the response of the people in the singular. This cannot be discerned from any English translation because of the ambiguity of its word "you," but it is plain in the Latin.

The priest's prayer that concludes the renewal of promises is the same one that appeared when the rite was first introduced in 1951. However, the 1969 draft supplied an alternative: the traditional collect for the vigil Mass,[270] which the same draft had eliminated. As noted above in paragraph 32, this collect was kept in place through a change in the verb, making it more appropriate for the prebaptismal part of the vigil.

56. The priest sprinkles everyone with water. All sing *Vidi aquam* ("I saw water"), or some other song with a baptismal character. The notes for the chant appear now for the first time in the third edition of the Missal.

The sprinkling of the faithful has appeared in other sources—for example, *Ordo Romanus* 30B, where the bishop used his hand to sprinkle the people with the blessed water.[271] The V*idi aquam* was suggested for this rite from the drafts of the postconciliar reform.[272] Another similar song was always permitted in the drafts. The third edition now specifies that a replacement song should have a baptismal character.

57. During the sprinkling, the newly baptized are brought to their place among the faithful. If they were baptized by immersion, they may need a little time to dry off and change clothes.

If the parish has a font, but the blessing took place in the sanctuary to provide visibility for the people, the deacon and ministers carry to the font the container in which the blessed water sits. If there is no deacon, this would logically be done by other ministers, so that the priest does not need to leave the sanctuary. As with many other similar rubrics, the deacon's role has been added in the third edition.

If there is no font in which people will be baptized in this location, the blessed water is put aside in an appropriate place. If it is not in the way, it could remain in the sanctuary. But if it needs to be put aside, perhaps the sacristy is the best choice.

The 1969 draft called for the candelabra around the altar to be lighted after the water rite concluded. This would have put focus on the altar as the Liturgy of the Eucharist was getting underway. However, this did not carry into the published postconciliar rite. All the candles are to be lighted during the Gloria.

58. The priest goes to his chair. The Creed is omitted. He leads the universal prayer (the prayer of the faithful). The newly baptized participate in this for the first time. This rubric, borrowed from the initiation rites,[273] presumes that, as catechumens, these individuals were dismissed from the assembly before the Liturgy of the Eucharist began. Some parishes maintain this practice, but very few among the newly baptized are people who are literally participating in the prayer of the faithful for the first time in their lives. It is their first time as baptized members of the Christian faithful. In the early church, though, it would truly have been the first occasion for them to experience the entire Liturgy of the Eucharist.

A note in the 1968 draft for the postconciliar liturgy made a point that never appeared in the Missal:

> The prayer of the faithful after baptism has great importance for the newly baptized, not so much therefore that the whole Church prays for them, as that they themselves pray as members of the church with

their brothers and sisters for the first time. In the time of Hippolytus catechumens were expressly forbidden to pray with the baptized faithful or to give the peace. But "afterwards they pray now together with all the people, not praying with the faithful for the first time until all these rites (baptism and confirmation) have been completed. And after they pray, they offer the kiss of peace" (*Apostolic Tradition*, 21; ed. Botte, p. 54). For this reason the prayer for the newly baptized is not expressly proposed, lest it overshadow the greatest importance of the new union with the church.[274]

The practical advice from this is the surprising idea that the church *not* pray for the newly baptized in the prayer of the faithful at the Easter Vigil. The newly baptized, rather, should be praying with and for the church.

In the preconciliar liturgy, which had no prayer of the faithful, this is when the second half of the litany took place.[275] It concluded with the *Kyrie*, which set the stage for singing the Gloria and the beginning of the Easter Mass.

The drafts of the postconciliar Missal made several attempts to hone this part of the service. As mentioned above, the 1965 draft suggested that the prayer of the faithful should conclude with what had been the collect for the vigil Mass because of the place of baptism in the sequence of liturgical actions.[276] However, the collect was retained earlier in the service with a small change to its text.

Fourth Part: The Liturgy of the Eucharist

59. The priest goes to the altar, and the Liturgy of the Eucharist begins as usual. This seems straightforward enough, but the preconciliar revision had the priest kiss the altar upon reaching it, as he does at the beginning of Mass. This was retained even in the 1969 draft for the postconciliar liturgy.[277] But since it is now understood that the Mass begins at the very beginning of the vigil and not here, the kiss was eliminated.

In the preconciliar revisions, all of the following took place after the Old Testament readings, the litany in two parts, the blessing of water, and the renewal of baptismal promises: the priest kissed the altar and prayed the collect, then the epistle was read (in this case Col 3:1-4), followed by the Alleluia, tract, and the gospel.[278] In the postconciliar revision, the complete Liturgy of the Word takes place before baptism.

60. It is desirable that the newly baptized bring forth the bread and the wine, or that the parents or godparents of newly baptized infants do so. The third edition has added the reference to newly baptized

infants. This should have been understood, but in practice many seem unaware that the Rite of Baptism for Children promotes celebrating the baptism of infants at the Easter Vigil.[279] The implications of such a celebration are brought to light in a clarified rubric such as this one.

61. In the prayer over the offerings, the priest asks the Lord to accept the prayers of the people that the paschal mysteries may bring the healing of eternity. This prayer originated as the second of two options in the Gelasian Sacramentary's Easter Vigil.[280] It has been the prayer of choice for this part of the vigil throughout the life of the pre- and postconciliar Missal.

62. The first preface of Easter is prayed at this Mass. It is the second of two prefaces in the Gelasian Sacramentary's Easter Vigil[281] and has long been the preface at this Mass. In the place where there are options pertaining to the time of day, the words "on this night above all" are to be used. The third edition of the Missal puts the title of the preface in place here, as it has done on similar pages throughout Holy Week.

This preface inspired one of the memorial acclamations from the first English translation: "Dying you destroyed our death, rising you restored our life. Lord Jesus, come in glory."

The complete text is not found on this page, as is often the case. One must look for it among the collection of prefaces or the texts at Mass for Easter Day.

63. During the eucharistic prayer, the community prays for the baptized and their godparents. The texts to be inserted are found in the back of the Missal under "Ritual Masses," "For the Conferral of the Sacraments of Christian Initiation," "For the Conferral of Baptism." There one finds insertions for the four main eucharistic prayers. However, Eucharistic Prayer IV is not to be used at the Easter Vigil because its preface cannot be replaced with a seasonal one, and the preface for this Mass is so important to hear. The previous editions of the postconciliar Missal said the insertion was made into the Roman Canon (Eucharistic Prayer I), but the third edition clarifies that an insertion is to be made no matter which of the eucharistic prayers is offered. The insert for the first eucharistic prayer is nearly identical, word for word, to the one given in the Gelasian Sacramentary for this occasion, [282] and it is even closer to the text in the Gregorian.[283] The others were composed for the postconciliar Missal.

The rubric here neglects to mention it, but Eucharistic Prayer I has one other insert for the Easter Vigil in paragraph 86. This section of the prayer has always allowed some variation on some of the most important days in the liturgical year in order to explain why the community has gathered. It functions somewhat like the preface. If Prayer I is chosen, then, the priest needs to remember two inserts. The second is repeated at paragraph 87 within the body of Eucharistic Prayer I, but it is an abbreviated version of the one from the Ritual Mass for the Conferral of Baptism. It would more logically be used if no one was baptized at the Easter Vigil this year. These inserts may be repeated at all Masses during the Easter Octave, including next Sunday.

The Circular Letter encourages singing the entire eucharistic prayer, together with its embolisms (insertions),[284] but the Missal provides no music for the embolisms. The presider will have to improvise these or rely on the compositional skills of others to assist.

In the preconciliar liturgy, the kiss of peace and the Agnus Dei were omitted at this Mass. The absence of the kiss of peace in the eighth century probably had to do with the anticipatory nature of the vigil: The next morning, Easter Day, the day that the risen Christ appeared to his disciples and greeted them with peace, morning prayer began with the kiss of peace.[285] The restoration of the peace and the *Agnus Dei* to the vigil liturgy was among the first changes proposed in the postconciliar drafts.[286]

64. Before giving the invitation to Communion, the priest addresses the newly baptized who will be receiving their First Communion. Obviously, this does not apply to any infants who may have been baptized at this Mass, even though the Eastern Rites have the custom of administering communion to them on the occasion of their baptism. The priest improvises a text telling them "about the excellence of this great mystery, which is the climax of Initiation and the center of the whole Christian life." This has been borrowed from the same place in the Rite of Christian Initiation of Adults,[287] but it is newly placed here in the third edition. Here is what Pope Benedict XVI said at the Vatican's Easter Vigil in 2011:

> Dearest sons and daughters, I turn to you who in this glorious night, reborn by water and the Holy Spirit, receive for the first time the bread of life and the cup of salvation.

> May the Body and Blood of Christ the Lord always make you grow in his friendship and in communion with the whole Church, may it be the constant food for the journey of your life, and a pledge of the eternal banquet of heaven.[288]

65. It is desirable that the newly baptized receive Communion under both kinds, together with their catechists, godparents, and Catholic parents and spouses. With the consent of the diocesan bishop, it is appropriate that all the faithful be admitted to Communion under both kinds. All this is new to the third edition of the Missal. However, it can be found in the Rite of Christian Initiation of Adults[289] and in the Ceremonial of Bishops,[290] though without the reminder that "Catholic parents and spouses" are admitted to Communion—not those outside the faith. The Circular Letter added its support, while acknowledging the right of the local ordinary: "It is fitting that in the communion of the Easter Vigil full expression be given to the symbolism of the Eucharist, namely by consuming the Eucharist under the species of bread and wine. The local ordinaries will consider the appropriateness of such a concession and its ramifications."[291]

66. The communion antiphon is 1 Corinthians 5:7-8, "Christ our Passover has been sacrificed." Psalm 118 (117) may be sung with it. The text for this antiphon was new to the postconciliar Missal, and the third edition is the first to suggest this particular psalm with it.

In the preconciliar Missal, there was no communion antiphon as such. Instead, three Alleluias were sung as the antiphon for a psalm, but as part of Easter Morning Prayer, which was sung after Communion and before the dismissal.[292] That custom became optional after the council,[293] so an antiphon needed to be created. The drafts immediately proposed retaining the three Alleluias as the communion antiphon,[294] but these were replaced for the published edition of the Missal with this text from 1 Corinthians. It was a new antiphon for this part of the Mass, having no precedents in antiquity. Perhaps it was chosen for Communion because it mentions "unleavened bread." The same antiphon appears the next day, where it has served for many centuries.

67. In the prayer after Communion, members of the community ask for the Spirit of love, that they might be one in mind and heart. This is the same prayer from the preconciliar tradition;[294] it can be found even in the 1474 Roman Missal.

68. In the solemn blessing, the priest prays that the people be defended from every assault of sin, be endowed with immortality, and come to the feasts of eternal joy. The third edition has newly inserted this blessing here. It was always permitted, but one had to search for it among the texts of Easter Day (where it was found in the English translation but not in the Latin original) or in the collection of solemn

blessings. Now it is right on the page with other texts for the vigil. This blessing was newly composed for the postconciliar Missal. The conclusion is a little fuller than it was in previous editions.

The third edition also now permits replacing this final blessing with one from the Rite of Christian Initiation of Adults or the Rite of Baptism for Children. Actually, there is no such final blessing in the first of these sources, but there are examples in the second.[295] The Ceremonial of Bishops more correctly permits the blessings from the Rite of Baptism for Children,[296] saying nothing of the rite for adults.

69. The deacon sings or says the dismissal; in his absence, the priest does so. A double alleluia is added to the dismissal and to the response. The Latin third edition now offers four options for the dismissal formula at any Mass, but its vigil still provides only the traditional one, *Ite, missa est.* However, the revised English translation supplies two alternatives, taken from the possible four: "Go forth, the Mass is ended, alleluia, alleluia," and "Go in peace, alleluia, alleluia." The double alleluia is retained throughout the Easter Octave, including next Sunday. It returns on Pentecost to close the season of Easter.

The third edition clarifies who says or sings the dismissal. The previous editions of the postconciliar Missal could have been understood to say that either the deacon or the priest may sing it. Actually, the priest sings only in the absence of the deacon. The third edition now provides the musical notation for both parts of this dialogue. The earliest reference to the practice of singing a double alleluia here comes from the Pontifical of Durandus in the thirteenth century.[297]

70. The paschal candle is lighted in all the more solemn liturgical celebrations of the Easter season. This is new to the third edition, but it was stated this way in the Circular Letter: "The paschal candle has its proper place either by the ambo or by the altar and should be lit at least in all the more solemn liturgical celebrations of the season until Pentecost Sunday, whether at Mass or at Morning and Evening Prayer."[298] So even though daily Mass may seem less solemn than Sunday Mass, the candle should be aflame.

AT THE MASS DURING THE DAY

71. The Mass on Easter Sunday opens with one of two choices for the entrance antiphon. The first is the traditional one from the preconciliar Missal. The community sings it as though Jesus Christ himself were singing: "I have risen and I am still with you." That verse (Ps

139 [138]:18) is probably a mistranslation of "at the end I am still at your side," but the mistranslation has been used for this purpose on Easter Sunday morning for many centuries. The group preparing the postconciliar revision knew of the difficulties,[299] so they came up with another solution. They suggested taking the antiphon from the Simple Gradual, but two other study groups combined to work on the antiphons and proposed four different ones for this Mass in 1969.[300] The first two are the ones that survived. The third came from an earlier collection of antiphons: "The Lord has risen from the dead as he said; let us all rejoice and be glad, for he rules forever." The last was based on John 10: "The Good Shepherd, who laid down his life for his sheep, has risen, and he was pleased to die for the sake of his flock."

The alternative antiphon that now appears in the Missal combines passages from Luke and the book of Revelation. It has the advantage of biblical authenticity.

The third edition of the Missal has added the information that the Gloria is said at this Mass. This has always been the case, but the instruction was added here for clarity.

Before ever the entrance music begins, the holy water stoups of the church should be filled with blessed water from the vigil. The Circular Letter also suggests that the penitential rite take the form of sprinkling with water blessed at the vigil;[301] however, in the United States, this Mass may include a sprinkling with water during the renewal of baptismal promises.

72. In the collect, members of the community pray that they may rise to the light of life through the renewal brought by God's Spirit. The prayer is based on the first of two options for this Mass in the Gelasian Sacramentary.[302] It has remained in use in the Roman Rite ever since.

The postconciliar Liturgy of the Word introduced Acts of the Apostles 10:34a, 37-43 to the repertoire of readings for Easter. It is an excerpt from the speech Peter gave on the day of Pentecost. In 1965 this had been proposed as one of the options for the epistle at the vigil.[303] In the redesign of the Lectionary, which features passages from Acts as the first reading throughout Easter Time, this excerpt was more appropriately moved here. The responsorial is the classic psalm for Easter: 118 (117):1-2, 16-17, 22-23. These are exactly the verses for the extended gospel acclamation at the vigil. For the second reading, a choice is offered between Colossians 3:1-4, which was the epistle at the vigil in the preconciliar liturgy,[304] and 1 Corinthians 5:7-8, which was the epistle for this Mass of Easter Day in the preconciliar liturgy.[305] The traditional gospel reading from the preconciliar Missal was Mark 16:1-7, which is now offered during Year B at the Easter Vigil. It was included in the earliest lists of gospels, dating to the seventh century.[306] In its place today, the gospel for Easter Day comes from John (20:1-9), the only evangelist who does not have an entire year devoted to his writings but who shows up at important times throughout the three-year cycle, such as Easter Sunday morning. There are other options for the gospel: the repetition of the vigil gospel or Luke's account of the journey to Emmaus (Luke 24:13-35), which is more appropriate for evening Mass on this day because that is the time of day in the story as told by Luke.

After the second reading the sequence is sung. It is obligatory on Easter Sunday [307] but optional for all the days of the octave, including next Sunday.[308] The authorship is ascribed to Wipo of Burgundy, an eleventh-century poet and historian. The opening verses command Christians to sing praises to the paschal victim. Later the verses engage Mary Magdalene in a dialogue, "What did you see along the way?" It concludes with a prayer, "Have mercy on us, Victor King."[309]

The Creed is recited at this Mass. As with the Gloria, this should be obvious, but the Missal clarifies the point. Incidentally, the third edition now calls for the Creed every day of the Easter Octave, whereas its predecessors did not. The Creed is normally said on solemnities,[310] so this corrects what was probably an oversight.

Ever since the postconciliar liturgy has been celebrated in English, the Creed for this Mass in the United States has been replaced with the renewal of baptismal promises and sprinkling with blessed water, probably out of a pastoral concern for those who do not participate in the Easter Vigil. The Latin postconciliar Missal never included this variation, but the third edition of the Missal in English now permits it as an option in the United States.

73. This prayer over the offerings is not so much a prayer as a statement to God. Its structure is very unusual. The community tells God that they offer the sacrifice by which the church is reborn and nourished. It is found in the Gelasian Sacramentary on Easter Monday[311] and replaces the text from the preconciliar Missal. It was probably favored because of its allusion to the Easter sacraments of baptism and the Eucharist.

74. The preface is the traditional one for this day, the same one that is offered at the vigil. The third edition gives its title, as it does in other

instances of the prefaces during Holy Week. It also provides the chant notation right on the page. Whether this Mass is celebrated during the day or in the evening, the appropriate time is inserted into the variable text.

If the Roman Canon is used (Eucharistic Prayer I), it takes proper forms in paragraph 86 and paragraph 87. The first identifies the special nature of the day, and the second refers to the newly baptized. According to an old tradition, the newly baptized participated in the Masses throughout the Octave of Easter and received their mystagogical catechesis at that time. The texts of the Mass in the Easter Octave still presume that the neophytes are there, even though the Rite of Christian Initiation of Adults never mentions the practice. As noted above in the Easter Vigil, these inserts can be traced to the Gelasian Sacramentary.

75. The communion antiphon, 1 Corinthians 5:7-8, is the traditional one for this day. It was copied over to fill the vacancy in the Easter Vigil (see above, p. 163). The third edition adds a second Alleluia to the end of this antiphon. The previous editions of the postconciliar Missal had only one Alleluia. The preconciliar Missal had three.

76. In the prayer after Communion, the faithful ask God to look on them with love and favor so that they may come to the glory of the resurrection. This prayer originated in the Ambrosian Rite, and it was added to the postconciliar Missal to replace a previous prayer.

77. For the solemn blessing, the priest may use the one from the Easter Vigil. This is new to the third edition in Latin. However, in the previous English translation, the priest found the entire solemn blessing in place here. Today, he has to locate it among the texts of the vigil or in the collection of blessings.

78. The dismissal with the double alleluia is the same as for the vigil. In this case, the third Latin edition gives two options for the blessing formula, where its predecessors gave only one. Even though the third edition now has four options for the dismissal formula in the Order of Mass, only these two have been translated into English for Easter Day. Musical settings appear on the pages dedicated to the vigil.

The previous editions of the postconciliar Missal indicated here that the dismissal with the double octave is repeated throughout the Octave of Easter. This notice was moved from this location more appropriately to the concluding of the Easter Vigil.

Afterword

To celebrate Holy Week according to the third edition of the post–Vatican II Roman Missal is to enter a world of death and resurrection. Faithful Christians have observed these ceremonies in a variety of ways. Individual parishes have created ways to make the universal norms work in their locale. During the revisions in the last half of the twentieth century, many ideas were brought forth. Some were maintained, others discarded. Some elements of history, once lost, have been restored. Some new approaches have been added. The rituals themselves provide evidence of the central story of every human life. People are born once in order to be born again, and they die in order to rise. Along the way, each person faces the cross, and each one receives the promise of glory.

Notes

Palm Sunday of the Passion of the Lord—pages 1–20

[1] John Walton Tyrer, *Historical Survey of Holy Week: Its Services and Ceremonial*, Alcuin Club Collections 29 (London: Oxford University Press, 1932), 45–46.

[2] Roman Missal, Fifth Sunday of Lent.

[3] Congregation for Divine Worship and the Discipline of the Sacraments, Circular Letter Concerning the Preparation and Celebration of the Easter Feasts, Prot. N. 120/88, 20 February 1988. In *The Liturgy Documents: A Parish Resource*, vol. 2 (Chicago: Liturgy Training Publications, 1999), 59–80.

[4] CL, 31.

[5] Hermanus A. P. Schmidt, *Hebdomada Sancta* (Rome: Herder, 1957), 662–64. Unless otherwise noted, all translations of non-English works are my own.

[6] Nicola Giampietro, *The Development of the Liturgical Reform as Seen by Cardinal Ferdinando Antonelli from 1948 to 1970* (Fort Collins: Roman Catholic Books, 2009), 288.

[7] Ibid., 299.

[8] This was the time given in the Roman-Germanic Pontifical, #2; Schmidt, 561.

[9] Schmidt, 954.

[10] Ibid., 46.

[11] Study Group 17, appointed by the Consilium for the Implementation of the Constitution on the Sacred Liturgy, forbade a circular procession, partly because Jesus did not have one and partly because the true goal of the procession of Jesus was the holy City of God. Schemata, no. 278, 21 martii 1968, Declarationes, D1. All translations of ICEL's Schematas are my own.

[12] Ibid., D3.

[13] *Ordo Romanus* 14 (Mabillon); Schmidt, 704.

[14] CL, 29, says, "The palms should be taken home, where they will serve as a reminder of the victory of Christ."

[15] Ceremonial of Bishops (Collegeville, MN: Liturgical Press, 1989), 264.

[16] CB, 268.

[17] Giampietro, 274.

[18] Schmidt, 35, 52.

[19] Ibid., 36.

[20] Ibid.

[21] Ibid., 561.

[22] Schemata no. 278, D3, ad 6. Pope Paul VI established a consilium, or committee of liturgical experts, for implementing the vision of the Second Vatican Council. That group appointed numerous study groups to revise the rites. Holy Week was assigned to number 17.

[23] Schemata no. 304, "De ritibus peculiaribus in anno liturgico: de hebdomada sancta, de ritu candelarum, in festo praesentationis Domini, de ritu cinerum initio Quadragesimae, 2.IX.1968," p. 7, footnote "ad 17."

[24] CB, 266.

[25] *Sacrosanctum Concilium* (Constitution on the Sacred Liturgy), in Vatican Council II: The Basic Sixteen Documents, ed. Austin Flannery (Northport, NY: Costello, 1996), 11, 14, 30, and 48.

[26] GIRM, 5, 18, and 386.

[27] Schmidt, 41.

[28] CB, 267.

[29] Schmidt, 700.

[30] The Roman-Germanic Pontifical supplies an example of this practice; Schmidt, 561.

[31] Schmidt, 564.

[32] The Roman-Germanic Pontifical included Exod 15:27; 16:1-10 because it says that Moses camped near an area with seventy palm trees.

[33] Section 23:16–20. *Les Ordines Romani du haut moyen age*, vol. 5, ed. Michel Andrieu (Louvain: Spicilegium Sacrum Lovaniense Administration, 1961), 169–71.

[34] Schemata no. 278, D3, ad 6.

[35] Schmidt, 42.

[36] Schemata no. 278, D4, ad 7.

[37] Schmidt, 472.

[38] CB, 269.

[39] Schmidt, 46.

[40] Schemata no. 278, D4, ad 8.

[41] Schemata no. 304, p. 6.

[42] CB, 270.

[43] Schmidt, 46.

[44] Ibid.

[45] Ibid.

[46] Ibid.

[47] *Le Liber Ordinum en usage dans l'église wisigothique et mozarabe d'espagne du cinquième au onzième siècle*, ed. Marius Férontin (Rome: CLV Edizioni Liturgiche, 1996), 178–79.

[48] Schmidt, 701.

[49] Schemata no. 278, D4, ad 11.

[50] Schemata no. 304, p. 6, ad 9.

[51] Schmidt, 663.

[52] Ibid., 565–66.

[53] J. D. Crichton, *The Liturgy of Holy Week* (Dublin: Veritas, 1983), 23.

[54] Schmidt, 43–44.

[55] Ibid., 48–49.

[56] Ibid., 568.

[57] This possibility was considered all throughout the development of the revised Holy Week services. See, for example, Schemata no. 278, D5, ad 13.

[58] However, Rite of Marriage, paragraph 20, imagines only a single piece of music, the entrance antiphon, and the musical shifts that actually take place in a wedding procession usually mark the different ranks of participants. In the Palm Sunday procession, the music marks the stages of the procession toward the main church.

[59] CB, 271.

[60] Schmidt, 52.

[61] Ibid., 568.

[62] Schemata no. 304, p. 17, ad 12–15.

[63] Schemata no. 278, D4, ad 11.

[64] See, for example, GIRM, 49.

[65] Giampietro, 299.

[66] Ibid., 292–93.

[67] Schemata no. 278, D5–6, ad 15.

[68] Ibid., D6, ad 15.

[69] Schemata no. 278, p. 5, indicated that the introit and *Kyrie* were retained in this form, but not the act of penitence. Schemata no. 304, p. 7, ad 17, omitted everything between the greeting and the collect, even in the simple entrance. But these instructions have not been retained.

[70] See GIRM, 48, 31, in which he may incorporate the antiphon into his opening remarks on occasions when it is not otherwise sung or recited.

[71] Schmidt, 565.

[72] Ibid., 47.

[73] See Schemata no. 278, D7, ad 21.

[74] Schmidt, 348.

[75] Giampietro, 63–64.

[76] See also Lectionary for Mass, 38.

[77] GIRM, 175, 275b.

[78] Schmidt, 457, 674.

[79] Ibid., 480.

[80] Ibid., 53.

[81] Ibid., 457.

[82] Ibid., 514.

[83] Lectionary for Mass, 38.

[84] CL, 33.

[85] See paragraph 20 above. In 1955 a proposal to move the passion to Monday of Holy Week was made and denied, though it prompted the reduction of verses; see Giampietro, 286–87.

[86] Schmidt, 54.

[87] Ibid., 59, 62–63.

[88] Ibid., 461.

[89] Ibid., 55.

[90] Ibid., 677.

[91] Walter D. Miller, *Revised Ceremonial of Holy Week* (New York: Catholic Book Publishing Co., 1971), 40.

[92] J. B. O'Connell, *The Ceremonies of Holy Week: Solemn Rite and Simple Rite, A Commentary* (Westminster: The Newman Press, 1958), 12, citing the Sacred Congregation of Rites, 4044 and 2169.

[93] CB, 273.

[94] Schmidt, 55.

[95] Ibid.

[96] Schemata no. 278, D8, ad 22.

[97] CL, 34.

[98] Schemata nos. 278, p. 6, ad 22; and 304, p. 8, ad 24. No reason is given. Perhaps it was struck as one of the measures of simplifying this liturgy.

[99] Tyrer, 47–48.

[100] Rite of Christian Initiation of Adults, 148, 157.

[101] Schemata no. 278, p. 6, ad 22.

[102] *Sacramentarium Veronense*, ed. Leo Cunibert Mohlberg, Rerum Ecclesiasticarum Documenta (Rome: Herder Editrice e Libreria, 1978), 628.

[103] Schmidt, 55.

[104] Giampietro, 218.

[105] *Le Sacramentaire Grégorien, ses principals forms d'après les plus anciens manuscrits*, ed. Jean Deshusses (Freiburg: Éditions Universitaires, 1979), 1585. Schmidt, 422, refers to the Fulda Gelasian from the late tenth century.

[106] Schemata no. 278, p. 7.

[107] Schmidt, 480.

[108] GIRM, 87.

[109] Schmidt, 349.

[110] Gregorian Sacramentary, 327.

Weekdays—pages 21–29

[1] Congregation for Divine Worship and the Discipline of the Sacraments, Circular Letter Concerning the Preparation and Celebration of the Easter Feasts, Prot. N. 120/88, 20 February 1988. In *The Liturgy Documents: A Parish Resource*, vol. 2 (Chicago: Liturgy Training Publications, 1999), 27.

[2] CL, 37.

[3] John Walton Tyrer, *Historical Survey of Holy Week: Its Services and Ceremonial*, Alcuin Club Collections 29 (London: Oxford University Press, 1932), 34, 37, cites Epiphanius and Egeria.

[4] Ibid., 74.

[5] Hermanus A. P. Schmidt, *Hebdomada Sancta* (Rome: Herder), 480.

[6] Schemata no. 338, die 14 februarii 1969, De Missali no. 60, p. II.

[7] Schmidt, 688–89.

[8] Schmidt, 458, citing the *Evangeliorum Capitulare Romanum A.*

[9] Schemata no. 176, 25 iulii 1966, De Missali no. 25, pp. 45–46.

[10] Schmidt, 349.

[11] Ibid., 688–89.

[12] Ibid., 421–22.

[13] Schemata no. 246, 13 novembris 1967, p. 3, ad 3.

[14] Schmidt, p. 904.

[15] *Sacramentarium Veronense*, ed. Leo Cunibert Mohlberg, Rerum Ecclesiasticarum Documenta (Rome: Herder Editrice e Libreria, 1978), 871.

[16] *Liber Sacramentorum Romanae aeclesiae ordinis anni circuli*, ed. Leo Cunibert Mohlberg (Rome: Casa Editrice Herder, 1981), 282.

[17] Schmidt, 688.

[18] Verona Sacramentary, 904.

[19] Ibid., 639.

[20] Schemata no. 104, 10 septembris 1965, De Anno Lit., 3, p. 5.

[21] Schmidt, 59.

[22] Ibid., 690.

[23] Ibid., 59.

[24] Schemata no. 176, p. 46; Schmidt, 457.

[25] Schmidt, 458.

[26] Ibid., 59.

[27] Gelasian, 341.

[28] Schmidt, 60.

[29] Ibid., 489.

[30] Ibid., 60.

[31] Schemata no. 246, p. 4.

[32] *Le Sacramentaire Grégorien, ses principals forms d'après les plus anciens manuscrits*, ed. Jean Deshusses (Freiburg: Éditions Universitaires, 1979), 322.

[33] Schemata no. 246, p. 4.

[34] Schmidt, 906.

[35] Ibid., 383.

[36] Ibid., 62.

[37] Ibid., 458.

[38] Schemata no. 176, p. 46.

[39] Schmidt, 664–65.

[40] Ibid., 474.

[41] Ibid., 62–63, 458. Tyrer, 74, says that Leo the Great preached on the passion on Wednesday of Holy Week.

[42] *Ordo Romanus* 24:26; Schmidt, 515.

[43] Schmidt, 350.

[44] Ibid., 63, 907.

[45] Ibid., 63.

[46] Ibid., 372.

[47] Ibid., 350.

Thursday of Holy Week [Holy Thursday]—pages 30–54

[1] GIRM, 380.

[2] Order of Christian Funerals, 177–203.

[3] Schmidt, 67.

[4] Ibid., 757, 561.

[5] Paul Bradshaw, Maxwell E. Johnson, and L. Edward Phillips, *The Apostolic Tradition: A Commentary*, ed. Harold W. Attridge (Minneapolis: Augsburg Fortress, 2002), 112–13.

[6] Schmidt, 714.

[7] Gelasian, 375–90, 391–94.

[8] Gregorian, 328–37.

[9] Tyrer, p. 93. See also the eighth-century *Ordo* 24 in Schmidt, 513–14.

[10] Ferdinando Antonelli wrote, "The Chrism Mass, whose formulae are known from ancient sacramentaries, should of course be restored, but only for use in Cathedrals on the morning of Holy Thursday. It should be a matter of no more than a few alterations to simplify the very long rites, bearing in mind the ancient formulae." Nicola Giampietro, *The Development of the Liturgical Reform as Seen by Cardinal Ferdinando Antonelli from 1948 to 1970* (Fort Collins: Roman Catholic Books, 2009), 61.

[11] Schemata no. 51, 30 novembris 1964, De anno liturgico 1 ter, p. 3.

[12] Congregation for Divine Worship and the Discipline of the Sacraments, Circular Letter Concerning the Preparation and Celebration of the Easter Feasts, Prot. N. 120/88, 20 February 1988. In *The Liturgy Documents: A Parish Resource*, vol. 2 (Chicago: Liturgy Training Publications, 1999), 35. "Easter night" here obviously means "Easter Vigil."

[13] Schemata no. 192, 4 octobris 1966, De Pontificali, 14, p. 2.

[14] Schmidt, 762–63.

[15] Giampietro, 247–48.

[16] Ibid., 68.

[17] Ceremonial of Bishops (Collegeville, MN: Liturgical Press, 1989), 274.

[18] Schmidt, 69.

[19] Bradshaw, Johnson, and Phillips, 5:1–6:4, pp. 50–54.

[20] Tyrer, 99.

[21] Schemata no. 49, 18 novembris 1964, De Pontificali 2, pp. 1–2.

[22] Schemata no. 151, 2 aprilis 1966, De Pontificali 8, pp. 1–2.

[23] Schemata no. 158, 25 aprilis 1966, De Pontificali 9. CB, 274, says the purpose of the oil is for the anointing of catechumens; it makes no mention of infants.

[24] Schemata no. 151, pp. 1–2.

[25] Schemata no. 158.

[26] Giampietro, 247.

[27] Schemata no. 51, p. 3.

[28] Schmidt, 64.

[29] Ibid.

[30] Schemata no. 181, 25 augusti 1966, De Pontificali 13, p. 14.

[31] *The Roman Missal in Latin and English for Holy Week and Easter Week, including the Mass of the Chrism with the Blessing of the Oils* (Collegeville, MN: Liturgical Press, 1966), 92–95.

[32] Schmidt, 737.

[33] Schemata no. 51, pp. 1–2.

[34] CB, 281.

[35] The first copy of the English translation of the Roman Missal presented by Vox Clara to the Pope Benedict XVI in 2010, however, translated the 2002 version of this rubric, not the one from 2008. See paragraph 55 of the Easter Vigil.

[36] Schmidt, 355.

[37] Schemata no. 51, p. 6, referring to 999 and 96.

[38] See below, p. 68.

[39] *Holy Week and Easter Week*, 96–97.

[40] Schmidt, 358.

[41] Ibid., 69.

[42] The practice appeared even in the Gelasian Sacramentary; Schmidt, 358. But it was probably adopted from a place where the chrism Mass was the only Eucharist—or at least the last Eucharist—to be celebrated on the day before Good Friday.

[43] Giampietro, 247.

[44] Schemata no. 51, p. 3.

[45] Gregorian, 149, 204.

[46] Schmidt, 66.

[47] Schemata, no. 368, die 23 maii 1970, De Pontificali, 23, p. 1.

[48] Paul Turner, *The Meaning and Practice of Confirmation: Perspectives from a Sixteenth-Century Controversy*, American University Studies 7/31 (New York: Peter Lang, 1987), 208–09.

[49] Rite of Christian Initiation of Adults (Collegeville, MN: Liturgical Press, 1988), 102B.

[50] *Pastoral Care of the Sick: Rites of Anointing and Viaticum*, 123.

[51] Schmidt, 67.

[52] Ibid.

[53] *Apology* 1:65–67. See *Catechism of the Catholic Church*, 1345.

[54] Schmidt, 67.

[55] Schmidt, 582.

[56] *Holy Week and Easter Week*, 99.

[57] Schemata no. 368, p. 3, for example.

[58] CB, 128.

[59] Schmidt, 68–70. In reality, this is still practiced in some places, in spite of the rubrics here.

[60] This had already been done in the revised preconciliar liturgy of 1966. See *Holy Week and Easter Week*, 94–95.

[61] Schemata no. 48, 6 novembris 1964, De Pontificali, 1, ad no. 5.

[62] Schemata no. 181. A footnote indicates that this was done in the past, according to the Gregorian Sacramentary, the Gelasian Sacramentary, and the *Ordines Romani*.

[63] Schmidt, 67–68.

[64] Ibid., 71.

[65] Bradshaw, Johnson, and Phillips, 112–13.

[66] Schmidt, 68–70.

[67] Ibid., 65.

[68] Ibid., 70–71.

[69] Ibid., 582.

[70] F. J. E. Raby, *A History of Christian-Latin Poetry from the Beginnings to the Close of the Middle Ages* (Oxford: The Clarendon Press, 1953), 158.

[71] GIRM, 73, 178. See also CB, 145.

[72] Schmidt, 68, 70.

[73] Ibid., 70.

[74] *Holy Week and Easter Week*, 98.

[75] Schmidt, 722. *Le pontifical de Guillaume Durand*, ed. Michel Andrieu (Vatican City: Biblioteca Apostolica Vaticana, 1940), 65.

[76] Schemata no. 48, ad no. 6.

[77] *Holy Week and Easter Week*, 98–99.

[78] Ibid.

[79] Schmidt, 355–356.

[80] CB, 274.

[81] Schmidt, 580.

[82] Ibid., 69.

[83] Schemata no. 354, 22 octobris 1969, De Pontificali, 20, p. 9.

[84] Schmidt, 71.

[85] *Holy Week and Easter Week*, 100–101.

[86] For example, the Roman-Germanic Pontifical; Schmidt, p. 582.

[87] *Holy Week and Easter Week*, 100–101.

[88] Ibid., 100–111.

[89] Schmidt, 356–57.

[90] *Holy Week and Easter Week*, 100–101.

[91] Ibid., 110–11.

[92] Schmidt, 68, 75.

[93] *Holy Week and Easter Week*, 100–101.

[94] Ibid.

[95] Ibid., 108–9.

[96] As late as 29 September 1969, Schemata no. 352 of De Rituali, no. 36, p. 48, shows no indication of a text for blessing the oil of catechumens.

[97] *Holy Week and Easter Week*, 100–103.

[98] Ibid., 102–3.

[99] Schmidt, 583.

[100] Ibid.

[101] 354, 495.

[102] Schemata no. 49, 2, p. 3.

[103] Schmidt, 73.

[104] Ibid.

[105] Ibid., 356.

[106] Schemata no. 181, p. 18, no. 11, citing *Ordo Romanus* 31 in Adrieu, p. 494 (*sic*; it is on 495).

[107] Schmidt, 65, 74.

[108] Schemata no. 354, pp. 10–11.

[109] Schmidt, 74–75.

[110] *Holy Week and Easter Week*, 108–9.

[111] Schemata no. 49, p. 3.

[112] Schmidt, 76.

[113] Ibid., 77.

The Sacred Paschal Triduum—pages 55–56

[1] Augustine, *De consenus evangelistarum* 3.24, 66; PL 34:1199.

[2] The consultors preparing the postconciliar Holy Week liturgies had quite a conversation about when the Triduum should begin. Many believed it should begin on Good Friday with the paschal fast; others thought the Lord's Supper could not be separated from the meaning of the Triduum. They even discussed whether or not the chrism Mass served as the conclusion of Lent. Many interesting remarks can be found in Schemata no. 65, 15 martii 1965, De Calendario, 2, pp. 1–3.

[3] Ambrose *Epistola* 23.13; PL 16:1050.

[4] Canons 97, 1250–53.

[5] Congregation for Divine Worship and the Discipline of the Sacraments, Circular Letter Concerning the Preparation and Celebration of the Easter Feasts, Prot. N. 120/88, 20 February 1988. In *The Liturgy Documents: A Parish Resource*, vol. 2 (Chicago: Liturgy Training Publications, 1999), 27.

[6] CL, 75.

Thursday of the Lord's Supper—pages 57–77

[1] J. Gordon Davies, *Holy Week: A Short History* (Richmond: John Knox Press, 1963), 23, citing cap. xxii of the "Expositio fidei," the appendix to the *Panarion* of Epiphanius.

[2] Hermanus A. P. Schmidt, *Hebdomada Sancta* (Rome: Herder, 1957), 665.

[3] Davies, 38, citing Epistle 54:7 to Januarius.

[4] John Walton Tyrer, *Historical Survey of Holy Week: Its Services and Ceremonial*, Alcuin Club Collections 29 (London: Oxford University Press, 1932), 114.

[5] Nicola Giampietro, *The Development of the Liturgical Reform as Seen by Cardinal Ferdinando Antonelli from 1948 to 1970* (Fort Collins: Roman Catholic Books, 2009), 245.

[6] Ibid., 299.

[7] Schmidt, 78.

[8] Ibid., 510.

[9] Ibid., 317–18.

[10] *The Roman Missal in Latin and English for Holy Week and Easter Week, including the Mass of the Chrism with the Blessing of the Oils* (Collegeville, MN: Liturgical Press, 1966), 96–97.

[11] Sacra Congregatio Rituum, *Ordinationes et declarationes circa Ordinem Hebdomadae Sanctae instauratum*, die 1 februarii 1957, Acta Apostolica Sedis 49 (1957), 91–95; Schmidt, 955.

[12] Ibid., no. 11–12.

[13] See paragraph 33 below.

[14] GIRM, 305.

[15] Schmidt, 78.

[16] GIRM, 85.

[17] Schemata no. 304, p. 10, no. 30.

[18] Schmidt, 78.

[19] Ibid., 907.

[20] Ibid.

[21] See above, p. 24.

[22] *An Analysis of the Restored Holy Week Rites for Pastoral Use*, ed. Notre Dame Liturgical Committee (Notre Dame: University of Notre Dame Press, 1956), 13.

[23] Schmidt, 743.

[24] Ibid., 79.

[25] Ceremonial of Bishops (Collegeville, MN: Liturgical Press, 1989), 300.

[26] Schmidt, 79.

[27] *Musicam Sacram*, 81b and 83b.

[28] Walter D. Miller felt quite strongly about this: "Certainly the use of these noisemakers should stop! The pistol shot or Donald Duck quacking sounds that the noisemakers produce add absolutely nothing to the meaningful celebration of the Paschal mystery." *Revised Ceremonial of Holy Week* (New York: Catholic Book Publishing Company, 1971), 43n.

[29] Schmidt, 359.

[30] Schemata no. 278, D8, ad 29.

[31] Schmidt, 95.

[32] Schemata no. 278, D8, ad 30.

[33] Schmidt, 458, 737.

[34] Ibid., 665.

[35] Ibid., 459–60.

[36] Ibid., 80.

[37] Sacra Congregatio Rituum, *Ordinationes et declarationes*, 91–95; Schmidt, 955, no. 10.

[38] Schemata no. 304, p. 10, no. 36.

[39] Schmidt, 80.

[40] Schemata no. 304, p. 10, no. 37.

[41] Schmidt, 767–68.

[42] Kenneth Stevenson, *The Liturgical Meaning of Holy Week: Jerusalem Revisited* (Washington, DC: The Pastoral Press, 1988), 37.

[43] Schmidt, 769.

[44] Ibid. Crichton writes, "In Rome, however, where the rite had penetrated in the early twelfth century (and perhaps before) there was the washing of the feet of the poor in the Lateran when the prior presided. He and other members of the community washed the feet of a considerable number of people to whom they gave food, 'a dole of bread, a dish of beans and two eels'!" (42).

[45] Schmidt, 80–81.

[46] Giampietro, 245.

[47] *The Bishops' Committee on the Liturgy Newsletter*, 23 (February 1987): 1–2.

[48] Schmidt, 80.

[49] Ibid., 81.

[50] CB, 301.

[51] Schmidt, 81.

[52] *On Renewing the Holy Week Liturgy: A General Decree and Instruction of the Sacred Congregation of Rites by Which the Holy Week Liturgy is Renewed* (Washington, DC: National Catholic Welfare Conference, 1955), I:1b, p. 6.

[53] Schmidt, 585–86.

[54] The 1969 draft inexplicably omitted the traditional first antiphon, John 13:34, which begins with the word *mandatum* and gave the rite its name.

[55] Schmidt, 83–84.

[56] Schemata no. 278, p. 8, no. 33.

[57] Schmidt, 80.

[58] Schemata no. 278, p. 6, no. 35; Schemata no. 304, p. 11, no. 41.

[59] Congregation for Divine Worship and the Discipline of the Sacraments, Circular Letter Concerning the Preparation and Celebration of the Easter Feasts, Prot. N. 120/88, 20 February 1988. In *The Liturgy Documents: A Parish Resource*, vol. 2 (Chicago: Liturgy Training Publications, 1999), 52.

[60] Schmidt, 651.

[61] Ibid., 764.

[62] Ibid., 83.

[63] The decision was made rather late. Schemata no. 304 from 1969 still had the preconciliar prayer in this place, p. 11.

[64] *Sacramentarium Veronense*, ed. Leo Cunibert Mohlberg, Rerum Ecclesiasticarum Documenta (Rome: Herder Editrice e Libreria, 1978), 93.

[65] Anthony Ward, "Euchology for the Mass 'In Cena Domini' of the 2000 *Missale Romanum*," Notitiae 507–508 (December 2008): 611–34.

[66] GIRM, 149.

[67] Maurizio Barba, *La riforma conciliare dell "Ordo Missae": Il percorso storico-redazional dei riti d'ingresso, di offertorio e di comunione* (Rome: Edizioni Liturgiche CLV, 2008), 427.

[68] Joseph Jungmann, *The Mass of the Roman Rite: Its Origins and Development*, trans. Francis A. Brunner, vol. 2 (Westminster, MD: Christian Classics, Inc., 1992), 198.

[69] Schmidt, 85.

[70] Ibid., 85–87.

[71] *Holy Week and Easter Week*, 124–25.

[72] Schemata no. 304, p. 12, no. 45.

[73] CL, 53.

[74] Schmidt, 86.

[75] Ibid., 514.

[76] Ibid., 87.

[77] Schmidt, 89.

[78] CL, 55.

[79] Order of Mass, 139. This one is new to the third edition of the Missal.

[80] GIRM, 165.

[81] *Missale Gothicum (Cod. Vat. Reg. Lat. 317)*, ed. Leo Cunibert Mohlberg, Rerum ecclesiasticarum documenta, Series maior, Fontes 5 (Rome: Herder, 1961), 214.

[82] *Holy Week and Easter Week*, 124–25.

[83] Schmidt, 89.

[84] GIRM, 277.

[85] Schmidt, 89.

[86] GIRM, 277.

[87] Schmidt, 89.

[88] Ibid., 90.

[89] Schemata no. 304, p. 12, no. 47.

[90] Schmidt, 89.

[91] Ibid., 90.

[92] Ibid., 666.

[93] CB, 307.

94 *Holy Week and Easter Week,* 124–25, but it seems to presume that either of these options would be inside the main church.

95 CL, 49.

96 See paragraph 44 below.

97 J. D. Crichton, *The Liturgy of Holy Week* (Dublin: Veritas, 1983), 59.

98 Schmidt, 90.

99 Ibid.

100 Ibid., 358.

101 CB, 309.

102 CL, 57.

103 Schmidt, 90.

104 Ibid., 777.

105 James Monti, *The Week of Salvation: History and Traditions of Holy Week* (Huntington: Our Sunday Visitor Publishing Division, 1993), 56.

106 Ibid., 122.

107 Congregation for Divine Worship and the Discipline of the Sacraments, letter of March 14, 2000, Prot. N. 569/00/L.

108 Matt 26:36, 40-41; Mark 14:32, 37-38; Luke 22:40, 45-46.

109 CL, 56.

110 Schmidt, 586.

111 Congregation for Divine Worship and the Discipline of the Sacraments, Circular Letter Concerning the Preparation and Celebration of the Easter Feasts, Prot. N. 120/88, 20 February 1988. See, for example, *The Liturgy Documents: A Parish Resource,* vol. 2 (Chicago: Liturgy Training Publications, 1999), 54.

112 CL, 43.

Friday of the Passion of the Lord [Good Friday]—pages 78–110

1 Hermanus A. P. Schmidt, *Hebdomada Sancta* (Rome: Herder, 1957), 797.

2 Schemata no. 304, p. 13, no. 54.

3 Matt 9:15; Mark 2:20; and Luke 5:35.

4 Congregation for Divine Worship and the Discipline of the Sacraments, Circular Letter Concerning the Preparation and Celebration of the Easter Feasts, Prot. N. 120/88, 20 February 1988. In *The Liturgy Documents: A Parish Resource,* vol. 2 (Chicago: Liturgy Training Publications, 1999), 40.

5 CL, 61.

6 *Holy Week and Easter Week,* 130–31.

7 Schmidt, 667–69.

8 Matt 27:45; Mark 15:33; and Luke 23:44.

9 CL, 63.

10 Schmidt, 806.

11 Ibid., 92.

[12] Nicola Giampietro, *The Development of the Liturgical Reform as Seen by Cardinal Ferdinando Antonelli from 1948 to 1970* (Fort Collins: Roman Catholic Books, 2009), 241.

[13] Ibid., 292.

[14] Ibid., 300.

[15] *The Bishops' Committee on the Liturgy Newsletter* 34 (January 1998): 3.

[16] *Holy Week and Easter Week*, 130–31.

[17] John Walton Tyrer, *Historical Survey of Holy Week: Its Services and Ceremonial*, Alcuin Club Collections 29 (London: Oxford University Press, 1932), 121.

[18] Schemata no. 278, pp. D10–11, ad 43.

[19] Ceremonial of Bishops (Collegeville: Liturgical Press, 1989), 315.

[20] Rite of Ordination of a Bishop, paragraph 51.

[21] Matt 9:15; Mark 2:20; and Luke 5:35.

[22] CL, 65.

[23] Schmidt, 359.

[24] Ibid., 93 no. 4.

[25] *Holy Week and Easter Week*, 130–31.

[26] CB, 315.

[27] Schmidt, 93.

[28] GIRM, 49, 123, and 173.

[29] Schemata no. 278, D11, ad 44.

[30] CL, 65.

[31] GIRM, 43, *genuflectant*.

[32] Schmidt, 511.

[33] *Holy Week and Easter Week*, no. 5, 130–31.

[34] Order of Mass, 1.

[35] Schmidt, 93.

[36] Schemata no. 278, D11, ad 45.

[37] Schmidt, 359.

[38] Ibid., 349.

[39] Schemata no. 278, D 11, ad 45.

[40] Schmidt, 94.

[41] Ibid., 412.

[42] Ibid., 478.

[43] Schemata no. 278, p. 10, no. 46.

[44] Schemata no. 304, p. 13, no. 60.

[45] Schemata no. 278, D11, ad 46.

[46] Schmidt, 95.

[47] Schemata nos. 278, p. 10 and 304, ad 7, where a handwritten word, "difficult," appears next to this citation. Schemata no. 304, p. 14, no. 61.

[48] Philippians 2:8–9. Schemata no. 278, p. 10, ad 48.

[49] Schmidt, 680, citing *Ordo Romanus* 33.

[50] Ibid., 668.

[51] Ibid., 459, citing the *Evangeliorum Capitulare Romanum A*.

[52] Giampietro, 249.

[53] Schmidt, 95.

[54] *Holy Week and Easter Week*, 134–35.

[55] Schmidt, 512, citing *Ordo Romanus* 23.

[56] James Monti, *The Week of Salvation: History and Traditions of Holy Week* (Huntington: Our Sunday Visitor Publishing Division, 1993), 56.

[57] Ibid., citing *Plures locorum* of March 25, 1965.

[58] Ceremonial of Bishops (Collegeville: Liturgical Press, 1989), 319.

[59] PL 78:1214–15.

[60] CB, 319.

[61] Giampietro, 249.

[62] Schemata no. 304, p. 14, no. 63.

[63] *Holy Week and Easter Week*, 144–45, no. 12.

[64] Schemata no. 304, p. 14, ad 64.

[65] Ibid., p. 18, ad 85.

[66] Schmidt, 97–98.

[67] Ibid., 507.

[68] Schemata no. 278, p. 10 no. 49a.

[69] Ibid., D12, ad 50.

[70] In theory this could include a major superior, for example. See the Code of Canon Law, canon 134.

[71] CB, 320.

[72] Tyrer, 126.

[73] Schmidt, 359–61.

[74] Ibid., 513, 515, citing *Ordo Romanus* 24.

[75] Giampietro, 249.

[76] Schmidt, 361.

[77] Ibid., 546.

[78] Ibid., 98.

[79] *Holy Week and Easter Week*, 144–55.

[80] Schemata no. 278, D 11, ad 50.

[81] Ibid., D12, ad 52.

[82] GIRM, 149. See notes on the eucharistic prayer for Holy Thursday's evening Mass.

[83] Schemata no. 304, p. 14, ad 67.

[84] Schemata no. 278, D12, ad 54.

[85] Schmidt, 100.

[86] Ibid.

[87] Schemata no. 278, D12, ad 56, gives a commentary on this very point, including the observation that "without doubt our separated brethren think that *we* have erred in the faith." The new formula did not dwell on errors but on the universal church.

[88] Schemata no. 304, p. 16, 73.

[89] Schmidt, 100.

[90] *Holy Week and Easter Week*, 154–55.

[91] Ibid.; emphasis mine.

[92] Ibid., 154.

[93] Schmidt, 100–101.

[94] Schemata no. 304, p. 16. The text was inspired by Rom 1:20 and Wis 13:3.

[95] Schemata no. 278, D12, ad 53.

[96] Ibid., D12, ad 55. The revised translation names travelers "pilgrims," making the connection to sailors more difficult to see.

[97] Schmidt, 667, says in the year 326.

[98] Ibid., 791.

[99] Ibid., 667.

[100] Ibid., 511, 515.

[101] Tyrer, 128.

[102] *Liber officialis* I, I, c. 14, 10. *Amalarii episcopi opera liturgica omnia*, ed. John Michael Hanssens, Studi e Testi 139, vol. 2 (Vatican City: Biblioteca apostolica Vaticana, 1948), 102.

[103] Schmidt, 101–2.

[104] Schemata no. 278, D9.

[105] Kenneth Stevenson, *The Liturgical Meaning of Holy Week: Jerusalem Revisited* (Washington: The Pastoral Press, 1988), 65.

[106] Schemata no. 278, D9–10.

[107] The question first surfaced on page 6 of Schemata no. 104 in 1965.

[108] Schemata no. 278, D13, ad 59.

[109] Schemata no. 104, p. 6, no. 2.

[110] *Summa Theologica* III, q. 25, a. 4.

[111] Schemata no. 278, p. 14; emphasis in the original.

[112] Schmidt, 102.

[113] Ibid., 101–2.

[114] Ibid., 101.

[115] Ibid.

[116] Schemata no. 304, p. 16, no. 77.

[117] Schmidt, 101.

[118] Ibid., 102.

[119] Ibid., 485, 939.

[120] Ibid., 498.

[121] Ibid., 361.

[122] Ibid., 515.

[123] Ibid., 793.

[124] Ibid., 102–3.

[125] Ibid., 546–47.

[126] *The Monastic Constitutions of Lanfranc*, ed. David Knowles (London: Thomas Nelson and Sons Ltd, 1951), 40–41.

[127] Monti, p. 234, citing Liber II, Caput 25, no. 23, p. 253 (1902 printing).

[128] Schmidt, 102.

[129] Ibid.

[130] Ibid., 103–4.

[131] CB, 321.

[132] Schemata no. 278, p. 14, no. 50.

[133] J. D. Crichton, *The Liturgy of Holy Week* (Dublin: Veritas, 1983), p. 58.

[134] Schemata no. 304, p. 17, ad no. 80.

[135] Schemata no. 278, D16, ad 60.

[136] Schmidt, 103–4.

[137] Ibid., 103.

[138] Ibid.

[139] Ibid.

[140] Ibid.

[141] CB, 322.

[142] Schmidt, 104.

[143] Ibid., 511, 515.

[144] Giampietro, 300–301.

[145] Schemata no. 104, p. 6.

[146] Schmidt, 490, 494, 593, 795.

[147] Ibid., 796.

[148] *Le pontifical de Guillaume Durand*, ed. Michel Andrieu (Vatican City: Biblioteca Apostolica Vaticana, 1940), 585.

[149] Schmidt, 940.

[150] Ibid., 546–47, 793.

[151] Ibid., 490, 591, 794.

[152] Ibid., 794, 943.

[153] Monti, 232.

[154] Schemata no. 278, p. 14.

[155] See comments on Wednesday of Holy Week above.

[156] *Le Liber Ordinum en usage dans l'église wisigothique et mozarabe d'espagne du cinquième au onzième siècle*, ed. Marius Férontin (Rome: CLV Edizioni Liturgiche, 1996), 194.

[157] Schmidt, 547, 794.

[158] Schemata no. 304, p.18, no. 85.

[159] Schmidt, 109–10.

[160] CB, 325.

[161] Schmidt, 110.

[162] Schemata no. 278, D15, ad 61.

[163] Schmidt, 797.

[164] Ibid., 512.

[165] Ibid., 361.

[166] Ibid, 111.

[167] Ibid., 799. See, for example, *Ordo Romanus* 24, 515–16.

[168] Tyrer, 140, citing the Congregation of Rites.

[169] Giampietro, 249.

[170] Ibid., 250.

[171] Ibid., 67.

[172] Schmidt, 798.

[173] Ibid., 112.

[174] Schemata no. 304, p. 18, no. 86.

[175] Ibid.

[176] Schmidt, 113.

[177] Ibid.

[178] CL, 70.

[179] Schmidt, p. 113.

[180] Schemata no. 304, p. 18, no. 88 and ad 87 (however the footnote is incorrectly numbered 87; it should be 88).

[181] Schmidt, 114.

[182] CL, 70.

[183] Schmidt, 516.

[184] Ibid., 593.

[185] See, for example, the ninth-century *Antiphonale Rhenaugiense* in Schmidt, 485.

[186] Schemata no. 278, no. 14. The consultors wondered, "Would it be more in keeping with the special character of this Day if communion took place in silence?" Schemata no. 278, D15, ad 62.

[187] Schemata no. 304, p. 18, no. 89.

[188] Schmidt, 116.

[189] CL, 71.

[190] See below, Holy Saturday, paragraph 3.

[191] Schmidt, 115.

[192] Schemata no. 304, p. 19, no. 91.

[193] Schmidt, 115.

[194] Giampietro, 250.

[195] CB, 330–31.

[196] GIRM, 274.

[197] CL, 71.

Holy Saturday—pages 111–12

[1] Congregation for Divine Worship and the Discipline of the Sacraments, Circular Letter Concerning the Preparation and Celebration of the Easter Feasts, Prot. N. 120/88, 20 February 1988. In *The Liturgy Documents: A Parish Resource*, vol. 2 (Chicago: Liturgy Training Publications, 1999), 74.

[2] CL, 73.

³ Rite of Christian Initiation of Adults (Collegeville: Liturgical Press, 1988), 185–205.

⁴ CL, 75.

⁵ CL, 61.

Eastertime: Easter Sunday of the Resurrection of the Lord— pages 113–67

¹ Exod 12:42.

² Congregation for Divine Worship and the Discipline of the Sacraments, Circular Letter Concerning the Preparation and Celebration of the Easter Feasts, Prot. N. 120/88, 20 February 1988. In *The Liturgy Documents: A Parish Resource*, vol. 2 (Chicago: Liturgy Training Publications, 1999), 80.

³ J. D. Crichton, *The Liturgy of Holy Week* (Dublin: Veritas, 1983), 69–70. J. Gordon Davies, *Holy Week: A Short History* (Richmond: John Knox Press, 1963), 17.

⁴ Nicola Giampietro, *The Development of the Liturgical Reform as Seen by Cardinal Ferdinando Antonelli from 1948 to 1970* (Fort Collins: Roman Catholic Books, 2009), 49.

⁵ Ibid., 229.

⁶ CL, 91.

⁷ Ceremonial of Bishops (Collegeville: Liturgical Press, 1989), 334.

⁸ *Sermo* 219, PL 38:1088.

⁹ CL, 95.

¹⁰ CL, 94.

¹¹ Kathleen Hughes, "Synodus II S. Patricii," in Latin Script and Letters: A.D. 400–900, ed. John J. O'Meara and Bernd Naumann (Leiden: E. J. Brill, 1976), 141–47.

¹² Cf. John Walton Tyrer, *Historical Survey of Holy Week: Its Services and Ceremonial*, Alcuin Club Collections 29 (London: Oxford University Press, 1932), 147.

¹³ Schmidt, 669.

¹⁴ Ibid., 875.

¹⁵ Ibid.

¹⁶ *Sermo* 219, PL 38:1088.

¹⁷ Schmidt, 873.

¹⁸ Crichton, 73.

¹⁹ Giampietro, 39.

²⁰ Ibid., 220

²¹ Ibid., 230.

²² Ibid., 51.

²³ Ibid., 252.

[24] Schmidt, 956, citing Sacra Congregatio Rituum, *Ordinationes et declarationes circa Ordinem Hebdomadae Sanctae instauratum*, die 1 Februarii 1957, Acta Apostolica Sedis 49 (1957).

[25] Schemata no. 278, D17, ad 65.

[26] CL, 78.

[27] Schmidt, 365.

[28] Schemata no. 246, p. 19, no. 62.

[29] Schemata no. 278, D 17, "In genere."

[30] Schemata no. 304, p. 20, no. 95.

[31] GIRM, 208.

[32] Schmidt, 120–21.

[33] Schemata no. 278, p. 15, no. 66.

[34] Schmidt, 126–27.

[35] Ibid., 118–19.

[36] Schemata no. 304, p. 21, no. 102.

[37] Tyrer, 148, citing *Vita Constantini*, iv. 22; and *Procat.* 15.

[38] Ibid., 148–49, citing *Life* by Muirchu Maccu Mactheni; and Tirechan's *Collectanea* (i. 8).

[39] Schmidt, 361–62.

[40] Ibid., 809.

[41] Ibid., 518.

[42] Schemata no. 278, D17, ad 66.

[43] Schemata no. 104, p. 7.

[44] Schmidt, 120–21.

[45] CB, 338.

[46] Giampietro, 50, citing *Il Triduum Sacrum*.

[47] CB, 339.

[48] John 11:51-52.

[49] CB, 340.

[50] Schmidt, 121–23.

[51] Schemata no. 304, p. 21, no. 103.

[52] Schmidt, 120–23.

[53] Ibid., 362.

[54] Ibid., 628, citing 32.10.

[55] Giampietro, 39.

[56] Schmidt, 122–23.

[57] Ibid., 124.

[58] Rev 22:13.

[59] Schemata no. 304, pp. 21–22, for example.

[60] Schemata no. 278, D18, ad 67.

[61] CL, 82.

[62] *The Pontifical of Egbert, Archbishop of York, A.D. 732–766, Now First Printed from a Manuscript of the Tenth Century, in the Imperial Library, Paris* (Durham: The Surtees Society, 1853), 130.

[63] Schmidt, 363.

[64] For example, Andrieu, *Le Pontifical Roman au moyen-âge: Le Pontifical Romaine de XIIe siècle*, 239–40.

[65] Schmidt, 137.

[66] Schmidt, 124.

[67] For example, Schemata no. 304, p. 21.

[68] Schemata no. 278, D18, ad 67.

[69] Schemata no. 278, p. 15, no. 68.

[70] Schemata no. 246, 4 octobris 1967, p. 21, no. 68.

[71] Schmidt, 126.

[72] Schemata no. 278, D18, ad 69.

[73] CL, 83.

[74] Schemata no. 304, p. 22.

[75] Ibid.

[76] CB, 340.

[77] Schmidt, 126–27.

[78] Giampietro, 226.

[79] Schmidt, 128–29.

[80] Ibid., 128–31.

[81] CL, 83.

[82] Schemata no. 278, D18, ad 70.

[83] Schmidt, 128–29.

[84] Ibid., 507.

[85] Andrieu, *Le Pontifical Romain du XIIe siècle*, 241.

[86] Schmidt, 129.

[87] Ibid., 128.

[88] CB, 343.

[89] Schemata no. 304, p. 22, no. 105.

[90] Schmidt, 128–29.

[91] Schemata no. 278, p. 16, no. 69.

[92] Schmidt, 130.

[93] Kenneth Stevenson, *The Liturgical Meaning of Holy Week: Jerusalem Revisited* (Washington: The Pastoral Press, 1988), 88–89.

[94] Schmidt, 133.

[95] GIRM, 277.

[96] Schemata no. 304, p. 22, no. 107.

[97] *Diaconus, incensatis libro et cereo, annuntiat . . .*

[98] *Holy Week and Easter Week*, 178–79.

[99] Schmidt, 132–33.

[100] *Holy Week and Easter Week*, 178–79.

[101] Giampietro, 51.

[102] Schmidt, 626.

[103] Ibid., 640–44.

[104] Ibid., 138–39.

105 For example, Num 3:6.

106 Schmidt, 644.

107 PL 14:1116.

108 Schmidt, 644–45.

109 Ibid. See Rita Ferrone, "Virgil and the Vigil: The Bees Are Coming Back to the Exsultet," *Commonweal* 136, no. 7 (April 10, 2009): 12–13, http://www.commonwealmagazine.org/virgil-vigil-0.

110 Schemata no. 278, D19, ad 72.

111 Ibid.

112 Schmidt, 139.

113 Schemata no. 278, D19, ad 72.

114 Schemata no. 304, pp. 23–24, no. 108.

115 Much of this commentary is based on notes in Schmidt, 644–45.

116 Giampietro, 48 and 226.

117 Schmidt, 138–39.

118 *Sermo* 219, PL 38:1088.

119 CL, 77.

120 General Norms for the Liturgical Year and Calendar, 21.

121 CL, 85.

122 Schemata no. 278, p. 19.

123 Schmidt, 138–39.

124 CB, 346.

125 CL, 86.

126 Schmidt, 143.

127 GIRM, 31, 128.

128 Lectionary for Mass, 42.

129 Maurizio Barba, *Institutio Generalis Missalis Romani: Textus Synopsis, Variationes*, Monumenta Studia Instrumenta Liturgica (Vatican City: Libreria Editrice Vaticana, 2006), 422.

130 Schemata no. 278, p. 18.

131 Schemata no. 304, p. 26, no. 112.

132 CL, 86.

133 Schmidt, 669.

134 Thomas J. Talley, *The Origins of the Liturgical Year* (New York: Pueblo Publishing Company, 1986), 48–49.

135 Aemiliana Löhr, *The Great Week: An Explanation of the Liturgy of Holy Week* (London: Longmans, Green, 1958), 164–65.

136 Schmidt, 459, citing the *Evangeliorum Capitulare Romanum A.*

137 Ibid., 363–65, 143–51.

138 Ibid., 141.

139 Giampietro, 40, 227.

140 Ibid., 231.

141 Ibid., 40.

[142] Schemata no. 104, p. 8, no. 2.

[143] It should be Ezek.

[144] Schemata no. 104, pp. 8–9, no. 2.

[145] Schemata no. 278, pp. 18–19, no. 73–84.

[146] Ibid. 278, p. 18.

[147] Ibid., 278, D19, ad 73.

[148] Schemata no. 278, D16, "In genere."

[149] Ibid., 278, D16–17, "In genere."

[150] Ibid., 278, D19, ad 73.

[151] Schemata no. 304, p. 26, ad n. 112.

[152] Schemata no. 278, D19, ad 73. See paragraph 30 below.

[153] Ibid., 278, D20, ad 86.

[154] Ibid., 278, D20, ad 87.

[155] Schmidt, 143.

[156] Schemata no. 304, p. 27, no. 115.

[157] Schemata no. 278, D20, ad 72.

[158] Schemata no. 304, p. 27, no. 116.

[159] Schmidt, 365.

[160] Schemata no. 278, p. 19, no. 84.

[161] Schemata no. 304, p. 28, no. 117.

[162] Schmidt, 365.

[163] Schemata no. 246, p. 22.

[164] Schmidt, 363.

[165] *Sacramentarium Veronense*, ed. Leo Cunibert Mohlberg, Rerum Ecclesiasticarum Documenta (Rome: Herder Editrice e Libreria, 1978), 94.

[166] Schmidt, 155.

[167] Ibid., 367.

[168] Ibid., 867.

[169] Ibid., 516.

[170] Ibid., 170–71.

[171] Ibid., 172–73.

[172] Schemata no. 246, p. 24.

[173] Ibid., p. 24, no. 77.

[174] Schemata no. 278, D20, ad 87.

[175] Schemata no. 304, p. 29, ad 120.

[176] Schmidt, 173.

[177] Ibid., 367–68.

[178] Schemata no. 104, p. 9, no. 2.

[179] Schemata no. 278, p. 19.

[180] Schemata no. 304, p. 33, no. 131.

[181] Schmidt, 175.

[182] James Monti, *The Week of Salvation: History and Traditions of Holy Week* (Huntington: Our Sunday Visitor Publishing Division, 1993), 353.

[183] Schemata no. 104, p. 9, no. 102.

[184] Schemata no. 278, p. 19, no. 88.

[185] Monti, 354.

[186] CB, 352.

[187] Ibid.

[188] Matt 21:42; Mark 12:10-11; and Luke 20:17.

[189] Acts 4:11.

[190] Schmidt, 485, citing the *Antiphonale Rhenaugiense*.

[191] Ibid., 175. See also Schemata no. 278, D20, ad. 88.

[192] Ibid., 516.

[193] Ibid., 459, citing the *Evangeliorum Capitulare Romanum A*.

[194] Ibid., 175.

[195] Schemata no. 304, p. 29, no. 123.

[196] Schmidt, 175.

[197] Schemata no. 304, p. 29, ad 123.

[198] Schmidt, 669.

[199] Schemata no. 246, p. 7, no. 3, citing the *Missale Gothicum*, 250. See also Schemata no. 278, D21, ad 90.

[200] Schemata no. 304, p. 30, no. 125.

[201] See, for example, the Ordination of a Bishop, paragraph 42, in the *Rites of Ordination of a Bishop, of Priests, and of Deacons*.

[202] Schmidt, 863.

[203] *De corona*, 3.

[204] CL, 88.

[205] Schemata no. 278, D20, ad 90.

[206] Schmidt, 861. Giampietro, 40.

[207] Schmidt, 861–66.

[208] Ibid., 863. Giampietro, 40.

[209] Schmidt, 150–53.

[210] Ibid., 170–73.

[211] Schemata no. 104, pp. 7, 9.

[212] Schemata no. 246, p. 27, no. 84.

[213] Schemata no. 278, p. 20, no. 90.

[214] Schemata no. 304, pp. 30–31, no. 127.

[215] Schmidt, 155.

[216] See Tyrer, 163.

[217] Schmidt, 155.

[218] Tyrer, 162.

[219] Schmidt, 365–67.

[220] Ibid., 412, citing the *Sacramentarium Gelasianum Augiense*.

[221] Schemata no. 246, p. 26, no. 80.

[222] Schemata no. 278, D21, ad 91.

[223] Giampietro, 40.

[224] Schmidt, 152–63.

[225] Rite of Christian Initiation of Adults (Collegeville: Liturgical Press, 1988), General Introduction, 21.

[226] Schemata, no. 246, 20 novembris 1967, De anno liturgico 4, p. 2.

[227] Schemata no. 278, p. 22, no. 91.

[228] Schemata no. 304, p. 32, no. 129.

[229] See RCIA, 224, and Rite of Baptism for Children (Collegeville: Liturgical Press, 2002), 57. For a full treatment of the rubrics in those ritual books, see Paul Turner, *Celebrating Initiation: A Guide for Priests* (Chicago: World Library Publications, 2007).

[230] CB, 362.

[231] Davies, 33.

[232] RCIA, 33/7.

[233] Schmidt, 164.

[234] See RCIA 225, RBC 58.

[235] Schmidt, 367.

[236] *Baptism* 6.13. See Paul Turner, *The Hallelujah Highway: A History of the Catechumenate* (Chicago: Liturgy Training Publications, 2000), 29.

[237] RBC, 62.

[238] RBC, 65.

[239] RCIA, 197.

[240] CB, 365, citing RBC, no. 28, 3.

[241] Giampietro, 228.

[242] Schemata no. 104, p. 10, no. 3.

[243] See Paul Turner, *When Other Christians Become Catholic* (Collegeville, MN: Liturgical Press, 2007).

[244] Canon 883/2 and 885/2.

[245] RCIA, 232.

[246] Turner, *The Hallelujah Highway*, 168.

[247] CB, 367.

[248] For example, *Ordo Romanus* 24; Schmidt, 516.

[249] See RCIA, 215.

[250] Ibid., 232.

[251] Schemata no. 304, p. 31, no. 128.

[252] In April 2010, Vox Clara, a consultative body to the Congregation for Divine Worship and the Discipline of the Sacraments, concluded its work on the revision of the translation of the third edition of the Missal and presented a copy to Pope Benedict XVI. The International Commission on English in the Liturgy (ICEL), for which the author of this book has done some work, had prepared the proposed translation. Bishops from the member conferences of ICEL had voted on that work and approved it. The text from Vox Clara was leaked online in the fall of 2010. A number of typographical errors were apparent. For example, in the section dealing with Holy Week, the short rubric

at the head of paragraph 45 of the Easter Vigil was completely missing. Here in paragraph 55, the text referred the reader to paragraph 48. However, the apposite reference occurs in paragraph 49. The third edition of the Roman Missal, which was published in Latin in 2002, was republished in 2008 with some emendations. One of them occurred here, changing the incorrect reference from 48 to 49. This suggests that Vox Clara and the Congregation were not always consulting the most recent versions of the texts before finalizing their work.

[253] Giampietro, 50.

[254] Ibid., 220.

[255] Schmidt, 156.

[256] Giampietro, 227–28.

[257] Ibid., 231.

[258] Schmidt, 168–69.

[259] *Holy Week and Easter Week*, 208–09.

[260] Schmidt, 164–65.

[261] Schemata no. 104, p. 10, no. 3.

[262] Schemata no. 278, D21, ad 93.

[263] Schmidt, 164.

[264] Schemata no. 278, p. 22, no. 94.

[265] Schemata no. 304, p. 32, no. 131 and footnote ad 131.

[266] Schmidt, 166.

[267] Schemata no. 246, p. 26, no. 82.

[268] Schmidt, 175.

[269] Schemata no. 278, p. 22, no. 94; Schemata no. 304, p. 32, no. 131.

[270] Schmidt, 175

[271] Ibid., 541.

[272] Schemata no. 246, p. 26, no. 83.

[273] RCIA, 241.

[274] Schemata no. 278, D21, ad 96.

[275] Schmidt, 168–71.

[276] Schemata no. 104, p. 10, no. 3.

[277] Schemata no. 304, p. 33, no. 134.

[278] Schmidt, 172–75.

[279] RBC, 9.

[280] Schmidt, 368.

[281] Ibid., 368.

[282] Ibid., 368–69.

[283] Ibid., 873.

[284] CL, 91.

[285] Schmidt, 867, citing the Roman *Ordos* 30A, 30B, and 31.

[286] Schemata no. 104, p. 10, no. 4.

[287] RCIA, 243.

[288] "Domenica di Pasqua Risurrezione del Signore. Veglia Pasquale Nella Notte Santa. Presieduta dal Santo Padre Benedetto XVI," accessed July 4, 2011, http://www.vatican.va/news_services/liturgy/libretti/2011/20110423_veglia.pdf, p. 83.

[289] RCIA, 243.

[290] CB, 370.

[291] CL, 92.

[292] Schmidt, 178–79.

[293] Morning Prayer can be appended to any celebration of the Eucharist.

[294] Schemata no. 104, p. 10, no. 4.

[295] Schmidt, 178–79.

[296] RBC, 70, 247, 248, 249.

[297] CB, 370.

[298] *Le pontifical de Guillaume Durand*, ed. Michel Andrieu (Vatican City: Biblioteca Apostolica Vaticana, 1940), 593.

[299] CL, 99.

[300] Schemata no. 313, p. 9.

[301] Schemata no. 383, die 14 februarii 1969, De Missali no. 60; p. 29.

[302] CL, 97.

[303] *Liber Sacramentorum Romanae aeclesiae ordinis anni circuli*, ed. Leo Cunibert Mohlberg (Rome: Casa Editrice Herder, 1981), 76, no. 463.

[304] Schemata no. 104, p. 9, no. 102.

[305] Schmidt, 175.

[306] See, for example, the 1474 Roman Missal.

[307] Schmidt, 458.

[308] GIRM, 64.

[309] Lectionary for Mass, appendix I.

[310] Ibid.

[311] GIRM, 68.

[312] *Liber Sacramentorum*, 77, no. 470.

Bibliography

An Analysis of the Restored Holy Week Rites for Pastoral Use. Edited by Notre Dame Liturgical Committee. Notre Dame: University of Notre Dame Press, 1956.

Barba, Maurizio. *La riforma conciliare dell' "Ordo Missae": Il percorso storico-redazional dei riti d'ingresso, di offertorio e di comunione.* Rome: Edizioni Liturgiche CLV, 2008.

Bradshaw, Paul, Maxwell E. Johnson, and L. Edward Phillips. *The Apostolic Tradition: A Commentary.* Edited by Harold W. Attridge. Minneapolis: Augsburg Fortress, 2002.

Ceremonial of Bishops. Collegeville, MN: Liturgical Press, 1989.

Congregation for Divine Worship and the Discipline of the Sacraments. Circular Letter Concerning the Preparation and Celebration of the Easter Feasts. Prot. N. 120/88, 20 February 1988. In *The Liturgy Documents: A Parish Resource.* Vol. 2. Chicago: Liturgy Training Publications, 1999.

Crichton, J. D. *The Liturgy of Holy Week.* Dublin: Veritas, 1983.

Davies, J. Gordon. *Holy Week: A Short History.* Richmond: John Knox Press, 1963.

Ferrone, Rita. "Virgil and the Vigil: The Bees Are Coming Back to the Exsultet." *Commonweal* 136, no. 7 (April 10, 2009): 12–13. http://www.commonwealmagazine.org/virgil-vigil-0.

Giampietro, Nicola. *The Development of the Liturgical Reform as Seen by Cardinal Ferdinando Antonelli from 1948 to 1970.* Fort Collins: Roman Catholic Books, 2009.

The International Commission on English in the Liturgy. Schemata no. 48, 6 novembris 1964, De Pontificali, 1.

———. Schemata no. 49, 18 novembris 1964, De Pontificali.

———. Schemata no. 51, 30 novembris 1964, De Anno Liturgico 1 ter.

———. Schemata no. 65, 15 martii 1965, De Calendario, 2.

———. Schemata no. 104, 10 septembris 1965, De Anno Liturgico.

———. Schemata no. 151, 2 aprilis 1966, De Pontificali.

———. Schemata no. 158, 25 aprilis 1966, De Pontificali.

———. Schemata no. 176, 25 iulii 1966, De Missali.

———. Schemata no. 181, 25 augusti 1966, De Pontificali 13.

———. Schemata no. 192, 4 octobris 1966, De Pontificali.

———. Schemata no. 246, 13 novembris 1967.

———. Schemata no. 278, 21 martii 1968.

———. Schemata no. 304, "De ritibus peculiaribus in anno liturgico: De hebdomada sancta, De ritu candelarum in festo praesentationis Domini, De ritu cinerum initio Quadragesimae, die 2 septembris 1968."

———. Schemata no. 338, die 14 februarii 1969, De Missali.

———. Schemata no. 352 of De Rituali, n. 36.

———. Schemata no. 354, 22 octobris 1969, De Pontificali, 20.

———. Schemata no. 368, die 23 maii 1970, De Pontificali, 23.

Jungmann, Joseph. *The Mass of the Roman Rite: Its Origins and Development.* Translated by Francis A. Brunner. 2 vol. Westminster, MD: Christian Classics, Inc., 1992.

Le Liber Ordinum en usage dans l'église wisigothique et mozarabe d'espagne du cinquième au onzième siècle. Edited by Marius Férontin. Rome: CLV Edizioni Liturgiche, 1996.

Les Ordines Romani du haut moyen age. Edited by Michel Andrieu. 5 vol. Louvain: Spicilegium Sacrum Lovaniense Administration, 1931–61.

Le pontifical de Guillaume Durand. Edited by Michel Andrieu. Vatican City: Biblioteca Apostolica Vaticana, 1940.

Le pontifical Romano-germanique du dixième siècle. Edited by Cyrille Vogel, Reinhard Elze, and Michel Andrieu. 3 vol. Studi e testi 226, 227, 269. Vatican City: Biblioteca Apostolica Vaticana, 1963–72.

Le Sacramentaire Grégorien, ses principals forms d'après les plus anciens manuscrits. Edited by Jean Deshusses. Freiburg: Éditions Universitaires, 1979.

Liber Sacramentorum Romanae aeclesiae ordinis anni circuli. Edited by Leo Cunibert Mohlberg. Rome: Casa Editrice Herder, 1981.

Löhr, Aemiliana. *The Great Week: An Explanation of the Liturgy of Holy Week.* London: Longmans, Green, 1958.

Miller, Walter D. *Revised Ceremonial of Holy Week.* New York: Catholic Book Publishing Co., 1971.

Missale Gothicum (Cod. Vat. Reg. Lat. 317). Edited by Leo Cunibert Mohlberg. Rerum ecclesiasticarum documenta. Series maior, Fontes 5. Rome: Herder, 1961.

Monti, James. *The Week of Salvation: History and Traditions of Holy Week.* Huntington: Our Sunday Visitor Publishing Division, 1993.

O'Connell, J. B. *The Ceremonies of Holy Week: Solemn Rite and Simple Rite, A Commentary.* Westminster: The Newman Press, 1958.

Patrologia Latina. Edited by J. P. Migne. Paris: Apud Garnier, 1844.

Raby, F. J. E. *A History of Christian-Latin Poetry from the Beginnings to the Close of the Middle Ages.* Oxford: The Clarendon Press, 1953.

Rite of Baptism for Children. Collegeville, MN: Liturgical Press, 2002.

Rite of Christian Initiation of Adults. Collegeville: Liturgical Press, MN, 1988.

The Roman Missal in Latin and English for Holy Week and Easter Week, including the Mass of the Chrism with the Blessing of the Oils. Collegeville, MN: Liturgical Press, 1966. *Sacramentarium Veronense.* Edited by Leo Cunibert

Mohlberg. Rerum Ecclesiasticarum Documenta. Rome: Herder Editrice e Libreria, 1978.

Schmidt, Hermanus A. P. *Hebdomada Sancta.* Rome: Herder, 1957.

Stevenson, Kenneth. *The Liturgical Meaning of Holy Week: Jerusalem Revisited.* Washington, DC: The Pastoral Press, 1988.

Talley, Thomas J. *The Origins of the Liturgical Year.* New York: Pueblo Publishing Company, 1986.

Turner, Paul. *The Meaning and Practice of Confirmation: Perspectives from a Sixteenth-Century Controversy.* American University Studies 7/31. New York: Peter Lang, 1987.

———. *Celebrating Initiation: A Guide for Priests.* Chicago: World Library Publications, 2007.

———. *When Other Christians Become Catholic.* Collegeville, MN: Liturgical Press, 2007.

Tyrer, John Walton. *Historcial Survey of Holy Week: Its Services and Ceremonial.* Alcuin Club Collections 29. London: Oxford University Press, 1932.

Ward, Anthony. "Euchology for the Mass 'In Cena Domini' of the 2000 *Missale Romanum.*" *Notitiae* 507–8 (December 2008): 611–34.

Index

Aaron, 35, 52

Abraham, 134, 137, 149

acclamation, 49, 56, 87, 105, 125, 126, 129, 142, 143, 151, 152, 161, 165

Adam, 83

adore, -ation, 75–77, 79, 92–96, 98–102, 105, 107–9, 146

Agnus Dei (Lamb of God), 35, 70, 105, 162

Albareda, Anselmo, 84, 86, 115

Alleluia, 143, 144, 160, 163, 164, 167

Amalarius of Metz, 32, 93

Ambrose, 55, 115, 129, 130, 177

Ambrosian Rite, 28, 98, 167

Antonelli, Ferdinando, 104, 119, 169, 174, 178, 182, 187, 197

Apostolic Tradition, 31–32, 46, 150, 160, 174, 197

Aquinas, Thomas, 94

Augustine, 55, 57, 113–15, 129, 131, 177

balsam, 40, 45, 47, 50, 51

banquet, 72, 113, 162

baptism(s), 17, 21, 31, 32, 33, 34, 35, 39, 40, 41, 47, 51, 52, 53, 63, 90, 111, 114, 117, 132, 134, 136–62, 166, 193, 198

baptized, -s, 18, 21, 35, 37, 39, 41, 42, 56, 90, 111, 118, 132, 139, 145–47, 149, 151–56, 159–60, 162–63, 167

Bea, Agostino, 131, 134, 157

bells, 60, 61, 78, 112, 131, 140, 142

Benedict XVI, 162, 175, 193

Blessed Sacrament, 59, 72–77, 103, 108, 110

Book of the Gospels, 8, 9, 44, 50, 73

both kinds, 32, 33, 70, 163

British Joint Group, 127

Byzantine, 100, 143

Caiaphas, 120

cantor(s), 85, 101, 102, 128, 133, 143, 146–48

catechumen(s), 1, 17, 27, 30, 31, 33, 34, 39–41, 45–47, 50, 51, 88–90, 92, 104, 111, 117, 132, 145, 151, 152, 155, 159, 160, 175, 177

cathedral, 31, 56, 174

Ceremonial of Bishops, 4, 6, 33, 37, 49, 60, 87, 99, 103, 119, 120, 144, 152, 155, 164, 169, 174, 178, 182, 183, 187, 197

chasuble, 4, 11, 12, 64, 66, 73, 100, 117

chrism, 30–43, 45–47, 50–54, 57, 58, 118, 140, 151–53, 174, 175, 177, 178, 198

chrism Mass, 30–54, 57, 58, 140, 152, 174, 175, 177

Christus factus est, 62

Circular Letter, 2, 16, 17, 21, 31, 70, 72, 74, 76, 77, 78, 81, 105, 108, 110, 111, 113, 114, 116, 122, 124, 125, 131, 133, 147, 162, 163, 164, 165, 169, 172, 174, 177, 179, 181, 186, 187

cloth, 75, 79, 86, 103, 159

Code of Canon Law, 55, 154, 183

collect, 11–15, 22, 25, 27, 35, 61, 66, 67, 82, 83, 88, 106, 133, 140, 142, 143, 148, 158, 160, 161, 163, 165, 167, 169, 171, 173, 178, 182, 187, 199 commemoration, 1, 2, 37, 68

communion antiphon, 19, 23, 26, 28, 38, 71, 163, 167

concelebrate, -es, -tion, 32, 39, 43, 44, 48, 50, 53, 58, 116, 128

conference of bishops, 1, 41, 46, 50, 60, 87, 124, 129, 157

confirmation, -s, 21, 33, 35, 37, 39–41, 53, 153–55, 160, 175, 199

Congregation for Divine Worship and the Discipline of the Sacraments, 94, 102, 157, 169, 172, 174, 177, 179, 181, 186, 187, 193, 197

cope, 4, 11, 12, 73, 86, 92, 117

creed, 1, 17, 18, 37, 66, 158, 159, 166

cross, 1, 5, 6, 9, 10, 13, 15, 18, 19, 24, 27, 28, 50, 51, 54, 59, 62, 67, 73, 74, 75, 76, 79, 80, 82, 84, 87, 92, 93, 94, 95, 96, 97, 98, 99, 101, 102, 103, 104, 105, 107, 108, 100, 109, 110, 118, 119, 120, 121, 122, 123, 126, 128, 130, 151, 156, 168

crucifix, 97

Cyprian, 150

Cyril of Jerusalem, 118, 152

Dante, Enrico, 85

David, 5, 36, 39, 52

Decentius of Gubbio, 78

dialogue, 7, 8, 16, 36, 52, 56, 87, 94, 96–98, 104, 105, 107, 125–27, 129, 150, 164, 166

Didache, 56

dismissal, -ed, 2, 73, 77, 119, 159, 163, 164, 167

door(s), 3, 12, 59, 75, 76, 97, 123–26

Easter Sunday, 113, 116, 164–66, 187

Easter Vigil, 1, 15, 31, 39, 42, 56, 57, 58, 60, 76, 108, 110, 112, 113–64, 166, 167, 174, 175, 194

Eastern Rites, 104, 109, 111, 162

Edom, 28

Egbert, 122, 188

Egeria, 2, 3, 7, 9, 28, 57, 62, 74, 79, 84, 92, 93, 99, 115, 133, 145, 173

Egypt, 113, 116, 130, 131, 134, 137

entrance antiphon, 4, 10, 11, 13, 21, 24, 27, 34, 36, 59, 60, 164, 171

ephphetha, 153

Epiphanius, 57, 173, 178

Eusebius, 118

Exsultet (Easter proclamation), 114, 127, 128, 190

"faces (-ing) the people," 49, 51, 82, 96, 106, 107, 126

"Faithful Cross," 100

fast, -ing, 55, 56, 78, 83, 104, 111, 135, 146, 177

fire, 58, 115, 117–21, 123–26, 130, 144, 149

flowers, 58, 59

Fortunatus, Venantius, 75, 102

funeral, 30, 38, 78, 112, 174

Gelasian, 1, 14, 19, 21, 22, 23, 24, 25, 26, 28, 29, 31, 34, 35, 37, 38, 49, 50, 61, 76, 79, 83, 88, 89, 90, 91, 92, 96, 109, 116, 118, 122, 104, 121, 133, 135, 136, 137, 138, 139, 140, 141, 150, 152, 161, 165, 166, 167, 171, 172, 173, 174, 175, 176, 192

General Instruction of the Roman Missal (GIRM), 44, 48, 58, 59, 66, 81, 170, 171, 172, 174, 176, 178, 180, 182, 183, 186, 188, 189, 190, 195

General Norms for the Liturgical Year and Calendar, 131, 190

gibbet, 27, 101, 102

Gloria, 35, 60, 127, 131, 133, 136, 139–42, 159, 160, 165, 166

Gloria, laus, 9, 10

Good Friday, 1, 14, 15, 22, 24, 27, 28, 38, 55, 56, 59, 61, 62, 72, 75, 76, 77, 78–110, 112, 113, 118, 119, 120, 121, 175, 177, 181

Gothic Missal, 72, 129, 130, 146, 180, 192, 198

gradual, 15, 22, 27, 36, 46, 60, 62, 66, 100, 101, 140, 148, 165

Graduale, 46, 60, 100, 101, 140, 148

Gregorian Sacramentary, 19, 20, 23, 26, 29, 31, 38, 39, 137, 139, 141, 172, 176

Gregory the Great, 31, 133, 134

Hadrian Supplement, 19, 20, 26

Holy Saturday, 15, 56, 78, 104, 111, 112, 115, 118, 122, 124, 133, 152, 153, 186

Holy Thursday, 15, 24, 30–77, 84, 102, 110, 111, 113, 118, 119, 142, 174, 183

homily, 8, 17, 35, 36, 62, 63, 66, 68, 85, 86, 140, 142, 144, 145

image(s), 1, 50, 73, 76, 83, 91, 95, 97, 111, 117, 136

Innocent I, 78, 93, 104

incense, 7, 11, 12, 14, 16, 46, 54, 73, 75, 81, 84, 121, 122, 123, 124, 125, 127,128, 130, 144, 151

instruction on sacred music, 6, 61

International Commission on English in the Liturgy, the (ICEL), 101, 102, 169, 193

Isidore of Seville, 76

Jerome, 129

John Paul II, 78

Jounel, Pierre, 53

Judas, 16, 25, 28, 38, 61, 70, 105

Jungmann, Joseph, 69, 180, 198

Justin Martyr, 43

kiss, -ed, - ing, 17, 38, 63, 64, 70, 81, 92, 93, 97, 99, 110, 160, 162

Kyrie, 11, 12, 18, 101, 121, 140, 147, 148, 160, 171

Lanfranc, 97, 184

Leo the Great, 16, 174

Levite, 129

Life of Sylvester, 31

Litany of the Saints, 140, 147–49, 155

Lord's Supper, 21, 24, 30, 31, 36, 38, 39, 42, 54, 55, 56, 57, 62, 71, 72, 76, 119, 177, 178

Löw, Joseph, 131

lucernarium, 114, 118

mandatum, 65, 66, 179

Martimort, Aimé Georges, 54

Ministeria quaedam, 44

Monday (of Holy Week), 15, 21–23, 27, 28, 83

Moses, 34, 35, 52, 134, 149, 170

Mozarabic, 83, 97, 102

music, 6, 8, 9–12, 18, 61, 63, 75, 81, 87, 88, 97, 105, 107, 125, 140, 148, 149, 151, 154, 155, 162, 164, 165, 167, 171, 178

National Conference of Catholic Bishops, 152

Noah, 52, 134, 136, 138

"O Redeemer," 46, 54

oil of catechumens, 30, 31, 33, 39–41, 46, 47, 50, 51, 145, 151, 152, 177

oil of the sick, 30, 32–34, 39–42, 45–50

Order of Mass, 19, 20, 43, 68–70, 82, 101, 106–8, 141, 167, 180, 182

Ordinations and Declarations, 3, 63

Ordo Romanus 14, 85, 169

Ordo Romanus 16, 87, 126

Ordo Romanus 23, 58, 82, 99, 104, 183

Ordo Romanus 24, 71, 96, 99, 107, 140, 144, 174, 183, 185, 193

Ordo Romanus 26, 118

Ordo Romanus 27, 15, 52

Ordo Romanus 30B, 158

Ordo Romanus 31, 52, 88, 97, 101, 102, 177

Ordo Romanus 33, 183

Ordo Romanus 50, 6
organ, 61, 131

Palm Sunday, 1–20, 24, 26, 28, 62, 84, 107, 113, 171
Pange lingua, 74, 75, 102
paschal candle, 118–24, 126, 127, 144, 146, 150, 153, 164
paschal mystery, 1, 6, 11, 19, 21, 23, 25, 40, 59, 70, 83, 94, 108, 132, 151, 178
passion, 1, 2, 6, 11, 13, 14, 15, 16, 17, 18, 19, 21, 22, 23, 24, 25, 28, 62, 72, 78, 79, 81, 84, 85, 86, 87, 93, 94, 102, 107, 169, 172, 174, 181
Passover, 23, 61, 116, 119, 129, 130, 133, 134, 136, 163
Patrick, 114, 118
Paulinus, 115
Pontifical Commission for the Reform of the Sacred Liturgy, 3, 4, 32, 38, 57, 79, 125, 134
Pontifical of William Durandus, 47, 101, 146, 148, 164
Pope Paul VI, 32, 36, 44, 79, 170
prayer after communion, 19, 24, 26, 29, 39, 50, 72, 73, 108, 109, 163, 167
prayer over the offerings, 18, 23, 26, 28, 37, 39, 67, 83, 161, 166
prayer over the people, 6, 19, 20, 24, 26, 29, 108, 109
preface, 6, 18–20, 23, 26, 28, 30, 38, 52, 53, 61, 67, 68, 129, 139, 150, 161, 162, 166, 167
procession of the gifts, 43, 44, 46, 48, 50, 67
promises, 35–37, 40, 44, 53, 143, 145, 152, 156–58, 160, 165, 166
prostrate, -ion, 80–82, 97

Radegunda, Queen, 75
ring (bishop's), 80
Rite of Baptism for Children, 41, 145, 150, 152, 153, 161, 193, 198

Rite of Christian Initiation of Adults, 56, 111, 145, 148, 152, 154, 155, 162, 164, 167, 172, 175, 187, 193, 198
Rite of Reception of Baptized Christians, 154
Roman Canon (Eucharistic Prayer I), 33, 34, 44, 46, 48, 55, 68, 69, 70, 154, 161, 162, 167, 183, 193
Roman-Germanic Pontifical, 5,10, 9, 11, 14, 31, 44, 51, 59, 63, 77, 100, 101, 107, 169, 170, 176
Roman Pontifical, 30, 33, 40, 121, 126

Sacramentary Supplement, 39
sacristy, 9, 43, 45, 50, 54, 59, 76, 80, 81, 95, 96, 108, 109, 118, 159
Sacrosanctum concilium, 56, 170
sanctuary, 4, 12, 42, 43, 45, 50, 59, 60, 70, 76, 81, 93, 95–100, 107, 126, 127, 129, 145, 146, 154, 155, 159
Sanctus, 19, 67
Sequence (Easter), 166
shoes, 85, 99, 100
sign of the cross, 5, 6, 13, 73, 82, 119, 120, 123, 156
silence, -d, 6, 7, 17, 60, 61, 80, 82, 86, 87, 95, 97, 100, 103, 107, 108, 109, 132, 133, 142, 186
solemn blessing, 3, 19, 20, 109, 163, 167
Stabat mater, 102
Stations of the Cross, 80, 102
Study Group 17, 5, 7, 8, 9, 13, 17, 24, 169
Study Group 21, 34

tabernacle, 59, 74–76, 81, 104, 107, 108, 110
Tantum ergo, 75
Tenebrae, 58, 78
Tertullian, 115, 146, 152
Theodulf of Orleans, 9
"these or similar words," 8, 120, 158
Triduum, 21, 23, 25, 32, 55, 56, 57, 59, 77, 119, 177, 188

Trisagion, 101, 121
Tuesday (of Holy Week), 16, 22–29, 60

Ubi caritas, 67, 75
United States Conference of Catholic
    Bishops, 64

veil, 1, 9, 71, 73, 74, 76, 90, 91, 93,
    95–97, 103, 107, 110, 117
Verona Sacramentary, 18, 24, 37, 61,
    67, 139, 173
vessel(s), 38, 43–48, 50, 51, 54, 64, 106,
    145
vestment(s), vesture, 4, 11, 12, 24, 57,
    58, 76, 80, 96, 117, 132, 135
Viaticum, 108, 112, 175
Vidi aquam, 154, 158, 159

violet, 1, 4, 11, 76, 95, 96, 117, 132
Virgil, 130, 190, 197
Vogel, Cyrille, 52, 198
Vox Clara, 175, 193, 194

washing of feet, 63, 65, 66, 77
water, 6, 7, 43, 45, 52, 64, 76, 121,
    130, 134, 138, 139, 145–51, 154–56,
    158–60, 162, 165, 166
Wednesday (of Holy Week), 15, 16,
    19, 22, 23, 77, 88, 174, 178
Wipo of Burgundy, 166
Wright, Cardinal John, 36
Wurzburg Lectionary, 15

Zachariah, 118